Cornerst

eks

Georgia History

A Way Down South
James Cobb

Bible Belt - Mencken

Chap 8 & 9 Feb. 14
  March 28 Chap 10, 13, 14
  April 11 - Chap 15, 16
  April 25 - Chap 17, 18
  May 9 - Summary

Cornerstones

of

Georgia History

Documents
That Formed
the State

EDITED BY THOMAS A. SCOTT

The University of Georgia Press

Athens and London

© 1995 by the University of Georgia Press
Athens, Georgia 30602
All rights reserved
Set in 10 on 14 Electra
by Tseng Information Systems, Inc.

Printed and bound by Thomson-Shore
The paper in this book meets the guidelines
for permanence and durability of the
Committee on Production Guidelines for
Book Longevity of the Council on Library
Resources.

Printed in the United States of America
10 09 08 07 06 P 10 9 8 7 6

Library of Congress Cataloging-in-
Publication Data
Cornerstones of Georgia history : documents
that formed the state / edited by
Thomas A. Scott.
xiii, 265 p. ; 25 cm.
ISBN: 0-8203-1706-3 (alk. paper);
ISBN: 0-8203-1743-8 (pbk. : alk. paper)
Includes bibliographical references and index.
1. Georgia — History — Sources. I. Scott,
Thomas Allan.
F281 .C74 1995
975.8 — dc20   94-21880
Paperback ISBN-13: 978-0-8203-1743-4

British Library Cataloging-in-Publication
Data available

To the memory of my father,

W. Hubbard Scott,

a master storyteller,

who awakened my interest in history;

and to the memory of LeRoy P. Graf,

of the University of Tennessee, Knoxville,

my mentor of graduate school days;

and for George H. Beggs,

dean emeritus at Kennesaw State College,

who taught me what it means

to be a professional.

CONTENTS

PREFACE

᳀ ᳀ ᳀

During the last fifteen years, while teaching Georgia history at Kennesaw State College, I have tried to find materials that students can enjoy, understand, and remember. KSC's Center for Excellence in Teaching and Learning has helped me immensely in this quest. Several years ago, after CETL awarded me a summer stipend to collect primary sources for my Georgia history classes, I was delighted to discover that students liked the documents and found them easy to understand. The readings generated far more spirited and sophisticated classroom discussions than I had ever encountered before. Student reactions helped improve my selection of primary sources. This volume is the final product of that effort.

For at least a century U.S. historians have been divided over the value of textbooks as pedagogical tools. Most instructors have championed the thoroughness of general survey volumes while conceding their undeniable dullness. As far back as the 1890s, "source-textbooks" began to appear for the minority of teachers who wished to introduce primary documents.

While attending graduate school at the University of Tennessee, I became aware over two decades ago of Bruce Wheeler's success in using primary documents to provoke discussion in his introductory U.S. history course. Some years back Wheeler, along with Susan Becker, published a popular reader for survey classes entitled *Discovering the American Past*. The present work differs in significant ways from Wheeler and Becker's reader but owes to them the idea that students might find documents fun and profitable.

This book is based on the assumption that good history is about the present, not just the past. Most college students want courses to be relevant to their lives. In my classes they respond well to my feeble attempts at presenting historical foundations of contemporary social problems. They clearly want to know who we Georgians are as a people and how we got where we are. It has become my belief that students form sounder historical judgments when they are exposed to the materials and methodologies that research historians use. As valuable as textbooks and lectures may be in introducing a subject, they are of little assistance to students who want to go beyond an expert's interpretation and form independent opinions of their own. Many good students have told me that the documents approach revolutionized their view of history. Before, they found the subject boring, and consequently they never had much success in the classroom. The chance to evaluate conflicting primary sources seemed to empower them to think and form their own viewpoints.

Cornerstones of Georgia History does not attempt to present a single, unified interpretation of the past. Rather, it tries to provide both sides of issues about which Georgians argued at crucial points of the state's history. It is my hope that this approach will stimulate discussion and enable readers better to develop their personal understanding of pivotal events and issues. Some of the documents present the views of white, male "elites." Governors are quoted such as Joseph E. Brown, Ellis Arnall, and Jimmy Carter. But also integrated into the book are the views of less politically powerful people, including women, Native Americans, and African-Americans.

A virtually forgotten part of Georgia history is the presence of the Spanish in this area in the 1500s and 1600s and the sometimes stormy relationship between Franciscan brothers and the natives. With Georgia's Spanish-speaking population today well over one hundred thousand, the role of Spanish people in early Georgia takes on increasing significance. The first chapter explores the Guale revolt of 1597 which cost several missionaries their lives and resulted in a magnificent captivity narrative written by the one survivor. The second chapter contains several Cherokee myths that, among other things, introduce Native American beliefs regarding nature. These documents provide perspective for the last chapter of the book, which examines an environmental issue of the 1980s and 1990s, the alleged need for a hazardous waste facility in Taylor County.

From time to time Georgia has had fascinating debates on burning social and political issues. Many of these controversies provide unique case studies of major national questions. For example, the trustees planned a colony built on free labor, but "clamorous malcontents" demanded slavery, and both sides produced books and petitions presenting their viewpoint. A few decades later Georgians divided on the wisdom of rebelling against Britain and presented their respective cases in the provincial newspaper, the legislature, and other places. In the last two centuries Georgians have debated Indian removal, secession, women's suffrage, civil rights, and other issues.

A chapter on slavery presents various views of former bondsmen and bondswomen. A discussion of the Civil War centers on the homefront experiences of North Georgia women. Postwar poverty is examined from the perspectives of social critics Clare de Graffenried and W. E. B. Du Bois, as well as leading politicians Joseph E. Brown and Tom Watson. Anti-Semitism is explored in the Leo Frank case. The changing role of African-Americans in the mid-twentieth century is seen through the eyes of a black female worker at the Bell Aircraft

Company, a pioneer of the Civil Rights movement in Savannah, a parent challenging the segregated Atlanta school system, and one of the first black students to attend the University of Georgia.

It will be obvious to readers that my opinions and biases have entered into this work through my selection of issues and documents and my introductions to the various chapters. Nonetheless, it has been my desire to be fair to all sides. On the pivotal topics covered in this book, I hope that readers will have enough information to determine right and wrong for themselves, to analyze critically why the state followed the paths it took, and to decide how the actions of the past still influence us today.

ACKNOWLEDGMENTS

I would like to acknowledge my debts to many people who made this work possible. My wife, Kathleen Sherlock Scott, read each chapter as it was produced and has consistently given invaluable advice and support. Librarians and archivists have been most helpful, especially at Kennesaw State College, the Cobb County Public Library System, the Georgia Department of Archives and History, the National Archives-Southeast Region, the Library and Archives of the Martin Luther King, Jr. Center for Nonviolent Social Change, the Hargrett Rare Book and Manuscript Library at the University of Georgia, the Georgia Government Documentation Project at Georgia State University, and the Atlanta History Center. Cliff Kuhn of Georgia State University made available an oral history interview from his private collection, and the Georgia Hazardous Waste Management Authority gave me access to documents from the Taylor County controversy.

Numerous authors and publishers gave permission to copy parts of their works. They are mentioned at the appropriate places throughout the book. Editors and readers at the University of Georgia Press have suggested many valuable changes and have always been helpful and courteous in shepherding the book toward publication. I owe a huge debt to President Betty L. Siegel and the faculty of Kennesaw State College for honoring teaching and research related to classroom instruction. I have received much encouragement and support from Ann Ellis Pullen, Chair of KSC's History and Philosophy Department, and George H. Beggs, former Dean of the School of Arts, Humanities and Social Sciences. Donald W. Forrester and the Center for Excellence in Teaching and Learning provided the crucial initial support for this project. The Senior Secretary of the History Department, Selena Creasman, and a number of student assistants have helped in the work's preparation. Perhaps I owe the most to the students who have taken my Georgia history classes. They have read and discussed various drafts of the chapters and given their constructive criticisms. If they had not responded so enthusiastically when I first started, I certainly would have abandoned my efforts long ago.

1

Spain and the Native Americans:
The Guale Revolt, 1597

The era of Georgia history about which the public knows the least is undoubtedly the century and a half of Spanish domination. The first European to see Georgia was possibly Juan Ponce de León during his 1513 journey to Florida. The honor of establishing the first permanent settlement within the present U.S. boundaries goes to the gifted Spanish soldier, Pedro Menéndez de Avilés. In 1565 he established the Florida town of St. Augustine as part of an expedition to destroy French influence in the area. The following year he journeyed northward, stopping probably at St. Catherine's Island, where the natives, impressed by Spanish power, offered their friendship. Taking the name of the local peoples, the Spanish called the area along the Georgia coast Guale.

On the same voyage Menéndez established a major settlement at Santa Elena (Port Royal) in present South Carolina. Spanish presidios were soon erected all along the Atlantic shoreline, and expeditions, such as that of Pardo and Boyano, created small outposts in the interior. Nonetheless, permanent Spanish settlers stayed away from the Guale province. Opulent Mexico and Peru were too tempting for those whose ambitions ran toward material possessions, and no one seemed interested in living where riches could not be found immediately. Thus, the Spanish hit on the bright idea of letting the missionaries do the work of colonizing, by turning converted Indians into their settlers.

The Jesuits were the first seriously to make the attempt, but the most successful Christianizers in Guale were the Franciscans. The latter's greatest influence came after 1593, following the arrival in Florida of twelve missionaries led by Fray Juan de Silva. The friars soon spread out along the coast, half locating in Guale, where missions were established at principal Indian towns. Within three years the Franciscans had about fifteen hundred converts whom they instructed in religion and in the European lifestyle. Troubles came in 1597, however, when a rebellious Indian named Juanillo murdered Fray Pedro Corpa, the missionary at Tolomato, near present Darien. As the revolt spread, four other friars were martyred and one, Fray Francisco de Ávila, taken captive. Father Ávila remained in bondage for about ten months until rescued by the Spanish. Now, almost four hundred years later, historians, anthropologists, and Roman Catholic clergy have prepared materials for the Vatican Congregation for Sainthood Causes.[1]

The uprising was quickly put down by the Spanish governor at St. Augustine, who sent an army up to Guale to subdue the Indians. Having reasserted their authority, the Spanish returned to the task of civilizing and Christianizing their backsliding charges. They were marvelously successful, and the first half of the seventeenth century became the golden age of Spanish settlement in the Southeast. At the peak, the Franciscans served about twenty-five thousand converts located near thirty-eight missions spread throughout the region. According to Ray Allen Billington in his *Westward Expansion*, "The mission stations won southeastern North America for Spain. . . . The Franciscans gave their church and king a monopoly in the Florida country which latecomers would have to break."[2]

☙ ☙ ☙

Speech of Juanillo

From the Spanish perspective, Juanillo was a troublemaker who would not give in to the priests' demand that he keep only one wife. When a position of mico (chief) came open, that post may have gone to this young Indian save for the intervention of Father Pedro Corpa. A sulking Juanillo sought revenge by murdering the meddling friar; then he called on the natives of Guale to expunge the land of all Spanish influence.

Juanillo's speech to the Indians, justifying his behavior, is the first document below.

Now the friar is dead. This would not have happened if he had allowed us to live according to our pre-Christian manner. Let us return to our ancient customs. Let us provide for our defense against the punishment which the governor of Florida will mete out; if he succeeds in punishing us, he will be as rigorous in avenging the death of this single friar, as for the death of all. For he will punish us as severely for having killed one friar as if we had killed them all.

Consequently since the punishment for killing one friar must be equally severe as for killing all, let us restore our [ancient] liberty of which these friars deprive us. They give us promises of good things which they themselves have not seen but for which they hold out hope. We who are called Christians, experience only hindrances and vexations. They take away from us our women, allowing us but one, and that, in perpetuity, forbidding us to exchange them for others. They prohibit us from having our dances, banquets, feasts, celebrations, games and wars, in order that, being deprived of these, we might lose our ancient valor and skill, which we have inherited from our ancestors. They persecute our old men, calling them wizards. They are not satisfied with our labor for they hinder us from performing it on certain days. Even when we are willing to do all they tell us, they remain unsatisfied. All they do, is to reprimand us, treat us in an injurious manner, oppress us, preach to us and call us bad Christians. They deprive us of every vestige of happiness which our ancestors obtained for us, in exchange for which they hold out the hope of the joys of Heaven. In this deceitful manner, they subject us, holding us bound to their wills. What have we to hope for except to become slaves? If we kill them all now, we will throw off this intolerable yoke without delay. The governor will perceive our valor and will be forced to treat us well, in the event that he should get the better of us.[3]

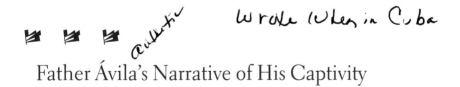

Father Ávila's Narrative of His Captivity

In the clash of two cultures, the Spanish, of course, had another point of view. The missionaries were men who gave up everything of material value, risking life and limb in the service of God and country. They clearly believed that their religion and culture were gifts of priceless value. The second document reproduced below is Father Ávila's written account of his captivity, as copied by Luis Hierónimo de Oré, O.F.M., *Relación de los mártires que ha habido en las Provincias de la Florida*, completed about 1617.

To relate once more how God delivered me from the hands of the Indians, I declare as follows: When they found me among the rushes where I had hid myself, they shot arrows at me. Then they held me for the period of an hour, leaving me with an Indian to guard me while the Indians were busy sacking and robbing the church and house. Soon there came the *cacique* who had liberated me, with three or four Indians, and at that hour of the night, they took me to their town which was two leagues from there, over a poor road. But since I was wounded, I could only walk with great difficulty; yet they urged me on, pretending they were taking me to their town to cure me and to provide for me. Finally, perhaps about twelve o'clock at night, we arrived where they threw me among some common reed-grass in the hut until morning. Some guards were placed over me, and I passed the time amid great annoyance. When morning arrived, the *cacique* came, despoiling me of my habit which I had, leaving me my undergarments. He said the habit was very bloody and he wanted to wash it. In the meanwhile I wore a small coat which he left with me. This is the clothing in which the Indians go about. So I was like an Indian with regard to my exterior, while all of them made fun of me and mocked me.

The *cacique* convoked all the boys and women, saying to them: "Come kiss the hand of your father; receive his blessing." Since we had taught them this good custom and mark of good breeding, the *cacique* commanded that they practice this custom on me in mockery. After the Indians had satisfied themselves by this amusement and had made fun of me, the *cacique* ordered that two Indians should tie my hands with a rope and take me to Tulafina, which was the first mission or post where I had been.[4] It was distant six leagues through swamps and mire so that one had to go through them up to the hips. Moreover the Indians said that I had declared that the land of Tulafina was bad and that the Indians were very bad. "Therefore," said the *cacique*, "I wish you to go there; and they will treat you as you deserve." So with great cruelty they soon took me there, without considering my wounds. And since the roads were so bad, I fell at almost every step and stuck in the mire. For them it was the occasion of so much satisfaction and delight that they could not hide it, for they made fun of me with gestures and grimaces, and played with me by slapping me on the neck. If God had not given me sufficient strength and relief, this journey would have been enough to bring on death, for I was sick and wounded. But God who wished to liberate me from their hands gave me sufficient strength to bear it.

At about four in the afternoon, we arrived at a very large town called Ufalage. This town is on the way to Tulafina. Many Indians, men and women, came out to meet me, all of whom were painted, and who made a great show and mockery of me. In this manner they took me to their hut where they made me sit down on the ground, while they all stood around laughing and ridiculing me. I was very tired and hungry and on this account I would have preferred to remain there that night. This, however, was not to their liking, so that night they took me to Tulafina because they alleged that the Indians there were awaiting me. Tulafina was distant two leagues from there. The journey was over a worse road than the previous one and in many parts, the water reached to the waist. Nevertheless, God gave me strength, and before nightfall we arrived at Tulafina. A little before arriving there we encountered a great number of painted Indians, their faces smeared with red earth, and fitted out with bows and arrows. They seemed to be numberless and looked like demons. They all came out to receive me, and amid great mockery and fun, led me to their habitation. When I arrived at the door of the hut, I found they had erected a large cross, while on one side there was a large whip which was a green rod with many branches which they use when at first they make the blood flow. On the other side of the cross was a rod to be used as a firebrand having a pine branch before it with the head-skin of a small animal. They commanded me to sit down at the foot of the cross. Thereupon they tied my hands; my arms being already bent because of the arrow shots in the shoulder, arm and hand. They also tied my neck strongly to the same cross so that they almost hung me. When this was done, a *cacique* came, who was the commander of the dwelling, and said: "Do you know what this is? The cross which is erected here, is an invention of yours so we shall have to place you on it. The torch is to be bound to your body to burn you; the whip is to beat you; and this skin which is here, is a sign that you have to die. Tomorrow all this will be put into execution." Then an Indian dressed in a chasuble, went about in mockery, mimicking the Mass. Another Indian came and placed a book before me and when I did not reverence it, a principal *cacique* came and with the book struck me on the head and cheek with a blow so hard that it left me senseless.

I was stark naked for they did not even let me have a poor coat. Another Indian came with a cord, one of those with which we gird ourselves, knotted and doubled, and gave me three or four strokes so hard that I was left like dead. While they were engaged in this, a *cacique* arose and carried a little bit of burning wood and threw it on my back. Since I was tied, I could not throw it from me very quickly. It left a deep mark on my body and caused me much pain. Soon the Indians began to dance around me as if they were passing in review before me, and if it struck someone's fancy, he gave me a heavy blow with a *macana* [club]. In this manner they danced for three hours, while they made a thousand incantations. When they were tired of dancing, they sat down a little and when I saw there was a little quiet, I asked them if they, for the love of God, would have the kindness to untie my arms for a little while (for they were in the bent position) and though they were going to kill me, I asked them to show this mercy to me. Just then they did not wish to heed my request, but they soon began to treat among themselves about showing me some mercy. They remembered that there was in the city of St. Augustine, a boy who was the heir to the caciquedom and they reasoned that if they would not kill me, they could sometime exchange him for me. Others said that those who had entered that hut were immune from death; still others said that the daughter of the sun had appeared to them and had told them that they should not kill me. This is one of their practices of witchcraft.

Finally, confronted with all these opinions, they decided to let me live and so a *cacique* arose and said to me: "Do you wish me to unbind you? Do you wish to live or die? We leave it in your hands. You may have what you wish. But I tell you that if we do not kill you, you will have to stay here among us, serving us by carrying water and wood, and by digging at times, and by attending to all that we tell you."

When the *cacique* said this to me, I was half dead. Nevertheless, I answered: "Do what you desire for my body is in your hands; but if you do not kill me, I shall do what you tell me and will be good, for you see that I cannot stir." This seemed good to him and I said much in a seasonable time. And so he untied me. Then they commanded me to sit down on the ground, having placed me against a bench. They gave me two *mazorquillas* of cooked maize to eat. But I was in such a condition that although it was good and substantial food, I could not eat it; but in order to satisfy them, I forced myself to eat. I asked them to give me one of those cane beds that I might sleep. This they did and placed an Indian with me who was to be in my presence in case I needed anything. But how could I sleep in those knotted canes, being naked and wounded and so illtreated? I only say that unless God had given me strength, it would have been impossible to live. In this manner I was in this hut for ten days, while the Indians danced till midnight, without showing any desire to heal my wounds. But God who is merciful permitted that within a short time, without any curative means, they were healed and I became well.

Fairer days succeeded and they allowed me to go from one house to another, though always naked even during the worst cold of winter. I was the laughingstock because when they held a feast, they sent for me and hurled nicknames at me. Thus they received pleasure from the feast and they were glad they had not killed me so that they could have someone to entertain them. They made me dig and stand guard over the huts in order that the birds would not eat the grain. All had dominion over me; whoever wished, hit me with a stick. Particularly the boys employed their scorn upon me. I had suffered much hunger and need because the Indians had nothing to eat and if they had anything, they first attended to their needs, rather than to mine. And so often I found it necessary to satisfy my hunger and need on the leaves of wild grapes and plants having a sour juice, for in this land there were no better fruits.

They tried to use force on me to make me abandon my law and accept that of the Indians, and to marry an Indian after their manner. This I answered with contradiction and with great spirit and feeling, confounding the Indians in such a way that they marvelled at the spirit and liberty I used in speaking to them and in contradicting them. After that they tried to make me serve in cleaning the house of the demon, for such we call it. They, however, call it a tomb. There they placed food and drink for the dead which the dead are supposed to find at the morning meal. The Indians believe that the dead eat this food. However, they are already persuaded that the dead do not eat it, because the wizards eat it themselves, as they know by experience, for we have made this known to them. The same wizards themselves have confessed this and we have made good Christians of them. To this I answered that although they cut me to a thousand pieces, I would not enter that house but I would rather go and burn it. When they saw me so strong in my resolve, they left me.

When affairs reached this stage, the Indians wished to take the crown from me by saying: "You will never see the Spaniards again, nor they, you; leave your law and become an Indian and you will enjoy what we enjoy; you will have a wife or more, if you wish; furthermore, in the other life you will enjoy what you enjoy here, for we know that he who has been miserable and mean in this life, will be the same in the other, and as many wives as one had in this life, so many will he have in the other. This is our belief. Give up the things you teach us for they are foolish. Here we are bringing this Indian woman, young and beautiful; marry her and you will have a happy life and thus reward yourself." While they were speaking and acting in this manner, the Indian girl brought decayed palm leaves from the woods, similar to straws, made a bed for [me] and called [me] to dine. As soon as I saw this, I perceived the persecution of the devil who did not leave any occasion pass, in order to tempt me and make me disconsolate. I had recourse to God in prayer on this occasion and with tears that fell from my eyes, begged Him to give me the grace to deliver me from so diabolical a temptation. God gave me such persuasiveness and such spirit that by means of them

I convinced the Indians and in order to safeguard myself from all this, I fled to the woods where I remained for four days, sustaining myself on herbs and roots. Nor did I return to that town, but betook myself to another, and since then they never spoke to me of such things.

One day while I was going along leisurely, I passed by a hut where some Indians were digging. Under the inspiration of the devil, they took their heavy rods and six Indians conjointly gave me so many strokes that they left me for dead. This renewed my wounds and caused many new ones as well, but God was pleased that they should be healed in a short time without any curative means. Ten months I was in this state of captivity during which the Lord delivered me from great dangers, giving me such good health and strength that never in my life have I experienced the same.

On a certain occasion when the Indians had determined to declare war against some enemies of theirs, they came to him and said: "See, here we have ten arquebuses without powder and bullets. Make us some powder and bullets and if you do not we have to kill you." He excused himself, saying that he did not know how. To this the Indian answered: "Do not excuse yourself for you do know how; your books tell you how you can make them." Father Ávila answered: "I have no books because you have taken them from me." They said: "We shall bring them to you." Then they brought him a *Summa* and a prayer book for religious, those by Fray Luís de Granada, and a breviary, all of which were a great consolation for him in his solitude. He hid them in the cavity of an oak tree where he went to read them and to console himself with their contents. The breviary, however, he always carried publicly but the boys tore out the pages. In order to answer them in this matter of the powder and bullets concerning which they molested him and pressed him, he asked for the necessary materials of which there were none in that country. Thus they understood that it was not because he was unwilling, but for lack of the materials, that he failed to make them. And so they left him.

This story of the powder and bullets, Father Ávila did not write in his *Relacion* but it was given to me by a religious who dealt with Father Ávila before and after his captivity and who spoke and conferred with him a great deal. He relates this incident and divers others, which I pass over in order to avoid prolixity.[5]

NOTES

1. Barbara King, " 'Georgia Martyrs' Changing Lives," *The Georgia Bulletin*, October 21, 1993, p. 1.

2. Ray Allen Billington, *Westward Expansion: A History of the American Frontier*, 4th ed. (New York: Macmillan, 1974), 40–41.

3. The source for this remarkable oration is Andres G. Barcía Carbillido y Zuniga, *Ensayo cronológico para la historia general de la Florida* (Madrid, 1737), translated by Rev. Maynard Geiger, O.F.M., for his doctoral dissertation, *The Franciscan Conquest of Florida (1573–1618)* (Catholic University of America, 1937). Geiger maintains (p. 90), "this speech may be only 'poetically true,' but it certainly characterizes the situation." A similar version comes from the Indian Lucas of Tupique in his confession to Spanish authorities at St. Augustine shortly after the uprising. Lucas asserted that the Indian leaders killed one of the priests "because he was artful and took away their enchantment or witchcraft, and would not allow them to have more than one wife." Another Indian captive, Bartolomé of Tolomato, attributed the killings to the fact that the priests "reproved them [the Indians]; that the priests were crafty, and did not care for them, and did not wish to have more than one wife." See Miss A. M. Brooks and Mrs. Annie Averette, *The Unwritten History of Old St. Augustine* (St. Augustine: The Record Co. [1909?]), 41, 46.

4. According to John Tate Lanning, Father Ávila's mission was on Jekyll Island (called Ospo at the time). Tulafina was apparently near the Altamaha River, not far inland from the present city of Darien. *The Spanish Missions of Georgia* (Chapel Hill: University of North Carolina Press, 1935), 71, 253.

5. Again, the translator is Maynard Geiger, who published Ore's important work under the title *The Martyrs of Florida (1513–1616)* (New York: Joseph F. Wagner, 1936).

2

Cherokees and Creeks:
Traditional Cultures and the
Anglo-Saxon Encounter

As we saw in the previous chapter, Europeans such as Father Ávila had little appreciation for the Indian cultures they encountered along the Atlantic coast. Indigenous lifestyles and religious concepts seemed to them backward and barbaric. Had Caucasians been willing to learn from the natives, however, they would have discovered much of value. For example, the Native American's reverence for nature stood in sharp contrast to the typical white colonizer's desire to exploit the environment. It is true that Indians farmed, set fires to control underbrush, and otherwise manipulated nature to their advantage. At the same time, however, they recognized that people could be happy only when they lived in harmony with the total creation. To the Indians all animals had spirits, as did many inanimate objects, and failure to show proper respect for those spirits could bring dire consequences. The two Cherokee myths below are examples of the Native American's high regard for nature. The first explains how man was responsible for the origin of disease; the second is a creation story.[1]

Origins of Disease and Medicine

In the old days the beasts, birds, fishes, insects, and plants could all talk, and they and the people lived together in peace and friendship. But as time went on the people increased so rapidly that their settlements spread over the whole earth, and the poor animals found themselves beginning to be cramped for room. This was bad enough, but to make it worse Man invented bows, knives, blowguns, spears, and hooks, and began to slaughter the larger animals, birds, and fishes for their flesh and their skins, while the smaller creatures, such as the frogs and worms, were crushed and trodden upon without thought, out of pure carelessness or contempt. So the animals resolved to consult upon measures for their common safety.

The Bears were the first to meet in council in their townhouse under Kuwahi mountain, the "Mulberry place," and the old White Bear chief presided. After each in turn had complained of the way in which Man killed their friends, ate their flesh, and used their skins for his own purposes, it was decided to begin war at once against him. Some one asked what weapons Man used to destroy them. "Bows and arrows, of course," cried all the Bears in chorus. "And what are they made of?" was the next question. "The bow of wood, and the string of our entrails," replied one of the Bears. It was then proposed that they make a bow and some arrows and see if they could not use the same weapons against Man himself. So one Bear got a nice piece of locust wood and another sacrificed himself for the good of the rest in order to furnish a piece of his entrails for the string. But when everything was ready and the first Bear stepped up to make the trial, it was found that in letting the arrow fly after drawing back the bow, his long claws caught the string and spoiled the shot. This was annoying, but someone suggested that they might trim his claws, which was accordingly done, and on a second trial it was found that the arrow went straight to the mark. But here the chief, the old White Bear, objected, saying it was necessary that they should have long claws in order to be able to climb trees. "One of us has already died to furnish the bowstring, and if we now cut off our claws we must all starve together. It is better to trust to the teeth and claws that nature gave us, for it is plain that man's weapons were not intended for us."

No one could think of any better plan, so the old chief dismissed the council and the Bears dispersed to the woods and thickets without having concerted any way to prevent the increase of the human race. Had the result of the council been otherwise, we should now be at war with the Bears, but as it is, the hunter does not even ask the Bear's pardon when he kills one.

The Deer next held a council under their chief, the Little Deer, and after some talk decided to send rheumatism to every hunter who should kill one of them unless he took care to ask their pardon for the offense. They sent notice of their decision to the nearest settlement of Indians and told them at the same time what to do when necessity forced them to kill one of the Deer tribe. Now, whenever the hunter shoots a Deer, the Little Deer, who is swift as the wind and cannot be wounded, runs quickly up to the spot and, bending over the blood-stains, asks the spirit of the Deer if it has heard the prayer of the hunter for pardon. If the reply be "Yes," all is well, and the Little Deer goes on his way; but if the reply be "No," he follows on the trail of the hunter, guided by the drops of blood on the ground, until he arrives at his cabin in the settlement, when the Little Deer enters invisibly and strikes the hunter with rheumatism, so that he becomes at once a helpless cripple. No hunter who had regard for his health ever fails to ask pardon of the Deer for killing it, although some hunters who have not learned the prayer may try to turn aside the Little Deer from his pursuit by building a fire behind them in the trail.

Next came the Fishes and Reptiles, who had their own complaints against Man. They held their council together and determined to make their victims dream of snakes twining about them in slimy folds and blowing foul breath in their faces, or to make them dream of eating raw or decaying fish, so that they would lose appetite, sicken, and die. This is why people dream about snakes and fish.

Finally the Birds, Insects, and smaller animals came together for the same purpose, and the Grubworm was chief of the council. It was decided that each in turn should give an opinion, and then they would vote on the question as to whether or not Man was guilty. Seven votes should be enough to condemn him. One after another denounced Man's cruelty and injustice toward the other animals and voted in favor of his death. The Frog spoke first saying: "We must do something to check the increase of the race, or people will become so numerous that we shall be crowded from off the earth. See how they have kicked me about because I'm ugly, as they say, until my back is covered with sores"; and here he showed the spots on his skin. Next came the Bird—no one remembers now which one it was—who condemned Man "because he burns my feet off," meaning the way in which the hunter barbecues birds by impaling them on a stick set over the fire, so that their feathers and tender feet are singed off. Others followed in the same strain. The Ground-squirrel alone ventured to say a good word for Man, who seldom hurt him because he was so small, but this made the others so angry that they fell upon the Ground-squirrel and tore him with their claws, and the stripes are on his back to this day.

They began then to devise and name so many new diseases, one after another, that had not their invention at last failed them, no one of the human race would have been able to survive. The Grubworm grew constantly more pleased as the name of each disease was called off, until at last they reached the end of the list, when someone proposed to make menstruation sometimes fatal to women. On this he rose up in his place and cried: "Wadan'! [Thanks!] I'm glad some more of them will die, for they are getting so thick that they tread on me." The thought fairly made him shake with joy, so that he fell over backward and could not get on his feet again, but had to wriggle off on his back, as the Grubworm has done ever since.

When the Plants, who were friendly to Man, heard what had been done by the animals, they determined to defeat the latter's evil designs. Each Tree, Shrub, and Herb, down even to the Grasses and Mosses, agreed to furnish a cure for some one of the diseases named, and each said: "I shall appear to help Man when he calls upon me in his need." Thus came medicine; and the plants, every one of which has its use if we only knew it, furnish the remedy to counteract the evil wrought by the revengeful animals. Even weeds were made for some good purpose, which we must find out for ourselves. When the doctor does not know what medicine to use for a sick man the spirit of the plant tells him.

🦋 🦋 🦋

How the World Was Made

The earth is a great island floating in a sea of water, and suspended at each of the four cardinal points by a cord hanging down from the sky vault, which is of solid rock. When the world grows old and worn out, the people will die and the cords will break and let the earth sink down into the ocean, and all will be water again. The Indians are afraid of this.

When all was water, the animals were above in Galunlati, beyond the arch; but it was very much crowded, and they were wanting more room. They wondered what was below the water, and at last Dayunisi, "Beaver's Grandchild," the little Water-beetle, offered to go and see if it could learn. It darted in every direction over the surface of the water, but could find no firm place to rest. Then it dived to the bottom and came up with soft mud, which began to grow and spread on every side until it became the island which we call the earth. It was afterward fastened to the sky with four cords, but no one remembers who did this.

At first the earth was flat and very soft and wet. The animals were anxious to get down, and sent out different birds to see if it was yet dry, but they found no place to alight and came back again to Galunlati. At last it seemed to be time, and they sent out the Buzzard and told him to go and make ready for them. This was the Great Buzzard, the father of all the buzzards we see now. He flew all over the earth, low down near the ground, and it was still soft. When he reached the Cherokee country, he was very tired, and his wings began to flap and strike the ground, and wherever they struck the earth there was a valley, and where they turned up again there was a mountain. When the animals above saw this, they were afraid that the whole world would be mountains, so they called him back, but the Cherokee country remains full of mountains to this day.

When the earth was dry and the animals came down, it was still dark, so they got the sun and set it in a track to go every day across the island from east to west, just overhead. It was too hot this way, and Tsiskagili, the Red Crawfish, had his shell scorched a bright red, so that his meat was spoiled; and the Cherokee do not eat it. The conjurers put the sun another hand-breadth higher in the air, but it was still too hot. They raised it another time, and another, until it was seven handbreadths high and just under the sky arch. Then it was right, and they left it so. This is why the conjurers call the highest place Gulkwagine Digalunlatiyun, "the seventh height," because it is seven hand-breadths above the earth. Every day the sun goes along under this arch, and returns at night on the upper side to the starting place. . . .

Men came after the animals and plants. At first there were only a brother and sister until he struck her with a fish and told her to multiply, and so it was. In seven days a child was born to her, and thereafter every seven days another, and they increased very fast until there was danger that the world could not keep them. Then it was made that a woman should have only one child in a year, and it has been so ever since.

Gender Relationships

If Indian concepts about nature contrasted with those of Europeans, so did their understanding of the proper roles of men and women. The Indians of the Southeast were matrilineal in their social organization, with inheritance passing through the female line. One's mother and father were always members of different clans, but the child identified only with the clan of the former. When divorces occurred, the children stayed with their mother, while the father returned to his mother's clan.

Some have argued that Indian women were better off before they became civilized. Females in the Southeast had clear economic roles as food gatherers and growers for the tribe. While males sometimes helped with crop cultivation, they were primarily responsible for hunting. The Native American quest for balance can be seen in this division of labor, where each gender performed essential economic functions. In contrast, the Europeans brought traditions where inheritance of wealth and family name came through the male line and where the property of a woman passed to her husband on their wedding day. The myth below is one of the stories James Mooney collected at the end of the nineteenth century. It explains why people have to work for a living.

Kanati and Selu: The Origin of Game and Corn

Another story is told of how sin came into the world. A man and a woman reared a large family of children in comfort and plenty, with very little trouble about providing food for them. Every morning the father went forth and very soon returned bringing with him a deer, or a turkey, or some other animal or fowl. At the same time the mother went out and soon returned with a large basket filled with ears of corn which she shelled and pounded in a mortar, thus making meal for bread.

When the children grew up, seeing with what apparent ease food was provided for them, they talked to each other about it, wondering that they never saw such things as their parents brought in. At last one proposed to watch when their parents went out and to follow them.

Accordingly next morning the plan was carried out. Those who followed the father saw him stop at a short distance from the cabin and turn over a large stone that appeared to be carelessly leaned against another. On looking closely they saw an entrance to a large cave, and in it were many different kinds of animals and birds, such as their father had sometimes brought in for food. The man standing at the entrance called a deer, which was lying at some distance and back of some other animals. It rose immediately as it heard the call and came close up to him. He picked it up, closed the mouth of the cave, and returned, not once seeming to suspect what his sons had done.

When the old man was fairly out of sight, his sons, rejoicing how they had outwitted him, left their hiding place and went to the cave, saying they would show the old folks that they, too, could bring in something. They moved the stone away, though it was very heavy and they were obliged to use all their united strength. When the cave was opened, the animals, instead of waiting to be picked up, all made a rush for the entrance, and leaping past the frightened and bewildered boys, scattered in all directions and disappeared in the wilderness, while the guilty offenders could do nothing but gaze in stupified amazement as they saw them escape. There were animals of all kinds, large and small—buffalo, deer, elk, antelope, raccoons, and squirrels; even catamounts and panthers, wolves and foxes, and many others, all fleeing together. At the same time birds of every kind were seen emerging from the opening, all in the same wild confusion as the quadrupeds—turkeys, geese, swans, ducks, quails, eagles, hawks, and owls.

Those who followed the mother saw her enter a small cabin, which they had never seen before, and close the door. The culprits found a small crack through which they could peer. They saw the woman place a basket on the ground and standing over it shake herself vigorously, jumping up and down, when lo and behold! large ears of corn began to fall into the basket. When it was well filled she took it up and, placing it on her head, came out, fastened the door, and prepared their breakfast as usual. When the meal had been finished in silence the man spoke to his children, telling them that he was aware of what they had done; that now he must die and they would be obliged to provide for themselves. He made bows and arrows for them, then sent them to hunt for the animals which they had turned loose.

Then the mother told them that as they had found out her secret she could do nothing more for them; that she would die, and they must drag her body around over the ground; that wherever her body was dragged corn would come up. Of this they were to make their bread. She told them that they must always save some for seed and plant every year.

Mary Musgrove

The most famous woman of the colonial era in Georgia was a Creek Indian named Coosaponakeesa, known to the whites as Mary Musgrove. According to historian Rodney Baine, Musgrove was born about 1708 to a Tuckabatchee Creek woman and a South Carolina trader named Edward Griffin. Coosaponakeesa learned the language and values of both parents' cultures. About 1725 she married a half-breed trader named Johnny Musgrove, and they ultimately developed a prosperous trading post on Yamacraw Bluff on the Georgia side of the Savannah River.[2] When Oglethorpe established Savannah nearby in 1733, the English colony builder used Mary Musgrove as an interpreter and ally in negotiating with the Creeks. She is credited with playing a crucial role in preserving the peace between the Indians and the infant Georgia colony. Her third husband was a former Anglican clergyman named Thomas Bosomworth. Together they successfully petitioned the English government for St. Catherines Island and other income that she claimed was owed to her but never paid. The document below is Thomas Bosomworth's summary of his wife's contributions to early Georgia.

A Statement of Mrs. Bosomworth's Case with respect to her services, losses, expenses, and demands of the colony of Georgia, received and read Jan. 7, 1761, C.O. 5/648, E. 11, enclosure A in Governor Ellis' June 27, 1760, letter to the Board of Trade.

That before the Charter for Establishing the Colony of Georgia Mrs. Bosomworth with her Family was settled on the river Savannah, a small space above where the Town of Savannah now stands, had large Credits from Merchants in Charles Town, South Carolina, and Carried on a Considerable Traffic with the Indians whereby she had already made very large Remittances in Skins, and was moreover Possess'd of a very Good Cowpen & Plantation upon the same River.

That Mr. Oglethorpe's Arrival with the first Adventures to settle a Colony under the aforesaid Charter gave great uneasiness to the Indians then upon the spot, who threatne'd [sic] to take up arms against them. Nor would they have permitted Mr. Oglethorpe & his people a Quiet Possession (as they look'd upon the White People's settling to the Southward of Savannah River contrary to the Treaty of Peace, enter'd into between the Indians & the Government of South Carolina after the Indian War in the year 1716) had not the Governor & Council wrote to Mrs. Bosomworth (by Mr. Oglethorpe) to use the utmost of her Interest with the Indians for that Purpose and to give the new settlers all the Aid & Assistance their Necessities might require. In Compliance with the request contain'd in that Letter, and from Motives of regard to the British Interest, Mrs. Bosomworth by her Influence, Quieted the Indians; allay'd all Animosity, obtain'd a present Asylum for the Adventures, and in about the space of twelve months, by her steady Adherence and good Offices settled and procur'd to be ratified a Treaty between the Indians & Mr. Oglethorpe in behalf of the Trustees for Establishing that Colony.

That by the Traffic she then carried on with the Indians there was no Impediment to her soon raising a Considerable Interest. Yet Mrs. Bosomworth could not unmov'd see a Colony (scarce begun) expos'd to the Incursions of the Spaniards & their Indians (the frequent & then late ravages of the frontier of Carolina) and whose Protection she well knew in their defenseless situation, could only be secur'd by the Friendship and Alliance with the Creek Indians she therefore upon Promises of adequate rewards from the Government Induc'd the Indians who were her Hunters and supplied her with Skins, most Generally to Employ themselves in Expeditions for the Public Service.

That in the Years 1736 & 1737 when Mr. Oglethorpe thought it Expedient to Improve the Southern Part of the Province, first by a settlement on the Island of St. Simon's, and by another settlement (of Scotch People) at Darian [sic] on the Altamaha River, the Assistance of the Creek Indians then became of so much greater Importance, as there were advices at that time that Spaniards were making Preparations to Disloge the Inhabitants of this new Colony & the more still effectually to further the Preservation & Growth of the frontier settlements. Mrs. Bosomworth at the Earnest request of General Oglethorpe (buoy'd up by Extensive Promises, & the Large Rewards so signal a Service for the public Welfare would Merit) settled a Trading House on the south side of the said River Altamaha about 150 miles up the same river by water at a Place call'd Mount Venture, the Intention of which settlement was that the Creek Indians, who would be constantly with her there might be an advanc'd Guard to prevent any Incursions of the Spaniards, or Indians in friendship with them, and be always more ready at hand when his Majesty's service requir'd their Assistance which throughly Answer'd the Intentions of the Public.

That after the Declaration of war against Spain the service of the Indians were so frequently requir'd that no Benefit could possibly arise from any Trade with them that might induce Mrs. Bosomworth's stay there, nevertheless so great was her zeal that without the least Prospect of Interest to herself she was daily expos'd at that Settlement, for the public Service, in keeping the Indians upon Excursions, and sending for her Friends & Relations from the nation to go to war whenever his Majesty's Service requir'd.

That at the time of Mr. Oglethorpe's first Arrival there being no House or Settlement on the Place except Mrs. Bosomworth's, She at the request of Mr. Oglethorpe, supplied the new Settlers and other Persons Employ'd on Public Services in their Greatest Wants not only with every thing her Plantation and store afforded but also with Liquor & other Necessari's, purchas'd on her own Credit from Merchants in Charles Town whereby she Loss'd in bad Debts so Contracted and acumalated the sum of 826 pounds sterling as can be Evidently prov'd from a state of her Books, and has been before amongst other Complaints, set forth & humbly represented to the Government.

That by Mrs. Bosomworth's Employing in his Majesty's service those Indians who used by Hunting, to supply her with Skins (the Chief support of herself & Family) her Trade naturally Decreas'd, and went nearly to ruin, a large Party of them who she prevail'd on assisted his Majesty's Arms & went to the siege of St. Augustine where many of them were kill'd, particularly her own Brother & other near Relations. By this Incident she greatly suffer'd in the Loss of Indian Debts amounting to several Thousand Weight of Leather for which she never yet received any satisfaction altho promiss'd it from time to time by Mr. Oglethorpe.

That from the time of settling the Southern Frontier aforementioned Mr. Oglethorpe was continually sending for Mrs. Bosomworth on all Affairs of Consequence with the Indians which expos'd her to many Dangers and Hardships the distance being Great & the Convenience for Passage being only in an open Boat, her own Affairs and Improvements on her land neglected & running to ruin, being left Intirely to the Management of Servants for Months at a Time. That in the Spring 1739/40 Mrs. Bosomworth had a Large Stock of Cattle at her Cowpen on Savannah River, but General Oglethorpe hearing that her Cowpen Keeper was a very Good Woodsman, in the absence of Mrs. Bosomworth at the Alatamaha Settlement, without her Consent or Knowledge, sent orders to the said Cowpen keeper to go directly as a Guide to a Troop of Rangers who were sent by Land to the Siege of St. Augustine which Orders he durst not to disobey, though sensible of the Loss would be to Mrs. Bosomworth's Interest, and, as it happen'd the Loss of his own Life; he being kill'd in that Expedition, by which means all Mrs. Bosomworth's Affairs at Savannah, Stock of Cattle, Improvements etc., which were very Considerable, went intirely to ruin, for which Losses no Satisfaction ever was made, although Constantly & solemnly Promissed her.

In the year 1742 Mrs. Bosomworth's then Husband, Captain Matthews, being taken sick at her settlement on the Alatamaha she was obliged to bring him from thence (On occasion of proper sustenance and Advice) to Savannah where he soon after died. Her Affairs on account of his Death demanding her stay in Savannah for some Time, The Indians at the Alatamaha were very uneasy and

Disgusted that she did not return, and on that Account left the place. The small Garrison that were there being in great want of Provisions & ammunition, a Party of Yamaseé, or Spanish Indians came upon them, and after committing several Barbarous Murthers, totally burnt and destroy'd the settlement and all Mrs. Bosomworth's Effects became a prey to the Enemy. . . .

That when General Oglethorpe was call'd home in the year 1743, He sent for Mrs. Bosomworth and then paid her 180 pounds in sola Bills which with a 20 pound Bill before receiv'd made 200 pounds on delivering her these Bills. He Gave her a Diamond Ring from his finger with Acknowledgement that he would never forget the service she had done him and the Public, and that the sum he then paid her was not intended for more than a years service, and he hop'd she would be pleas'd kindly to accept of it as all then in his Power to pay her (the Credit of his Bills being stop't in England) repeatedly Assuring her at Parting, that as soon as his Accounts were audited and paid by the Government she might draw upon him for 2000 pounds Sterling and he would Honour these Bills. This 200 pounds above mention'd is the sum total Mrs. Bosomworth ever receiv'd of Mr. Oglethorpe or any other Commanding Officer in the Province ever paid Her for all personal Services, her Interest with the Indians so frequently and with unabating ardour manifested, Salary as Interpretess (In which Capacity she was always Imploy'd by every Kings Commanding Officer in the Province) and all the various Losses sustain'd in her own private Affairs, and by neglect thereof on his Majesty's Service, which Losses, Expences, & Damages, in the Premises, moderately Computed have Annually, from the first Settlement of this Colony amounted to the Sum of two hundred Pounds sterling besides the Large Expences of two Voyages to England. . . .

Thomas Bosomworth

Savannah
23 July 1759.[3]

Views of an Indian Agent

Born in North Carolina in 1754, Benjamin Hawkins attended college at Princeton, served in the Continental Congress, and from 1790 to 1795 held one of North Carolina's seats in the U.S. Senate. In 1796 President Washington appointed him as Indian agent for all the territory south of the Ohio River. In time his responsibilities were reduced to working with the Creeks, among whom he lived until his death in 1816. A large part of Hawkins's job was to "civilize" the Indians by introducing them to the practices and customs of white Americans. The excerpts that follow come from his "Sketch of the Creek Country, in the Years 1798 and 1799." By then he was already forcing irrevocable changes in the native culture.

The towns on Chat-to-ho-che, generally called the Lower Creeks.

Cus-se-tuh[4] . . . The people of Cussetuh associate, more than any other Indians, with their white neighbors, and without obtaining any advantage from it; they know not the season for planting, or if they do, they never avail themselves of what they know, as they always plant a month too late.

This town with its villages is the largest in the Lower Creeks; the people are and have been friendly to white people, and are fond of visiting them; the old chiefs are very orderly men and much occupied in governing their young men, who are rude and disorderly, in proportion to the intercourse they have had with white people;[5] they frequently complain of the intercourse of their young people with the white people on the frontiers, as being very prejudicial to their morals; that they are more rude, more inclined to be tricky, and more difficult to govern, than those who do not associate with them. . . .

Au-put-tau-e; a village of Cussetuh, twenty miles from the river, on Hat-che thul-co; they have good fences, and the settlers under the best characters of any among the Lower Creeks. . . . At this village, and at the house of Tus-se-ki-ah Micco [a chief], the agent for Indian affairs [Hawkins] has introduced the plough; and a farmer was hired in 1797, to tend a crop of corn, and with so good success, as to induce several of the villagers to prepare their fields for the plough.[6] Some of them have cattle, hogs and horses, and are attentive to them. The range is a good one, but cattle and horses require salt; they have some thriving peach trees, at several of the settlements.

On Ouhe-gee creek, called at its junction with the river, Hitchetee, there is one settlement which deserves a place here. It belongs to Mic-co thluc-co, called by the white people, the "bird tail king." The plantation is on the right side of the creek, on good land, in the neighborhood of pine forest; the creek is a fine flowing one, margined with reed; the plantation is well fenced, and cultivated with the plough; this chief had been on a visit to New York, and seen much of the ways of white people, and the advantages of the plough over the slow and laborious hand hoe. Yet he had not firmness enough, till this year, to break through the old habits of the Indians. The agent paid him a visit this spring, 1799, with a plough completely fixed, and spent a day with him and showed him how to use it. He had previously, while the old man was in the woods, prevailed on the family to clear the fields for the plough. It has been used with effect, and much to the approbation of a numerous family, who have more than doubled their crop of corn and potatoes; and who begin to know how to turn their corn to account, by giving it to their hogs. This Micco and his family have hogs, cattle and horses, and begin to be very attentive to them; he has some apple and peach trees, and grape vines, a present from the agent. . . .

Government.

The Creeks never had, till this year, a national government and law. Every thing of a general tendency, was left to the care and management of the public agents, who heretofore used temporary expedients only; and amongst the most powerful and persuasive, was the pressure of fear from without, and *presents*. The attempt, in the course of the last and present year, to establish a national council, to meet annually, and to make general regulations for the welfare of the nation, promises to succeed. The law passed at the first meeting, to punish thieves and mischief-makers, has been carried into effect, in a few instances, where the personal influence of the agent for Indian affairs, was greatly exerted. On a trying occasion, the chiefs were called on to turn out the warriors, and to punish the leaders of the banditti, who insulted the commissioners of Spain and the United States, on the 17th of September. After this was repeatedly urged, and the agent agreed to be responsible for all the consequences, the chiefs turned out the warriors, and executed the law on the leader and a few of his associates, in an exemplary manner. While this transaction was fresh in the minds of the Indians, the agent for Indian affairs convened the national council, and made a report on the state of the nation to them, accompanied with his opinion of the plan indispensably necessary, to carry the laws of the nation into effect.

The council, after mature deliberation, determined that the safety of the nation was at stake; that having a firm reliance on the justice of the President of the United States, and the friendly attention of his agent for Indian affairs, they would adopt this plan. . . .

Government of the Towns.

The towns, separately, have a government and customs, which they derive from a high source. They have their public buildings, as well for business as pleasure; every town has a chief who presides over the whole; he is their *Mic-co*. . . .The Mic-co of the town superintends all public and domestic concerns; receives all public characters; hears their talks; lays them before the town, and delivers the talks of his town. The Mic-co of a town is always chosen from some one family. The Mic-co of Tuck-au-bat-che is of the eagle tribe, (Lum-ul-gee.) After he is chosen and put on his seat, he remains for life. On his death, if his nephews are fit for the office, one of them takes his place as his successor; if they are unfit, one is chosen of the next of kin, the descent always in the female line. . . .

Marriage.[7]

A man who wants a wife never applies in person; he sends his sister, his mother, or some other female relation, to the female relations of the woman he names. They consult the brothers and uncles on the maternal side, and sometimes the father; but this is a compliment only, as his approbation or opposition is of no avail. If the party applied to, approve of the match, they answer accordingly, to the woman who made the application. The bridegroom then gets together a blanket, and such other articles of clothing as he is able to do, and sends them by the women to the females of the family of the bride. If they accept of them the match is made; and the man may then go to her house as soon as he chooses. And when he has built a house, made his crop and gathered it in, then made his hunt and brought home the meat, and put all this in the possesion of his wife, the ceremony ends, and they are married; or as they express it, the woman is bound. From this first going to the house of the woman, till the ceremony ends, he is completely in possession of her.

This law has been understood differently, by some hasty cuckolds, who insist, that when they have assisted the woman to plant her crop, the ceremony ends, and the woman is bound. A man never marries in his own tribe.

Divorce.

This is at the choice of either of the parties. . . . Marriage gives no right to the husband over the property of his wife; and when they part she keeps the children and property belonging to them. . . .[8]

NOTES

1. All myths included in this chapter come from James Mooney, *Myths of the Cherokee* (Washington, D.C.: Government Printing Office, 1900), 239–40, 248–52.

2. Rodney M. Baine, "The Myths of Mary Musgrove," *Georgia Historical Quarterly* 76 (Summer 1992): 428–35.

3. The full documentation on the Bosomworth case can be found in Kenneth Coleman and Milton Ready, eds., *Colonial Records of the State of Georgia*, vol. 28, part 1, *Original Papers of Governors Reynolds, Ellis, Wright and Others, 1757–1763* (Athens: University of Georgia Press, 1976), 253–63.

4. Hawkins identified Cussetuh as a Lower Creek town along the east bank of the Chattahoochee River below the Fall Line (Benjamin Hawkins, "A Sketch of the Creek Country in the Years 1798 and 1799," *Collections of the Georgia Historical Society*, vol. 3, part 1 [Savannah: Georgia Historical Society, 1848; reprint, Spartanburg, S.C.: Reprint Company, 1974], 57.). The site is now part of Fort Benning Military Reservation. For a description and map of the location, see Mark E. Fretwell, *This So Remote Frontier: The Chattahoochee Country of Alabama and Georgia* (Tallahassee: Rose Printing Co., 1980), 11, 89, 106. The Indians living along the Ocmulgee, Flint, and Chattahoochee Rivers (roughly from present Atlanta south) were termed "Lower Creeks." Those living in Alabama around the Coosa and Tallapoosa Rivers were the "Upper Creeks."

5. Hawkins claimed that the Creeks called white Americans *E-cun-nau-nux-ulgee*: people greedily grasping after the lands of the red men. In contrast, Hawkins maintained that the Creeks called him *Iste-chate-lige-osetate-chemis-te-chaugo*: the beloved man of the Four [Indian] Nations. Hawkins, "A Sketch of the Creek Country," 9–10.

6. Before the arrival of Europeans, Indians lacked horses, mules, or oxen. Consequently, traditional Indian agriculture was done without plows. Cultivation centered around a series of hills, prepared by the Indians, each about a foot in diameter and three or four feet apart. The women used simple hoes to weed the growing crops.

7. In a letter from Cusseta (November 25, 1797) Hawkins gave this description of Creek women: "They have a great propensity to be obscene in conversation, and they call every thing by its name, and if the concurrant testimony of the white husbands may be relied on, the women have much of the temper of the mule, except when they are amorous, and then they exhibit all the amiable and gentle qualities of the cat." Once, when approached with a marriage proposal by the mother of a prospective bride, Hawkins explained that he expected his wife always to support and obey him and to be "at all times pleasing and agreeable when in company with me or with those who visit at my house." He reported that the woman "could not be prevailed on to acquiesce in the conditions proposed. She would not consent that the woman and children should be under the direction of the father, and the negotiation ended there" (letter of February 16, 1797). Benjamin Hawkins, "Letters of Benjamin Hawkins, 1796–1806," *Collections of the Georgia Historical Society*, vol. 9 (Savannah: The Morning News, 1916; reprint, Spartanburg, S.C.: Reprint Company, 1974), 83–84, 256.

8. "A Sketch of the Creek Country," 59–60, 67–70, 73–74.

3

Trustees and Malcontents:

The Colonial Controversy over

Slavery and Georgia's Future

The Spanish maintained a presence in Guale until the 1680s, when Englishmen and Indians from South Carolina invaded. At the time the Carolinians were strong enough to expel the Spanish, but not strong enough to replace them; so Georgia became "the debatable land" for half a century, with the English, French, and Spanish casting covetous eyes on the area. Ultimately, an English humanitarian named James Edward Oglethorpe ended the debate. A soldier of fortune and member of Parliament, Oglethorpe joined in 1732 with twenty friends and associates to receive from King George II a charter for a new colony. Georgia's initial purpose was spelled out in the opening lines of that document:

George the Second, by the Grace of God, To all To whom these Presents shall come: Greeting. Whereas wee are Credibly Informed that many of our Poor

Subjects are, through misfortunes and want of Employment, reduced to great necessities insomuch as by their labour they are not able to provide a maintenance for themselves and Families and, if they had means to defray the Charge of Passage and other Expenses incident to new Settlements, they would be Glad to be Settled in any of our Provinces in America, whereby Cultivating the lands at present vast and desolate, they might not only gain a Comfortable Subsistence for themselves and families, but also Strengthen our Colonies and Encrease the trade, Navigation, and wealth of these our Realms. And whereas our Provinces in North America have been frequently Ravaged by Indian Enemies, more especially that of South Carolina, which in the late war[1] by the neighboring Savages was laid wast with Fire and Sword and great numbers of English Inhabitants miserably Massacred, and our Loving Subjects who now Inhabit these by reason of the Smallness of their numbers will in case of any new war be Exposed to the like Calamities in as much as their whole Southern Frontier continueth unsettled and lieth open to the said Savages, and whereas wee think it highly becoming Our Crown and Royal Dignity to protect all our Loving Subjects. . . . Know yee therefore, that [the twenty-one individuals and their successors] shall be one Body Politick and Corporate, in Deed and in name, by the name of the Trustees for establishing the Colony of Georgia in America. . . .[2]

To carry out their mandate, the trustees granted fifty acres of land to persons settling in the New World at the colony's expense and as much as five hundred acres to those paying their own way and bringing at least ten white servants. The inhabitants, however, were denied the privilege of selling, leasing, or willing away their property to anyone but their eldest son. Having rescued the unfortunate from a life of poverty, the trustees felt justified in playing the role of loving father, leading irresponsible children not into temptation. If the people could not make easy profits from their land, neither could they lose it. Georgia was to be a place of hardworking small farmers, contentedly tending their own fields with no thought of the riches that might come to those who could buy and sell. Moreover, the beneficiaries of the trustees' largess were to defend the colony, providing a buffer for provinces to the north. Thus, for reasons of defense, farms needed to remain small and close together, with an arms-bearing man on each. To Oglethorpe and his companions, Georgia's military and humanitarian purposes dovetailed nicely.

Concerned that the colony remain true to its mission, Oglethorpe persuaded the trustees in 1735 to pass two laws that were highly unusual in the eighteenth century. One outlawed strong liquor, the other slavery. No other American colony had such laws. The preamble to the first law argued that rum and brandy made people sick and created problems with the Indians, frustrating the king's "good and fatherly Intentions" toward his subjects.

The exclusion of slavery was explained in the title: "an Act for rendering the Colony of Georgia more Defencible by Prohibiting the Importation and use of Black Slaves or Negroes in the same." The preamble went on to argue that the importation of slaves discouraged the migration of free whites who "alone can in case of a War be relyed on for the Defence and Security" of the settlement. Moreover, slaves were liable to rebel, especially in time of war, threatening a province with "utter Ruin." In the debates below, a number of additional anti-slavery arguments will be introduced. The Georgia founders were concerned not only with defense, but with implanting a strong work ethic in the settlers. They thought that Georgia would be best served by a class of virtuous, diligent white yeomen.

It did not take the inhabitants long to express their distaste for policies of well-meaning but poorly informed paternalists, trying to govern from three thousand miles away. Whatever their background, the people sensed limitless opportunities in a sparsely populated country. Only needless restrictions seemed to stand in their path to wealth. Bitter complaints soon assaulted the trustees' ears as the "clamorous malcontents" expressed their disapproval. At the same time, other Georgians petitioned their leaders not to deviate from the course. As the documents below reveal, the sharpest debate took place over slavery.

The Argument for Slavery

The first document is regarded by some as a classic of colonial protest literature. *A True and Historical Narrative of the Colony of Georgia in America* is a vehement indictment of Oglethorpe and others in positions of authority. The principal author, Patrick Talifer, migrated from Scotland in 1734, receiving a land grant of five hundred acres. The property was too far from Savannah, however, and he chose instead to practice medicine in town. According to Trevor Reese, Talifer became a highly respected physician and surgeon.[3] He added to his influence by marrying the sister of Robert Williams, one of Savannah's leading merchants. The coauthors of *A True and Historical Narrative* were also prominent. David Douglass was a merchant, and Hugh Anderson was inspector of Savannah's public garden. The leading malcontents were educated, influential men.

During his Georgia sojourn, Talifer helped organize the Scots Club, an organization composed primarily of Lowland Scots, which publicly and vigorously denounced trustee policies, viewing them as impractical for a military outpost and a hindrance to economic development. The Savannah physician remained in the province for only a few years, moving in 1740 to Charles Town. There Talifer, Anderson, and Douglass produced in 1741 the book for which they are famous. *A True and Historical Narrative* is a general critique of the entire plan of the trustees. The part reprinted below specifically addresses the economic and "medical" need for slavery.

But at Mr. *Oglethorpe's* going to England, the growing Fame of the Colony was thereby greatly increased, so that, as it has been before observed, People in abundance from all Parts of the World flock'd to *Georgia*. Then they began to consider, and endeavour, every one according to his Genius or Abilities, how they might best subsist themselves: Some, with great Labour and Expence, essayed the *making of Tar*: This, as it is well known to the Trustees, never quitted Costs: Others tried to make *Plank* and *Saw-Boards*; which, by the great Price they were obliged to sell them at, by reason of the great Expence of white Servants, was the chief Means of ruining those who thought to procure a Living by their Buildings in Town; for Boards of all kinds could always be bought in *Carolina* for half the Price that they were able to sell them at; but few were capable to commission them from thence, and those who were so were prevented from doing it, upon Pretence of discouraging the Labour of white People in *Georgia*. Those who had Numbers of Servants and Tracts of Land in the Country, went upon the *Planting of Corn, Pease, Potatoes*, etc. and the Charge of these who succeeded the best, so far exceeded the Value of the Produce, that it would have saved *three Fourths* to have bought all from the *Carolina Market*. The *Felling of Timber* was a Task very unequal to the Strength and Constitution of White Servants, and the *Hoeing the Ground*, they being exposed to the sultry Heat of the Sun, insupportable; and it is well known, that this Labour is one of the hardest upon the Negroes, even though their Constitutions are much stronger than white People, and the Heat no way disagreeable nor hurtful to them; but in us it created *inflammatory Fevers* of various kinds both *continued* and *intermittent, wasting* and *tormenting Fluxes*, most *excruciating Cholicks*, and *Dry Belly-Achs; Tremors, Vertigoes, Palsies*, and a long Train of *painful* and *lingering nervous Distempers*; which brought on to many a Cessation both from Work and Life; especially as *Water* without any Qualification was the chief Drink, and *Salt Meat* the only Provisions that could be had or afforded: And so general were those Disorders, that during the hot Season, which lasts from *March* to *October*, hardly one half of the Servants and working People were ever able to do their Masters or themselves the least Service; and the yearly Sickness of each Servant, generally speaking, cost his Master as much as would have maintained a Negroe for *four* Years. These things were represented to the Trustees in Summer 1735, in a Petition for the Use of Negroes, signed by about Seventeen of the better sort of People in *Savannah*: In this Petition there was also set forth the great Disproportion betwixt the Maintenance and Cloathing of white Servants and Negroes. This Petition was carried to *England* and presented to the Trustees by *Mr. Hugh Stirling*, an experienced Planter in the Colony; but no Regard was had to it, or to what he could say, and great Resentment was even shewn to *Mr. Thompson*, the Master of the Vessel in which it went. . . .[4]

🬔 🬔 🬔

The Trustees' Response

The trustees acutely resented the malcontents and the threats they posed to the original plan for Georgia. Benjamin Martyn, the board's secretary, became the Trustees' spokesman, relying on Oglethorpe and other provincial correspondents for the data contained in his *An Account Shewing the Progress of the Colony of Georgia in America From Its First Establishment.* His antislavery argument is printed below.

The trustees were induced to prohibit the Use of Negroes within *Georgia;* the Intention of his Majesty's Charter being to provide for poor People incapable of subsisting themselves at home, and to settle a Frontier for *South Carolina*, which was much exposed by the small Number of its white Inhabitants. It was impossible that the Poor, who should be sent from hence, and the Foreign persecuted Protestants, who must go in a manner naked into the Colony, could be able to purchase or subsist them, if they had them; and it would be Charge too great for the Trustees to undertake; and they would be thereby disabled from sending white People. The first Cost would pay the Passage over, provide Tools and other Necessaries, and defray the Charge of Subsistence of a white Man for a Year; in which Time it might be hoped that the Planter's own Labour would gain him some Subsistence; consequently the Purchase money of every Negro, (abstracting the Expence of subsisting him, as well as his Master) by being applied that way, would prevent the sending over a white Man, who would be of Security to the Province; whereas the Negro would render that Security precarious.

It was thought, that the white Man, by having a Negro Slave, would be less disposed to labour himself; and that this whole Time must be employed in keeping the Negro to Work, and in watching against any Danger he or his Family might apprehend from the Slave; and that the Planter's Wife and Children would by the Death, or even the Absence of the Planter, be in a manner at the Mercy of the Negro.

It was also apprehended, that the *Spaniards* at *St. Augustine* would be continually inticing away the Negroes, or encouraging them to Insurrections; that the first might easily be accomplished, since a single Negro could run away thither without Companions and would only have a River or two to swim over; and this Opinion has been confirmed and justified by the Practices of the *Spaniards*, even in Time of Profound Peace, amongst the Negroes in *South Carolina*; where, tho' at a greater Distance from *Augustine*, some have fled in Perriaguas and little Boats to the *Spaniards*, and been protected, and others in large Bodies have been incited to Insurrections, to the great Terror, and even endangering the Loss of that Province; which, though it has been established above Seventy Years, has scarce white People enough to secure her against her own Slaves.

It was also considered, that the Produces designed to be raised in the Colony would not require such Labour as to make Negroes necessary for carrying them on; for the Province of Carolina produces chiefly Rice, which is a Work of Hardship proper for Negroes; whereas the Silk and other Produces which the Trustees proposed to have the people employed on in *Georgia*, were such as Women and Children might be of as much Use in as Negroes.

It was likewise apprehended, that if the Persons who should go over to Georgia at their own Expence, should be permitted the Use of Negroes, it would dispirit and ruin the poor Planters who could not get them, and who by their Numbers were designed to be the Strength of the Province; it would make them clamorous to have Negroes given them; and on the Refusal, would drive them from the Province, or at least make them negligent of their Plantations; where they would be unwilling, nay would certainly disdain to work like Negroes; and would rather let themselves out to the wealthy Planters as Overseers of their Negroes.

It was further thought, That upon the Admission of Negroes the wealthy Planters would, as in all other Colonies, be more induced to absent themselves, and live in other Places, leaving the Care of their Plantations and their Negroes to Overseers.

It was likewise thought, that the poor Planter sent on Charity from his Desire to have Negroes, as well as the Planter who should settle at his own Expence, would (if he had Leave to alienate) mortgage his Land to the Negro Merchant for them, or at least become a Debtor for the Purchase of such Negroes; and under these Weights and Discouragements would be induced to sell his Slaves again upon any Necessity, and would leave the Province and his Lot to the Negro Merchant; in Consequences of which, all the small Properties would be swallowed up, as they have been in other Places, by the more wealthy Planters.

It was likewise considered, that the admitting of Negroes in *Georgia* would naturally facilitate the Desertion of the *Carolina* Negroes, thro' the Province of *Georgia*; and consequently this Colony, instead of proving a Frontier, and adding a Strength to the Province of *South Carolina*, would be a Means of drawing off the Slaves of *Carolina*, and adding thereby a Strength to *Augustine*.

From these several Considerations, as the Producers to be raised in the Colony did not make Negro Slaves necessary, as the Introduction of them so near to a Garison of the *Spaniards* would weaken rather than strengthen the Barrier, and as they would introduce with them a greater Propensity to Idleness among the poor Planters, and too great an Inequality among the People, it was thought proper to make the Prohibition of them a Fundamental of the Constitution. . . .[5]

The Son of a Prominent Official Calls for Slavery

Thomas Stephens was in his late twenties in 1737 when he came to Georgia as assistant to his father, William. The senior Stephens was the newly appointed secretary for the colony, sent over by the trustees when Oglethorpe failed to keep them adequately informed. The father steadfastly supported the policies of the Trust and eventually rose to the presidency of the colony. To William's chagrin, young Thomas became a major voice for the malcontents.

Returning to England in 1739, Thomas served as a lobbyist in Parliament, a body the trustees needed for financial support. Stephens received on one occasion a public reprimand in the House of Commons for making false and malicious charges against the trustees. Nonetheless, he seems to have prevailed in the long run in convincing the Trust that their cause was hopeless. According to Betty Wood, as long as the debate over slavery was merely between trustees and unhappy settlers, the former felt free to do as they pleased. Once Parliament became interested in the issue the trustees found themselves fighting a losing battle to show that their policies were in the national interest.[6] Part of Stephens's effort was the publication of *The Hard Case of the Distressed People of Georgia* (1742), from which the following passages are taken.

Besides these Discouragements in the Nature of the Tenures, and the Planter expending his Time, Money and Labour, on Lands, which, in a Course of Years, must revert to the Trust, he is even excluded from the necessary Means of raising a present Sufficiency of any kind of Produce for his Subsistence. The Use and Labour of Negroes has been found indispensably requisite for the Climate and Cultivation of Lands in *America*; and if in a Point of publick Utility so much contested, it may be allowed to produce in its Favour an Authority, which it is presumed none will object to, General *Oglethorpe*, a Gentleman of the Trust, (and one, who to all Appearances was as obstinately prejudiced against Negroes as any Man could be) is offer'd; who, 'tis plain, is now become reconciled to their Usefulness, as he keeps a Number of them on his Plantation, bordering on *Georgia*.[7]

And indeed the extraordinary Heats here, the extraordinary Difficulty and Danger there is in clearing the Lands, attending and Manufacturing the Crops, working in the Fields of Summer, and the *poor Returns of Indian Corn*, Pease, and Potatoes, which are as yet the only Chief Produces of the Land there, make it indisputably impossible for White Men alone to carry on Planting to any good Purpose. Besides, our Neighbours having such an Advantage, as the Privilege of Negroes, can always under-sell us in any Manufacture or Produce, which they are as well qualified for as we, should we ever be able to raise more than is necessary for home Consumption without them. The poor People of *Georgia*, may as well think of becoming Negroes themselves (from whose Condition at present they seem not to be far removed) as of hoping to be ever able to live without them; and they ought best to know, and most to be believed, who have made the Experiment.

'Tis objected, indeed, that the Introduction of Negroes might destroy the Colony; this, as it has never been tried, is but an idle Insinuation. That the Colony is already ruined is certain and evident; and it can't be said, that the Introduction of Negroes has brought this about. Besides, they were never intended to be admitted, but under such Limitations as the *Safety*, as well as the *Improvement* of the Colony, would be equally consulted and provided for.

'Tis said also, that Negroes being so near St. *Augustin* would desert thither. If they are as well and better treated in *Georgia* than they can be there, where is the Temptation? besides, their Desertion can affect but a few Individuals out of the Whole, except we admit it to be total; and their Labour is of general Use. Moreover, have we not a Land Army, Forts and Marines, and may not they be as honestly and usefully employed hereafter in *hunting* and *running down* fugitive Negroes, as they are now the distress'd *Georgians*, flying for Bread and Liberty to other Countries? May not these Troops also be of as important Service hereafter, as they have hitherto been judg'd, in defending Towns, etc. without Inhabitants, and protecting a People who have no Properties? Besides, it can be proved, that for every Negroe that has run away from *Augusta* in *Georgia*, or the Parts of *Carolina* bordering thereon (which are one hundred Miles distant from any Settlement on the Coast) that five to one white Servants have deserted their Masters, and even fled to *Augustin*, from the *meagre Hunger* and *frightful Oppressions*, which stared them in the Face in *Georgia*.

It is also presumed, that the admitting and substituting Negroes to the laborious Parts of Culture, etc., would make the white Men grow idle and lazy. It has been already shewn, that white Men are unequal to the Task, and yet it must be done. If, therefore, others may be found much fitter and abler for this Work, and who besides doing it better, shall save a Man all the Trouble, and put Money into his Pocket, is this a criminal or unreasonable Piece of Luxury? And as the Labours of the Field here supply but a small Share of that Variety and Stock, which goes to answer the common necessary Demands, may not white Men be still industrious, and to better Purpose, each Man furnishing that Part for which he is best qualified? Moreover, as the principal Springs to that Industry (which the Trustees so much contend for) besides Necessity, seem to be the *Possibility* of raising those Commodities which are necessary for Life, much cheaper and better at home; the Labour and Money therein employed, being thus turned to better Account, and the Assurance of Men enjoying themselves what they get, or of leaving it to their Children; has not this Government, in the very Foundation of it, entirely relaxed or broke off those Springs in every Motion? The only Difference between an industrious Man in their Sense, and an idle Man hitherto, has been that the former has taken the shortest Way to be ruined, and the latter may possibly hold out till he is put in a better.

It is lastly said, That this Colony, by the Numbers of white Men alone who should inhabit it, was design's to be the Barrier and Strength to the Northern Provinces in America, whose Safety was apprehended, from their Negroes. It were better, indeed, that it could be so established; but besides the Confirmations of an Experiment already made, it may be asserted, that there is no visible Way of doing it, but by making it a Garrison, and taking every Landholder, etc. into Pay; which could not be made effectual neither, for a much greater Sum every Year than has been given to the Trustees hitherto. . . .[8]

☙ ☙ ☙

The Human Rights Issue

The final two documents are an extraordinary petition to the trustees from the Scottish Presbyterians at Darien (originally named New Inverness) and a letter to his fellow board members penned by Oglethorpe while he was stationed at Frederica. The initial antislavery legislation and Benjamin Martyn's *Account* had argued against slavery as something bad for the white settlers and their defense. The Highlanders and Oglethorpe raised for the first time in Georgia the human rights issue, viewing slavery as something harmful to Africans and, therefore, morally wrong. Such arguments were rare anywhere in the early eighteenth century. For them to come from military outposts in the empire's backwaters was remarkable. Below is the Highlanders' petition, followed by an Oglethorpe letter.

"The Petition of the Inhabitants of New Inverness"

We are informed, that our neighbors of Savannah have petitioned your Excellency for the Liberty of having Slaves. We hope, and earnestly intreat, that before such Proposals are hearkened unto, your Excellency will consider our Situation, and of what dangerous and bad Consequence such Liberty would be of to us, for many Reasons;

I. The Nearness of the *Spaniard*, who have proclaimed Freedom to all Slaves who run away from their Masters, makes it impossible for us to keep them without more Labour in guarding them, than what we would be at to do their Work.

II. We are laborious, and know a White Man may be by the Year more usefully employed than a Negro.

III. We are not rich, and becoming Debtors for Slaves, in case of their running away or dying, would inevitably ruin the poor Master, and he become a greater Slave to the Negro Merchant, than the Slave he bought could be to him.

IV. It would oblige us to keep a Guard-duty at least as severe as when we expected a daily Invasion; and if that was the Case, how miserable would it be to us, and our Wives and Families, to have an Enemy without, and more dangerous ones in our Bosom!

V. It's shocking to human Nature, that any Race of Mankind, and their Posterity, should be sentenced to perpetual Slavery; nor in Justice can we think otherwise of it, than that they are thrown amongst us to be our Scourge one Day or other for our Sins; and as Freedom to them must be as dear as to us, what a scene of Horror must it bring about! And the longer it is unexecuted, the bloody Scene must be the greater. We therefore, for our own sakes, our Wives and Children, and our Posterity, beg your Consideration, and intreat, that instead of introducing Slaves, you'll put us in the way to get us some of our Countrymen, who with their Labour in time of Peace, and our Vigilance, if we are invaded, with the Help of those, will render it a difficult thing to hurt us, or that Part of the Province we possess. We will for ever pray for your Excellency, and are, with all Submission,

> New Inverness, 3d
> January 1738–9.   Your Excellency's most
> obliged humble Servants,
> [eighteen signatures] [9]

General Oglethorpe's Georgia

> Saint Simon's
> January 17, 1739

Gentlemen:

I have wrote already a letter upon the head of Negroes and shall only add that if we allow slaves we act against the very principles by which we associated together, which was to relieve the distressed. Whereas, now we should occasion the misery of thousands in Africa, by setting men upon using arts to buy and bring into perpetual slavery the poor people who now live free there.

Instead of strengthening we should weaken the frontiers of America, give away to the owners of slaves that land which was designed as a refuge to persecuted Protestants, prevent all improvement of silk and wine and glut the markets with more of the present American commodities which do already but too much interfere with English produce. I am persuaded therefore you will speedily reject the petition. And as soon as your resolution is known, the idle will leave the province and the industrious will fall to work, many of whom wait 'till they see the event of this application. . . . [10]

Conclusion

Despite the impassioned pleas of Oglethorpe and his supporters, Georgia's original blueprint was abandoned. The colony's unique legislation disappeared bit by bit, as the land rules and rum prohibition were lifted. By 1750 slavery had been made legal, and two years later the trustees gave up their charter. In the next quarter century Georgia became increasingly aristocratic, as large rice plantations developed along the coast and the sea islands. By 1776 an estimated half the population consisted of slaves.

Historian Betty Wood has described a colonial system that was extremely harsh.[11] Punishment of crimes committed by slaves was carried out in a manner that would "deter others from Offending in like manner." Consequently, the penalty for murder or robbery was often death by a public hanging or burning. Hangings were frequently followed by decapitation, with the head displayed on a pole for other bondsmen to see. For noncapital crimes public whippings were the preferred method of discipline. Except for the disappearance of burnings, punishments in the twenty years after the Revolution remained as barbaric as those before. The peculiar institution thus began its fateful career, lasting until the conquest of the state by an invading army a little over a century after Georgians rejected Oglethorpe's alternative.

NOTES

1. The Yamassee War, 1715.

2. Albert B. Saye, ed., *Georgia's Charter of 1732* (Athens: University of Georgia Press, 1942), 19–21. [Punctuation added].

3. Trevor R. Reese, ed., *The Clamorous Malcontents: Criticisms and Defenses of the Colony of Georgia, 1741–1743* (Savannah: The Beehive Press, 1973), viii–ix.

4. Ibid., 56–58.

5. Ibid., 190–92.

6. Betty Wood, *Slavery in Colonial Georgia, 1730–1775* (Athens: University of Georgia Press, 1984), 32.

7. Oglethorpe used slave labor on his plantation near Parachucla, South Carolina, some forty miles from Savannah. William Bacon Stevens, *A History of Georgia*, vol. 1 (New York: D. Appleton, 1847; reprint, Savannah: The Beehive Press, 1972), 288.

8. Reese, *Clamorous Malcontents*, 262–65.

9. Ibid., 249–50.

10. Mills Lane, ed., *General Oglethorpe's Georgia: Colonial Letters, 1733–1743*, vol. 2 (Savannah: The Beehive Press, 1975), 389.

11. Betty Wood, "'Until He Shall Be Dead, Dead, Dead': The Judicial Treatment of Slaves in Eighteenth-Century Georgia," *Georgia Historical Quarterly*, 71 (Fall 1987): 377–98.

4

Patriots and Loyalists: Georgia on the Eve of the Revolution

The baby of the Thirteen Colonies, Georgia had just begun to grow when the American provinces declared their independence from the mother country. Settled in 1733, Georgia spent two tumultuous decades under the Trust, then another twenty years of modest progress under royal government. The new regime of the 1750s not only permitted slavery but set in place a generous land policy, allowing family heads to claim headrights of one hundred acres for themselves and fifty additional acres for each family member, servant, or slave. The Governor in Council also occasionally sold at a bargain price an additional one thousand acres to those deemed able to use them. The new land laws contributed significantly to the growth of an aristocracy, but also attracted many small farmers. Between 1752 and 1776 the population expanded from well under four thousand to about forty thousand.

The colonial protest against English rule hardly existed before the conclusion in 1763 of the French and Indian War. An imperialistic struggle, pitting Great Britain against France and Spain, the Great War for Empire, as it has sometimes been called, drove the Spanish from Florida and the French from Canada and the trans-Appalachian West. The British, who absorbed all this territory, found their attention focused on America as never before. To keep troops and officials in the New World to govern their expanded domain, Parliament looked to the colonists for new sources of revenue. Unfortunately, the British failed to ask the provinces if they minded being taxed. The question of taxation without representation thus became one of several constitutional issues raised by discontented Americans, struggling to protect their rights as Englishmen.

For a variety of reasons, Georgians were less rebellious than colonists elsewhere. With most of the province held by Indians, the whites regarded British troops as protectors rather than potential oppressors. Even under royal rule, Parliament continued to appropriate funds for Georgia's benefit. The last of the royal governors, James Wright, was widely respected, gaining the people's gratitude by negotiating large tracts of land away from the Creeks and Cherokees and keeping South Carolina from claiming the coastal areas south of the Altamaha. Consequently, Georgia perhaps had little reason to complain.

A protest movement, nonetheless, existed in Georgia from the time of the Stamp Act crisis in 1765–66, when for the first time the Sons of Liberty took to the streets of Savannah. The Commons House of Assembly, Georgia's lower house, joined the other provinces in petitioning Parliament to repeal the measure. Governor Wright managed throughout the controversy to maintain law and order, becoming the only governor actually to collect stamp taxes. Parliament in 1766 backed down, keeping only the principle that they could legislate for the Americans in all matters.

For almost a decade after the Stamp Act upheaval, Governor Wright managed to work with the colonists in most cases. Life never returned entirely to normal, however, as one issue after another shattered the domestic tranquility. One of the last controversies began in 1773 when Parliament passed the Tea Act, designed to help the British East India Company. This measure would actually have reduced the price of tea by allowing the company to bypass middlemen in England and America, selling the drink directly through its own agents. Nevertheless, the cheaper tea still carried a tax, the last of the Townshend duties placed on American imports.

Imagining a British plot to deprive them of liberty, the American radicals took to the streets in several port cities, preventing any shipments from being unloaded. In Boston the famous "tea party" was held in which the Sons of Liberty dumped the tea in the harbor. The response from England was swift, as Parliament adopted a series of measures labeled by the Americans as the Intolerable Acts. The port of Boston was closed until the destroyed property was paid for. Troops moved from a fort in the harbor back into the city. Town meetings in Massachusetts were eliminated except for the purpose of electing representatives to the legislature. The trials of soldiers accused of crimes in the line of duty could be moved outside the colony where the crime was committed. Boston, in reality, became an occupied city.

Twelve of the thirteen colonies gathered in Philadelphia in 1774 to protest the Intolerable Acts and impose an import embargo on products from Great Britain. Due to disorganization and Indian problems at home, Georgia was the only colony not in attendance. Even in Georgia, however, a heated debate raged, as witnessed by the province's newspaper, the *Georgia Gazette*. Produced by a Scotsman named James Johnson, the paper was somewhat compromised by the subsidies it received from the government as the official printer. Johnson, nonetheless, possessed a desire to report both sides of issues and thus devoted space to the opinions of both patriots and Tories.

The first document is a letter to the editor by "Mercurius," arguing the side of Georgia's Tories. It is followed by a response from "A Freeholder." While both authors remained anonymous, "A Freeholder" was possibly John J. Zubly, the pastor of the Independent Presbyterian Church in Savannah. That, at least, is the conclusion of Marjorie Louise Daniel in her Ph. D. dissertation, "The Revolutionary Movement in Georgia, 1763–1777."[1] A pamphleteer in behalf of colonial rights, Zubly served as a delegate to the Second Continental Congress. His zeal for the American cause, however, stopped short of revolution, and the unhappy minister remained loyal to Britain when the war came. He died in Savannah in 1781, while a conflict he opposed raged throughout the land.

For the identity of "Mercurius," the editor is indebted to Gloria Murphy Graham, a student in his Georgia history class at Kennesaw State College. While engaged in genealogical research, Ms. Graham and her husband, Samuel, discovered that the Library of Congress possessed a transcription of a memorial of Haddon Smith, the Anglican priest at Christ Church in Savannah.[2] A Loyalist, forced to escape from Georgia to avoid tarring and feathering, Smith on April 4, 1776, petitioned the Bishop of London for financial relief. In that memorial he identified himself as "Mercurius" and argued that his suffering had resulted from his defense of the British cause. Thus, it would appear that the newspaper war was a battle of rival clergymen.

A Loyalist View

Georgia Gazette, August 10, 1774

It is said that Mercury held in his hand a golden wand, to shew the excellency of seasonable and friendly admonition. Never was admonition more necessary than at present. Whatever it may be in the *Northern Colonies*, it is undoubtedly extremely necessary to the Province of *Georgia*. We have an enemy at our backs, who but very lately put us into the utmost consternation. We fled at their approach; we left our property at their mercy; and we have implored the assistance of Great Britain to humble these haughty *Creeks*. And yet, no sooner is our panick a little subsided, but we insult our best and only friend, from whom alone we can expect protection. *Carolina*, it is certain, will give us none. And it is in vain to expect it from the Northern Provinces. In so precarious a situation as we are now in, it becomes us to be very cautious and circumspect in our conduct, not to enter rashly, and with precipitation, into measures, and form resolutions, before we are convinced of the propriety of them.

The author of the CASE STATED has not stated it as it really is. He says, *"The plain and single question is, whether the British Parliament have a right to levy what sums of money on the Americans they please, and in what manner they please."* But in this he is evidently mistaken. This question about *Taxation* is an old question; a question that has been upon the carpet ever since the *Stamp Act*; and has not the least connection with the present affair of the Bostonians [regarding the Tea Party and subsequent Intolerable Acts]. The arguments therefore upon the CASE STATED about *Taxation* are foreign to the present dispute: for the question is not now, whether the Parliament has a right to tax the Americans, *but whether the Americans have a right to destroy private property with impunity.*

That the *India Company* did send tea to Boston on their own account, is *undeniable*: that they had a *right* so to do, and to undersell the Merchants there (or rather the Smugglers) is quite undeniable. . . . Had the *Bostonians* any shadow of right to seize upon it, or to destroy it? Surely such an act . . . in the judgment of sober reason, be highly criminal, and worthy of exemplary punishment. . . .

[There follows a long defense of the Intolerable Acts.]

Since then nothing appears in the present affair of Boston, to affect our just rights and liberties, how unreasonable (not to say preposterous) it is to fly in the face of lawful authority. Our entering into resolutions against the Government, in the present case, can answer no end but to injure our infant province, by provoking the Mother Country to desert us. Great Britain is our only dependence:

If we deprive ourselves of that, we shall be as treacherous to our country as the daughter of *Nisas* to her father, who cut off his golden lock upon which the fortune of his Kingdom depended.

MERCURIUS

A Patriot Replies

The following is the conclusion to a letter appearing in the August 17, 1774, issue of the *Georgia Gazette*:

P.S. Mercury, we are told, *"held in his hand a golden wand to shew the excellency of seasonable and friendly admonition;"* but Dr. King informs us that this wand was wound about with two serpents, and his face half-black and half-bright, because he converses as well with infernal as celestial deities. The description our Georgian Mercury gives us of the consternation and flight of many in this province, among whom he includes himself, on a late Indian alarm, naturally made me recollect that Mercury has wings fixed to his hat and sides, and being curious to know what sort of a man he might have been, I met with this odd passage in a treatise of Dr. King aforesaid: He was a god much adored by shepherds, who thought he would preserve them from thieves, or at least help them to increase their flocks by stealing from other people.

Our own Mercurius saith, *"the question is not whether the Parliament has a right to tax the Americans;"* this question, in which he neither affirms nor denies is, "an old question, but all arguments about it are foreign to the present dispute:" And yet in Parliament it is said this is the ALL that lies at stake; fleets and armies are sent to enforce acts made for that purpose, and all America is in a ——— because they apprehend thus to have money raised on them for the purpose of a perpetual revenue is to reduce them to downright slavery. The Americans insist this is all that is in dispute, and Government will hardly thank or reward this writer for saying "the right of Parliament to tax the Americans is not now the question."

The question, according to him is, *"Whether the Americans have a right to destroy private property with impunity."* This question, which it must be owned, implies a very genteel compliment to the Americans in general, and may be taken as a decisive proof that the author is no American, nor a friend or acquaintance of such vile beings, I dare say every American will very readily answer: We no more think we have a right to destroy private property than we think you have a right to take our property from us without our consent; if you will determine the character of a whole people by an act of some individuals, perhaps yourselves may be the greatest sufferers by the comparison. What fair, candid, impartial reasoning, is this? A Boston mob has illegally destroyed some tea, and hence it is clear the Americans in general think private property may be destroyed with impunity. . . .

Admitting the destruction of the tea "to be highly criminal and worthy of exemplary punishment," what will be the consequence? Why that the offenders should be prosecuted and punished. But they were not known. Well, and was any reward offered by proclamation for their discovery? NO. What did the chief magistrate do, or what was he prevented from doing? Did any Military or Peace Officer interfere? Has the East-India Company been refused justice where the fact happened? NO. Did they ever even apply for it? NO. Did *they* make any application to Parliament? NO. But without any complaint from these supposed sufferers, without endeavoring to find out the offenders, without any hearing or time given for defense, the Town of Boston is blockaded, thousands utterly unconcerned in the matter complained of deprived of their property, their charter infringed, a military force sent among them, and laws previously made for the safety and protection of these soldiers if any murder should happen in enforcing these acts of revenue, and all this done with a profound intention to let the other provinces know that Great Britain "is roused and in earnest." . . .

From ideas of justice without a hearing, from punishments of supposed guilt without a trial by Peers, from the destruction of a whole province for the rashness of a few, from Judges that will not suffer the suspected to plead, and then compare the sufferers with men enduring torment because they will not put in a plea, — Good Lord deliver us. . . .

A FREEHOLDER

☙ ☙ ☙

The True Meaning of Liberty: Differing Views of Governor Wright and the Legislature

Georgia's colonial assembly consisted of two houses. The more radical was the Commons House of Assembly, whose members were required by law to possess at least five hundred acres of land, but who were elected by inhabitants owning as few as fifty acres. A fairly aristocratic body, the Commons House was at least chosen in a somewhat democratic fashion. The upper house, or Council, on the other hand, was appointed by the king and consisted of the wealthiest men in the colony. This group not only participated in the legislative process, but had administrative responsibilities as an advisory body to the governor.

Born in London in 1716, Georgia's last royal governor, James Wright, first came to America as a teenager, when his father was appointed chief justice of South Carolina. Young Wright returned to England for legal studies, but soon was back in Charleston, where he practiced law, held the post of attorney general, and became a wealthy planter. While serving briefly as South Carolina's agent to the mother country, he gained an appointment in 1760 as lieutenant governor of Georgia. The following year he was elevated to the gubernatorial post, following the resignation of Henry Ellis.

A strong and effective leader, he held that position through the troubled years when America and England grew increasingly apart. Always loyal to the king who had appointed him, Wright nonetheless identified strongly with his fellow Americans. By 1775 he was one of the richest planters of Georgia, with over five hundred slaves and about twenty-six thousand acres of land. In January 1776, one year after the address to the assembly reprinted below, the governor was arrested by the revolutionaries.

Breaking parole, he fled to England, where he stayed until the capture of Savannah by British troops in late 1778. Wright then returned for a final time, governing the parts of Georgia that the British could control. By July, 1782, the British pulled all soldiers out of their erstwhile colony, and Wright and other loyalists sailed away with them. Awarded an annual pension by the British government, Wright died in England in 1785, two years after the Anglo-American treaty recognizing American independence.

The passage that follows shows a politician of principle, who remained true to his definition of liberty, despite its rejection by many around him.

This day the General Assembly of this Province met here, when his Excellency, Sir James Wright, Baronet, Governor in Chief, &c., was pleased to deliver the following speech to both houses, viz:

Savannah, Geo.,

January 18, 1775
Honourable Gentlemen, Mr. Speaker, and Gentlemen of the Commons House of Assembly:
This being the first opportunity that has offered in General Assembly, I must not omit acquainting you that in consequence of the Petition of both Houses, his Majesty was graciously pleased to direct, that if this Province should be engaged

in any actual Indian war, we should have every proper succor and protection: and I was ordered to apply to the Commander-in-Chief of his Majesty's forces in America, for that purpose, who had received directions thereupon.

The alarming situation of American affairs at this juncture makes it highly necessary for me to say something to you on the subject; and it is with the utmost concern that I see by every account all the colonies to the northward of us, as far as Nova Scotia, in a general ferment; and some of them in such a state as makes me shudder when I think of the consequences which it is most probable will soon befall them. The unhappy disputes with the mother country are now become of the most serious nature, and I am much afraid the very extraordinary and violent measures adopted and pursued, will not only prevent a reconciliation but may involve all America in the most dreadful calamities.

Gentlemen, — I think myself very happy in having it in my power to say, that this Province is hitherto clear; and I much hope, by your prudent conduct, will remain so. Be not led away by the voices and opinions of men of overheated ideas; consider coolly and sensibly of the terrible consequences which may attend adopting resolutions and measures expressly contrary to law, and hostile to the mother country; especially at so late a season, when we may almost daily expect to hear the determination of Great Britain on the matters in dispute, and therefore, I conceive, can answer no purpose but that of throwing the Province into confusion: and I tremble at the apprehension of what may be the resolution and declarations of the new Parliament relative to the conduct of the people in some parts of America. You may be advocates for liberty, so am I; but in a constitutional and legal way. You, gentlemen, are legislators, and let me entreat you to take care how you give a sanction to trample on law and government; and be assured it is an indispensable truth, that where there is no law there can be no liberty. It is the due course of law. It is the due course of law and support of government which only can ensure to you the enjoyment of your lives, your liberty, and your estates; and do not catch at the shadow and lose the substance. I exhort you not to suffer yourselves to be drawn in to involve this Province in the distresses of those who may have offended; we are in a different situation, and on a very different footing from the other colonies. Do not consider me as speaking to you as the King's governor of this Province. As such, gentlemen, it is certainly my duty to support his Majesty's just right and authority, and preserve peace and good order within my government, and to contribute as much as possible towards the prosperity and happiness of the Province and people. Believe me, when I tell you I am at this time actuated by further motives than a show only of discharging my duty as the King's governor. I have lived amongst and presided over you upwards of fourteen years, and have other feelings. I have a real and affectionate regard for the people, and it grieves me that a Province that I have been so long in, and which I have seen nurtured by the Crown, at the least expense to the mother country, and grew up from mere infancy, from next to nothing, to a considerable degree of maturity and opulence, should, by the impudence and rashness of some inconsiderate people, be plunged into a state of distress and ruin. We have been most happy in, I hope, avoiding *Scylla*, and let me, in the strongest terms, conjure you to steer clear of *Charybdis*.

It is a most melancholy and disagreeable subject, and therefore I shall avoid making any observations on the resolutions adopted by the other colonies: but hope, through your prudence and regard for the welfare and happiness of this Province, of yourselves and your posterity, none will be entered into here. The strongest reasons operate against it, and as they must occur to every considerate person, I shall not mention any. . . .

On Friday, the 20th of January, the following Addresses were presented to his Excellency, viz.:—

To his Excellency, Sir James Wright, Baronet, Captain-General, Governor and Commander-in-Chief and over his Majesty's Province of Georgia, Chancellor and Vice-Admiral of the same.

The humble address of the Upper House of Assembly:—

May it please your Excellency,—We, his Majesty's most dutiful and loyal subjects, the Council of Georgia, in General Assembly met, beg leave to return your Excellency our most cordial thanks for your truly affectionate speech to both Houses of Assembly, at the opening of this session. We received with pleasure and gratitude the information you have been pleased to give us of the favorable reception the petition from both Houses met with from our most gracious Sovereign, and that his Majesty had been pleased to order troops for our protection, in case we had been unhappily engaged in an Indian War.

After having had the experience of your Excellency's prudent and equitable administration for upwards of fourteen years, we can have no doubt of your real and friendly concern for the true interest of this Province. The language of your Excellency's speech upon the subject, of the highest importance to the people of Georgia, is so truly paternal, that every unprejudiced person must be convinced of its being dictated by a heart warm with love and affection for the people over whom you preside: and we hope it will meet with that return of gratitude and attention which the affectionate spirit it breathes, and the great importance of the subject merits.

It is with the deepest concern we see the alarming lengths to which the present unhappy dispute between the mother country and the colonies is carried; lengths that threaten a dissolution of all good order and government, and of that union on which the happiness and prosperity of both countries depend.

But, whilst we lament these unhappy discussions, and disapprove of all violent and intemperate measures, and at the same time declare it to be our pride and glory to be constitutionally connected with Great Britain by the closest and most endearing ties and that we dread nothing more than a dissolution of those ties; yet, anxious for the present welfare of our country, and the interest of our posterity, our ardent wish is that his Majesty's American subjects may enjoy all the rights and privileges of British subjects, as fully and effectually, in all respects, as the inhabitants of Great Britain do; and to that end it now appears highly necessary that the constitutional rights of his American subjects may be clearly defined and firmly established, that so they may hold those inestimable blessings on such a footing as will unite the mother country and the colonies by a reciprocation of benefits, and on terms consistent with the spirit of the constitution, and the honor, dignity and safety of the whole empire. And we wish and hope to see a matter of such importance taken up in a constitutional way by both Houses of Assembly, not in the least doubting, but that if such prudent and temperate measures are adopted by the legislatures of other Provinces, we shall see them crowned with that success which may remove the unhappy division now subsisting, and bind us to our mother country by the tie of interest, love and gratitude, and establish the prosperity, power and grandeur of the British Empire, on foundations which may last till time shall be no more. Nor can we doubt of success, when we reflect that we are blessed with a King who glories in being the equal father of all his people; and therefore can and do submit our cause with full confidence to his royal wisdom and paternal goodness. Neither will we suppose that a British Parliament, that great and august body, who have so often generously asserted and defended the liberties of other nations, will disregard the equitable claims of their fellow-subjects.

We entirely agree with your Excellency in the opinion that where there is no law there can be no true liberty, and that it is the due and regular course of law and support of government which can alone ensure to us and our posterity the enjoyment of our lives, liberty and property.

We will cheerfully concur in the several matters recommended by your Excellency, and give them that serious attention which the utility of them requires.

By order of the House.

N. Jones.

(His Excellency's Answer.)

Honourable Gentlemen,—

The loyalty and affection expressed towards his Majesty, in this address, give me the greatest satisfaction, as it likewise does to see that your sentiments on the very important matters mentioned in many respects coincide with my own; and happy would it have been for America had the several legislatures proceeded in the manner you propose.

I return you my best thanks, gentlemen, for your kind opinion of my regard for, and wishes to serve this Province.

James Wright.

To His Excellency, Sir James Wright, Baronet, Captain-General, and Governor-in-Chief of his Majesty's Province of Georgia, Chancellor and Vice-Admiral of the same.

The address of the Commons House of Assembly: —

May it please your Excellency, — We, his Majesty's dutiful and most loyal subjects, the Commons of Georgia in General Assembly, return your Excellency our thanks for your speech to both Houses on the opening of this session.

We are greatly obliged to his Majesty for his gracious intentions: but allow us, sir, to observe, that we apprehended the Province was actually involved in a war, when we submitted our Petition for assistance; and, whilst we confess our real obligations to your Excellency for your conduct, assiduity, and perseverance, and render you our warmest acknowledgements for putting a happy end to that war, we cannot, but with horror, reflect on the dreadful crisis to which this Province must have been reduced, had we experienced no other resource than those dilatory succours which the administration meant conditionally to afford us.

We cannot be less affected by, and concerned for, the present alarming situation of our affairs between Great Britain and America, than your Excellency: we would be equally insensible not to feel our numerous grievances, and not to wish them redressed; it is that alone which every good American contends for; it is the enjoyment of our constitutional rights and liberties that softens every care of life, and renders existence itself supportable. At the same time, in all our proceedings, we shall studiously avoid every measure that shall not appear to us at once strictly consonant with our duty to his Majesty, and the interest, liberty, and welfare of our constituents. We shall, on all occasions, exert ourselves to accomplish every assurance we have already made, or may make to your Excellency, and will not fail to take into consideration the bill which you are pleased to point out and recommend. When the public accounts and estimates are laid before us, we will give them proper attention.

By order of the House.
William Young, *Speaker*

(His Excellency's Answer.)

Mr. Speaker and Gentlemen of the Commons House of Assembly:—

I am sorry that I must beg leave to differ with you in opinion with respect to the state we were in, when your Petition to his Majesty was given to me, and which I immediately transmitted. It is true several people had been murdered by Indians, but I conceive that that could by no means be called actually involved in a war with the Nation. There were murders committed by a small part only of Creek Indians, without the concurrence, or even the privity of the Nation, and disavowed by them as soon as they knew of it; and I apprehend something further was necessary, before we could be said to be involved in actual war with the Indians; and every account I received from them after this time was favorable, and showed rather a pacific than a hostile disposition; and which accounts I always transmitted to his Majesty's Secretary of State, as it was my duty to do. It gives me great pleasure to observe my conduct approved of by the Representatives of the people, and for which I thank you. I have every inducement to serve the Province, and to promote the welfare and happiness of the people, and which I shall continue to do to the utmost of my power; and on the other hand, I cannot doubt but you will also approve all my endeavors to discharge my duty to the Crown, with honor and integrity. And let me assure you, gentlemen, that no man can more wish his Majesty's American subjects the full and present enjoyment of their constitutional rights and liberties than I do.

James Wright[3]

NOTES

1. University of Chicago, 1935.

2. The following is part of Smith's letter to the bishop: "That upon the first breaking out of the present Trouble in America several very inflammatory Publications against Government appeared in the Georgia Gazette. That in order to counteract the evil Tendency of the said Publications, your Memorialist published several Letters in the said Gazette, under the Signature of Mercurius. That he verily believes the said Letters had the desired Effect, and were a principal Means of preventing the Province from entering at that time, into the Continental Association." Box 3, Virginia materials, Transcriptions from Archives of Bishop of London in Fulham Palace, Manuscript Division, Library of Congress.

3. George White, ed., "Governor Wright's Speech to the General Assembly and Their Answer," *Historical Collections of Georgia* (New York: Pudney and Russell, 1855; reprint of the 3d ed., Baltimore: Genealogical Publishing Company, 1969), 50–55.

5

The State of Georgia and the Cherokees: The Debate over Indian Removal

At the beginning of the nineteenth century most of the state still belonged to native Americans. The white population was found mainly along the coast and between the Savannah and the Oconee. The Creeks occupied the rest of south and central Georgia, and the Cherokees had the area north and west of the Chattahoochee. However, the Caucasian population was expanding rapidly. In 1800 there were a hundred thousand white Georgians; by 1830 the number had tripled and by 1840 quadrupled. In contrast, the 1835 Cherokee census enumerated a national total of little more than eighteen thousand, free and slave. The faster the white population grew, the greater the pressure on the Indians to step aside. Their misfortune was to have too much land and too few people.

The policy of the United States toward the Indians was at best contradictory. A host of treaties gave the Creeks and Cherokees perpetual jurisdiction over their lands; nevertheless, the federal government signed an agreement in 1802 with the state of Georgia, pledging to negotiate new treaties to remove the native peoples as soon as it could be done on reasonable terms. Meanwhile, the government suggested informally to the Indians that they might stay in the East if they became civilized, just like their white neighbors.

Both the Creeks and Cherokees made remarkable strides in adopting the culture of the newcomers, with the latter making greater progress than any other Indian nation. Assisted by Sequoyah's syllabary, the Cherokees during the 1820s adopted a written constitution and started a bilingual newspaper. Some prospered sufficiently in business and agriculture to build fine plantation houses and purchase black slaves. Missionaries were welcomed into the nation, and about a tenth of the Indians became Christians. Increasingly, the native Americans became indistinguishable in lifestyle from the whites who surrounded them.

Such changes, however, seemed to make Georgians more determined than ever to drive the Indians out. In a series of treaties, the Creeks gradually lost their Georgia lands; by 1827 all had been ceded to the whites. Then attention turned to the Cherokees. Beginning in 1829 whites rushed into the mountain region to profit from the discovery of gold. Georgia now claimed that the Indians had no jurisdiction in their own land and that Caucasians in Cherokee country had to swear allegiance to the state. The Cherokee territory was surveyed and distributed among Georgia citizens in gold and land lotteries.

Greatly outnumbered, the Cherokees fought back through the judicial system. After the Supreme Court refused in 1831 to hear a case brought by the Cherokee nation, the high court the following year considered a case involving two white missionaries, Samuel Worcester and Elizur Butler. The ministers, along with several colleagues, were arrested in 1831 for living among the Indians without Georgia's permission. Convicted in a Gwinnett County courtroom and sentenced to four years in jail, the clergymen were offered their freedom if they would take the Georgia loyalty oath or agree to stay away.

All but Worcester and Butler complied. These two, however, appealed to the federal courts, arguing that the Georgia law under which they were convicted was invalid, since it conflicted with federal treaties recognizing the sovereignty of the Cherokees. Whenever federal and state laws collide, the former, according to the Constitution, are always supreme. In the famous 1832 decision of *Worcester v. Georgia*, the Supreme Court agreed with the missionaries, arguing that Georgia had no jurisdiction within the territory given by federal treaty to the Indians. Unfortunately for the ministers and the Cherokees, however, the state of Georgia and the president of the United States chose to ignore the decision. Ultimately, Worcester and Butler gave up their appeal.

The two authors cited below were leaders of the rival sides in the Cherokee/Georgia dispute. For almost four decades John Ross was Principal Chief of the Cherokee nation. Seven-eighths Caucasian and educated at a white academy in Tennessee, Ross nonetheless identified strongly with the Indians. After 1827 he operated a ferry and ran a plantation at Rome, Georgia, while rising to power under the new Cherokee constitution. Ross and most of the Cherokee nation steadfastly struggled to keep their mountainous homeland, but in 1835 they were betrayed by a minority faction who signed with the federal government the Treaty of New Echota. This document gave up the Cherokee holdings in Georgia in exchange for cash and land in Indian territory (Oklahoma). Removed by force in 1838–39, many of the Cherokees, including Ross's wife, Quatie, died on the "Trail of Tears." In the West Ross continued to head the Cherokee nation until his death in 1866.

Perhaps no one played a greater role in the removal of the Cherokees and the development of North Georgia than Wilson Lumpkin. Lumpkin grew up in Oglethorpe County in northeast Georgia. A lawyer, he served several terms in Congress, where he was best remembered for his vigorous advocacy of Indian removal.

The speech below was delivered in support of President Andrew Jackson's general removal bill. Passed by Congress in 1830, the measure called for the peaceful uprooting of eastern tribes and their relocation in the West. Armed with this legislation, the Jackson administration worked vigorously to remove the Cherokees from Georgia. Allied with Andrew Jackson politically, Lumpkin served from 1831–35 as governor of Georgia. In that post he took the Jacksonian position of strongly opposing South Carolina's attempt to nullify federal tariff legislation. At the same time he received Jackson's support in his defiance of the Supreme Court's *Worcester v. Georgia* decision. After his two terms as governor he served for a while as a federal commissioner authorized to enforce the Treaty of New Echota. In 1837 he was elevated to the U.S. Senate, where he successfully headed off attempts to overturn the fraudulent treaty. With the Indians gone from Georgia, Lumpkin retired from political office in 1841, spending several years on the construction of the state-owned Western & Atlantic Railroad, which ran through the erstwhile Cherokee country, from Atlanta to Chattanooga. Eventually he retired to his Athens farm, which today is part of the campus of the University of Georgia.

Speech of the Hon. Wilson Lumpkin of Ga.

In Committee of the Whole House, on the State of the Union, on the Bill Providing for the Removal of the Indians. (1830)

Mr. Lumpkin rose and said:

Mr. Chairman: My life has never been free from care and responsibility; but, on no former occasion, have I ever felt more deeply impressed with a sense of that responsibility to *God and my country*, than I do at the present moment. The obligations which rest on me are common to every member of this House. The great importance which I attach to the decisions of this House upon the bill now under consideration, does not arise from any apprehension of material effects being produced in relation to any one of the states who are interested. It is true, your decision will have a strong bearing on their interest; but they have the capacity to some extent to take care of themselves. But to those remnant tribes of Indians whose good we seek, the subject before you is of vital importance. It is a measure of life and death. Pass the bill on your table, and you save them; reject it, and you leave them to perish. Reject this bill, and you thereby encourage delusory hopes in the Indians which their professed friends and allies well know will never be realized. The rejection of this bill will encourage and invite the Indians to acts of indiscretion and assumptions which will necessarily bring upon them chastisement and injury, which will be deplored by every friend of virtue and humanity. I therefore call upon you to avoid these evil consequences while you may. Delay is pregnant with great danger to the Indians; what you do, do quickly, before the evil day approaches.

I differ with my friend from Tennessee (Mr. Bell) in regard to Indian civilization. I entertain no doubt that a remnant of these people may be entirely reclaimed from their native savage habits, and be brought to enter into the full enjoyment of all the blessings of civilized society. It appears to me we have too many instances of individual improvement amongst the various native tribes of America to hesitate any longer in determining whether the Indians are susceptible of civilization. Use the proper means, and success will crown your efforts. The means hitherto resorted to by the Government, as well as by individuals, to improve the condition of the Indians, must, from the present state of things, very soon be withheld from these unfortunate people, if they remain in their present abodes, for they will every day be brought into closer contact and conflict with the white population, and this circumstance will diminish the spirit of benevolence and philanthropy towards them which now exists. . . .

Sir, before I pursue the course of the opposition any further, I will remark that I have so far confined myself principally to that part of the subject which relates to the interest of the Indians; but there are other interests which are entitled to a share of your considerations. The State of Georgia, one of whose Representatives I am, has, from my infancy till this day, been struggling with perplexing difficulties, strifes, and heart-burnings, upon the subject of her Indian relations.

Yes, sir, amongst my earliest recollections are the walls of an old fort, which gave protection to the women and children from the tomahawk and scalping knife of the Indians. And let me inform you that, while the Indians have receded thousands of miles before the civilized population, in other sections of the Union, the frontier of Georgia has comparatively remained stationary.

My present residence is not more than one day's travel from the place of the old fort to which I alluded. It is but part of a day's travel from my residence to the line of the Cherokee country.

In entering upon this branch of my subject, I find it necessary to summon up all the powers of philosophy to restrain feelings of indignation and contempt for those who are at this time straining every nerve and using every effort to perpetuate on the people whom I represent the evils which they have borne for so many years; and, whatever has or may be said of this Union, would have submitted, with equal patriotism, to the many ills and wrongs which we have received at the hands of those who were bound by the strongest human obligations to aid in relieving us from Indian perplexities, give us justice, and assist in the advancement of our peace, happiness, and prosperity.

Georgia, sir, is one of the good old thirteen States; she entered the Union upon an equal footing with any of her sisters. She claims no superiority, but contends for equality. That sovereignty which she concedes to all the rest, and would at any time unite with them in defending from all encroachment, she will maintain for herself. Our social compact, upon which we stand as a state, gives you the metes and bounds of our sovereignty; and within the limits therein defined and pointed out our state authorities claim entire and complete jurisdiction over soil and population, regardless of complexion.

The boundaries of Georgia have been defined, recognized, and admitted, by circumstances of a peculiar kind. Her litigations in relation to boundary and title to her soil may justly be considered as having been settled "according to law." Her boundaries are not only admitted by her sister states, but by this General Government, and every individual who administered any part of it, Executive or Legislative, must recollect that the faith of this Government has stood pledged for twenty-eight years past to relieve Georgia from the embarrassment of Indian population. It is known to every member of this Congress that this pledge was no gratuity to Georgia. No, sir, it was for and in consideration of the two entire states of Alabama and Mississippi.

I feel disposed to pity those who make the weak and false plea of inability, founded on the words *"reasonable and peaceable,"* whenever I hear it made.

Such pettifogging quibbles deserve the contempt of a statesman. No man is fit to be a Congressman who does not know that the General Government might many years ago, upon both reasonable and peaceable terms, have removed every Indian from Georgia.

But, sir, upon this subject this Government has been wanting in good faith to Georgia. It has, by its own acts and policy, forced the Indians to remain in Georgia, by the purchase of their lands in the adjoining states and by holding out to the Indians strong inducements to remain where they are, by the expenditures of vast sums of money, spent in changing the habits of the savage for those of civilized life. All this was in itself right and proper; it has my hearty approbation; but it should not have been done at the expense of Georgia. The Government, long after it was bound to extinguish the title of the Indians to all the lands in Georgia, has actually forced the Cherokees from their lands in other states, settled them upon Georgia lands, and aided in furnishing the means to create the Cherokee aristocracy.

Sir, I blame not the Indians; I commiserate their case. I have considerable acquaintance with the Cherokees, and amongst them I have seen much to admire. To me, they are in many respects an interesting people. If the wicked influence of designing men, veiled in the garb of philanthropy and Christian benevolence, should excite the Cherokees to a course that will end in their speedy destruction, I now call upon this Congress, and the whole American people, not to charge the Georgians with this sin; but let it be remembered that it is the fruit of cant and fanaticism, emanating from the land of steady habits; from the boasted progeny of the Pilgrims and Puritans.

Sir, my State stands charged before this House, before the Nation, and before the whole world, with cruelty and oppression towards the Indian. I deny the charge and demand proof from those who made it.

I have labored, as one of your Committee, day and night, in examining everything which has any connection with the history of this subject. Amongst other duties, we have examined all the various laws of the colonial and state governments in relation to the Indians. The selection made and submitted has long since been in the hands of every gentleman of this House. Let the laws of other states be compared with those which are the subject of complaint, and it must be admitted by every candid man that the states complained of stand pre-eminent in humanity, mildness, and generosity towards the Indians.

Georgia, it is true, has slaves; but she did not make them such; she found them upon her hands when she became a sovereign state. She never has, by her legislation, changed the state of freedom to slavery. If she has ever owned an Indian slave, it has never come to my knowledge; but more than one of the other states of this Union have not only treated them as brutes, destitute of any human rights—depriving them of their own modes of worshipping Deity—hunting them as wild beasts for slaughter—holding out rewards for their scalps, and even giving premiums for the raising of a certain breed of dogs, called bloodhounds, to hunt savages, that they might procure their scalps, and obtain the reward offered by Government for them. Sir, compare this legislation with that of Georgia, and let the guilty be put to shame. . . .

. . . I admit we do find in the Cherokee country many families enjoying all the common comforts of civil and domestic life, and possessing the necessary means to secure these enjoyments. Moreover, we find a number of schools and houses built for religious worship. Many of these comfortable families, too, are composed of natives born in the Cherokee country. But the principal part of these enjoyments are confined to the blood of the white man, either in whole or in part. But few, very few, of the real Indians participate largely in these blessings. A large portion of the full-blooded Cherokees still remain a poor degraded race of human beings. As to the proportion that are comfortable, or otherwise, I cannot speak from my own personal knowledge with any degree of certainty; but from what I have seen, I can readily conclude that but a very small portion of the real Indians are in a state of improvement, whilst their lords and rulers are white men and descendants of white men, enjoying the fat of the land, and enjoying exclusively the Government annuities upon which they foster, feed, and clothe the most violent and dangerous enemies of our civil institutions.

Whilst the smallest intrusion (as it is called) by the frontier citizens of Georgia on the lands occupied by the Cherokees excites the fiery indignation of the fanatics, from one end of the *chain of concert and coalition* to the other, do we not find an annual increase of intruders, from these philanthropic ranks, flocking in upon the poor Cherokees, like the caterpillars and locusts of Egypt, leaving a barren waste behind them? Yes, sir, these are the intruders who devour the substance which of right belongs to the poor, perishing part of the Cherokees.

They divide the spoil with the Cherokee rulers and leave the common Indians to struggle with want and misery, without hope of bettering their condition by any change but that of joining their brethren West of the Mississippi.

The inhumanity of Georgia, so much complained of, is nothing more nor less than the extension of her laws and jurisdiction over this mingled and misguided population who are found within her acknowledged limits.

And what, I would ask, is to be found in all this that is so very alarming? Sir, I have endeavored to tear the mask from this subject, that the character and complexion of this opposition might be seen and known. The absolute rulers of the Cherokee country, like other men, love office, distinction, and power.

They are enjoying great and peculiar benefits. They do not like the idea of becoming private citizens. It is with great reluctance they yield up their stewardship. They know they have not been faithful to the interest of the poor degraded Indians. They know the great mass of their people have been left to suffer in want and ignorance, whilst they have spent their substance in forming foreign alliances with an enthusiastic, selfish and money-loving people. These men, when incorporated into the political family of Georgia, cannot calculate on becoming at once the Randolphs of the State. And if they join the Western Cherokees they cannot carry with them their present assumed sovereignty and rule.

They will there find equals in many of their pioneer brethren. The Cadmus of the Cherokees, George Guess, and many others, are already there. Yes, sir, these Western Cherokees are in the full enjoyment of all the blessings of their emigrating enterprise, and there is but one opinion among them in regard to their relative comfort and prospect of future blessings. All the various emigrants to the West so far agree as to authorize the assurance that no inducement could be offered to them strong enough to bring them back again.

The Cherokees and Creeks are charmed with their country, and to the many things which attach to their comfort in it. The New England farmers who have emigrated to the fertile valleys of the West would as soon consent to return to the barren sand and sterile rocks of their native land as a Western Cherokee or Creek would return to the sepulchre of his forefathers.

Pages may be filled with the sublimated *cant* of the day, and in wailing over the departure of the Cherokees from the *bones* of their forefathers. But if the heads of these pretended mourners were waters, and their eyes were a fountain of tears, and they were to spend days and years in weeping over the departure of the Cherokees from Georgia, yet they will go. The tide of emigration, with the Indians as well as the whites, directs its course westwardly. . . .[1]

Annual Message of Chief John Ross

Fellow Citizens:

New Echota C.N. Oct. 13, 1828

In addressing you on this momentous occasion, we cannot, in justice to our feelings, forbear a solemn pause, and with grateful feelings meditate on the many blessings which a kind Providence has conferred on us as a people. Although we have had trials and tribulations to encounter, and in some instances, the sad effects of intemperance have been experienced within the circle of our citizens, yet, there is every reason to flatter us in the hope, that under wise and wholesome laws, the preponderating influence of civilization, morality and religion, will secure to us and our posterity, an ample share of prosperity and happiness.

Occupying your seats by the free suffrage of the people, under the privileges guaranteed by the Constitution, the various subjects requiring your deliberation the present session, will, necessarily be important. The organization of the new Government, the revision and amendments of the old laws, so as to make them in unison with the principles of the Constitution, will require your attention; and it cannot escape your wisdom, that the laws should be short, plain, and suitable to the condition of the people, and to be well executed. The Judiciary system demands your serious deliberation, and the mode for conducting suits in courts should be free from all complicated formalities, and no other *form* should be required than, to let both parties know distinctly, what is alleged, that a fair trial may be had.

A law should be passed requiring managers and clerks of all public elections to register the names of the persons voting as well as the names of the candidates to whom the votes are given, by observing such a course, illegal votes will be detected, and the elections conducted with more regularity, harmony and satisfaction.

The public press deserves the patronage of the people, and should be cherished as an important vehicle in the diffusion of general information, and as a no less powerful auxiliary in asserting and supporting our political rights. Under this impression, we cannot doubt, that you will continue to foster it by public support. The only legislative provision necessary for conducting the press, in our opinion, is to guard against the admission of scurrilous productions of a personal character, and also against cherishing sectarian principles on religious subjects. The press being the public property of the Nation, it would ill become its character if such infringements upon the feelings of the people should be tolerated.

In other respects, the liberty of the press should be as free as the breeze that glides upon the surface.

From the accompanying memorial, signed by several of our respectable citizens, together with the public Treasurer, you will discover that further indulgence is called for in behalf of the public debtors, and it is for your wisdom to determine whether it would be just and proper, that the laws requiring the Treasurer to call in all the money loaned out, should be amended so as to give further indulgence to the borrowers, that the payments may be made by reasonable installments. Owing to the extreme scarcity of money, from the general pressure in business, such indulgence would, no doubt, be a great relief; and the probable distress and ruin, from the sacrifices of property consequent from public sales, may be averted.

After receiving the Treasurer's report and ascertaining the true condition of the public funds, it will also be your province to determine the expediency of making suitable provisions for the erection of a National Academy, at New Echota. This subject, has for sometime past been agitated, and is anticipated with the warmest zeal by the reflecting part of our citizens, and it should receive your particular attention. By the Treaty of 1819, four tracts of land, equal to fifteen miles square were reserved for the purpose of creating a revenue for a school fund, to be applied under the direction of the President of the United States, for the education of the youths of this Nation. The lands were to have been sold under the direction of the President in the same manner as the lands of the United States, and notwithstanding the repeated and urgent requests which have been made for the sale of these lands, and the no less repeated promise on the part of the General Government to attend to it, for reasons unknown, they are not yet sold. We would recommend you to memorialize the President on this important subject, and respectfully to request that, the available funds may be applied to the support of the contemplated National Academy.

The several charity schools in the country under the immediate patronage of the benevolent societies of the several states should not escape your notice. Altho' the superintendents of these schools, under the direction of respective societies, have the right of conducting them, according to the dictates of their own discretion and judgments, yet, without presuming any disparagement to their regulations, we would suggest the expediency of selecting a visiting committee on the part of the nation, for the purposes of inspecting their examinations, & at such other times as said Committee may deem proper, and that they should be required to make a general report on the state of improvement &c. to be laid before the session of each General Council. Such a course pursued by the authorities of the Nation in relation to these institutions, would no doubt excite an interest among the pupils, and add to the vigilance of their preceptors, and at the same time produce general satisfaction. An indifferent course perhaps might eventually produce relaxation and apathy in their operations, and we should endeavor to avoid the dishonor of any circumstances which might possibly take place, that would defeat the fondest expectations of those, upon whose benefaction they are founded.

The circumstances of our Government assuming a new character under a constitutional form, and on the principles of republicanism, has, in some degree, excited the sensations of the public characters of Georgia, and it is sincerely to be regretted that this excitement should have been manifested by such glaring expressions of hostility to our true interests. By the adoption of the Constitution, our relation to the United States, as recognized by existing Treaties, is not in the least degree affected, but on the contrary, this improvement in our government, is strictly in accordance with the recommendations, views and wishes of the Great Washington under whose auspicious administration our Treaties of peace, Friendship and protection, were made and whose policy in regard to Indian civilization has been strictly pursued by the subsequent administrations.

The pretended claim of Georgia to a portion of our lands, is alleged on the following principles. First, by discovery. Secondly, by conquest. Thirdly, by compact.

We shall endeavor briefly to elucidate the character of this claim. In the first place, the Europeans by the skill and enterprise of their Navigators, discovered this vast Continent, and found it inhabited exclusively by Indians of various Tribes, and by a pacific courtesy and designing stratagems, the aboriginal proprietors were induced to permit a people from a foreign clime to plant colonies, and without the consent or knowledge of the native Lords, a potentate of England, whose eyes never saw, whose purse never purchased, and whose sword never conquered the soil we inhabit, presumed to issue a parchment, called a "Charter," to the Colony of Georgia, in which its boundary was set forth, including a great extend of country inhabited by the Cherokee and other Indian Nations.

Secondly, after a lapse of many years when the population of their Colonies had become strong, they revolted against their sovereign, and by success of Arm, established an Independent Government, under the name of "the United States." It is further alleged that the Cherokee Nation prosecuted a war at the same time against the Colonies.

3dly. Several years after the Treaties of peace, friendship and protection, which took place between the U.S. & Cherokee Nation, and by which the faith of the United States was solemnly pledged to guarantee to the Cherokee Nation forever, their title to their lands, a Compact was entered into between the United

States and the State of Georgia, by which the United States promised to purchase for the use of Georgia certain lands belonging to the Cherokee Nation so soon as it could be done on *reasonable* and *peaceable terms.*

Thus stands the naked claim of Georgia to a portion of our lands. The claim advanced under the plea of discovery, is preposterous. Our ancestors from time immemorial possessed this country, not by a "Charter" from the hand of a mortal King, who had no right to grant it, but by the Will of the King of Kings, who created all things and liveth for ever & ever.

The claim advanced on the second head, on the ground of conquest, is no less futile than the first, even admitting that the Cherokees waged a war with the Colonies, at the time they fought for their independence. The Cherokees took part in the war, *only* as the allies of Great Britain, and not as her subjects, being an independent Nation, over whose lands she exercised no rights of jurisdiction; therefore, nothing could be claimed from them, in regard to their lands by the conqueror over the rights of Great Britain. At the termination of the war, the United States negotiated with the Cherokees on the terms of peace as an Independent Nation, and since the close of that war, other wars took place, and at their terminations, other treaties were made, and in no one stipulation can there be found a single idea that our title to the soil has been forfeited, or claimed as the terms of peace; but, to the contrary, we discover that the United States solemnly pledged their faith that our title should be guaranteed to our Nation forever.

The third pretension is extremely lame. The United States enters into a compact with Georgia that they will purchase certain lands, which belong to us, for Georgia, so soon as they can do it on *peaceable* and *reasonable terms.* This promise was made on the part of the United States without knowing whether this nation would ever consent to dispose of those lands on any terms whatever; and the Cherokees not being a part in the compact, their title cannot be affected in the slightest degree. It appears astonishingly unreasonable, that all those hard expressions of denunciation which have been unsparingly lavished against our sacred rights and interests, by interested politicians, have arose from no other circumstance than our honest refusal to sell to the United States lands, for the fulfillment of their Compact with Georgia. Although our views & condition may be misrepresented—although we may be stigmatized with the appellation of "*nabobs,*" and should be represented as ruling with an "*Iron rod*" and "*grinding down into dust the wretched* and *abject mass*" of our citizens; and although we may be called *avaricious* for *refusing to sell our lands,* we should not be diverted from the path of rectitude. In all our intercourse with our neighboring white brethren, we should endeavor to cultivate the utmost harmony and good understanding, by strictly observing the relations which we sustain to the United States.

Owing to the various representations respecting us, we have been frequently called upon to make a treaty of cession. . . . We would recommend you as the immediate representatives of the people, to submit a respectful memorial to the Congress of the United States, expressive of the true sentiments of the people respecting their situation, and praying that measures may be adopted on the part of the United States for the adjustment of their Compact with the State of Georgia, otherwise than to anticipate any further cession of land from this nation.

William Hicks

John Ross[2]

NOTES

1. Wilson Lumpkin, *The Removal of the Cherokee Indians from Georgia, 1827–1841*, 2 vols. in 1 (New York: Dodd, Mead, 1907; reprint, New York: Augustus M. Kelley, Publishers, 1971), 1:57–88.

2. Gary E. Moulton, ed., *The Papers of Chief John Ross*, 2 vols. (Norman: University of Oklahoma Press, 1985), 1:140–45. For writings of other Cherokees and their white allies see *New Echota Letters*, ed. Jack Frederick Kilpatrick and Anna Gritts Kilpatrick (Dallas: Southern Methodist University Press, 1968); Elias Boudinot, *Cherokee Editor: The Writings of Elias Boudinot*, ed. Theda Perdue (Knoxville: University of Tennessee Press, 1983); and Jeremiah Evarts, *Cherokee Removal: The "William Penn" Essays and Other Writings*, ed. Francis Paul Prucha (Knoxville: University of Tennessee Press, 1981). There are numerous secondary accounts of the Cherokees' adoption of white civilization and Cherokee removal. Among the more useful are William G. McLouglin, *Cherokees and Missionaries, 1789–1839* (New Haven: Yale University Press, 1984), and Theda Perdue, *Slavery and the Evolution of Cherokee Society, 1540–1866* (Knoxville: University of Tennessee Press, 1979).

6

🏴 🏴 🏴

Slavery in Antebellum Georgia

On the eve of the Civil War, four of every nine Georgia residents lived in bondage. Almost half the capital in the state was invested in human property. A century earlier Georgians had debated the question of slavery. Now, the state was what Oglethorpe had feared: a rich land with resources concentrated in few hands. To be sure, numerous Georgians owned small farms, but about 20 percent of the free families possessed 90 percent of the wealth.

During the three decades before 1860, the "peculiar institution" was a topic of heated national discussion. Abolitionists saw slavery as a cruel, tyrannical violation of the rights on which the American republic was founded. To them, slavery was a sin because it destroyed families and denied freedoms and opportunities that other Americans took for granted. Southern apologists, on the other hand, spoke of a patriarchal society where fatherly masters protected contented, childlike servants, offering them cradle-to-grave security. The paternalists argued that their civilization was more humane than the free labor system of the North precisely because close personal bonds developed between master and slave.

The Sale of a Child

None were more qualified to speak about slavery than those who endured it. One example was John Brown, a runaway slave, who published his autobiography in London in 1855. According to the original preface, the book was designed "to advance the anti-slavery cause by the diffusion of information." John Brown, or Fed, as he was known as a bondsman, lived his early life near the Virginia–North Carolina border.[1] The following selection is a poignant account of a Georgia slave trader's purchase of young Brown, separating him from his mother.

I remained at James Davis's for nearly eighteen months. Once during that period, I remember he took me into the town to a tavern kept by one Captain Jemmy Duprey. There was a negro speculator there, on the look-out for bargains, but he would not have me. I did not know where I was going, when my master took me with him, but when I got back I told my mother, who cried over me, and said she was very glad I had not been sold away from her.

But the time arrived when we were to be finally separated. Owing to a considerable rise in the price of cotton, there came a great demand for slaves in Georgia. One day a negro speculator named Starling Finney arrived at James Davis's place.[2] He left his drove on the highway, in charge of one of his companions, and made his way up to our plantation, prospecting for negroes. It happened that James Davis had none that suited Finney, but being in want of money, as he was building a new house, and Finney being anxious for a deal, my master called me up and offered to sell me. I was then about or nearly ten years of age, and after some chaffering about terms, Finney agreed to purchase me by the pound.

How I watched them whilst they were driving this bargain! and how I speculated upon the kind of man he was who sought to buy me! His venomous countenance inspired me with mortal terror, and I almost felt the heavy thong of the great riding-whip he held in his hand, twisting around my shoulders. He was a large, tall fellow, and might have killed me easily with one blow from his huge fist. He had left his horse at the gate, and when the bargain for me was struck, he went out and led him to the door, where he took the saddle off. I wondered what this was for, though suspicious that it had something to do with me; nor had I long to wait before I knew. A ladder was set upright against the end of the building outside, to one rong of which they made a stilyard fast. The first thing Finney did was to weigh his saddle, the weight of which he knew, to see whether the stilyard was accurately adjusted. Having satisfied himself of this, a rope was brought, both ends of which were tied together, so that it formed a large noose or loop. This was hitched over the hook of the stilyard, and I was seated in the loop. After I had been weighed, there was a deduction made for the rope. I do not recollect what I weighed, but the price I was sold for amounted to three hundred and ten dollars. Within five minutes after, Finney paid the money, and I was marched off. I looked round and saw my poor mother stretching out her hands after me. She ran up and overtook us, but Finney, who was behind me, and between me and my mother, would not let her approach, though she begged and prayed to be allowed to kiss me for the last time, and bid me good bye. I was so stupified with grief and fright, that I could not shed a tear, though my heart was bursting. At last we got to the gate, and I turned around to see whether I could not get a chance of kissing my mother. She saw me, and made a dart forward to meet me, but Finney gave me a hard push, which sent me spinning through the gate. He then slammed it to and shut it in my mother's face. That was the last time I ever saw her, nor do I know whether she is alive or dead at this hour.

We were in a lane now, about a hundred and fifty yards in length, and which led from the gate to the highway. I walked on before Finney, utterly unconscious of anything. I seemed to have become quite bewildered. I was aroused from this state of stupor by seeing that we had reached the main road, and had come up with a gang of negroes, some of whom were hand-cuffed two and two, and fastened to a long chain running between the two ranks. There were also a good many women and children, but none of these were chained. The children seemed to be all above ten years of age, and I soon learnt that they had been purchased in different places, and were for the most part strangers to one another and to the negroes in the coffle. They were waiting for Finney to come up. I fell into the rank, and we set off on our journey to Georgia.

Li: bray g Congres w PA Slave Interview

⚡ ⚡ ⚡

The Paternalistic Viewpoint

One of the most distinguished clergyman of antebellum Georgia, Charles Colcock Jones, was also a wealthy Liberty County planter. His holdings included about twenty-six hundred acres and more than one hundred slaves. Rice and cotton were the primary crops. A graduate of Princeton Theological Seminary, the distinguished Presbyterian devoted his greatest clerical efforts to evangelizing the slaves. He reconciled his religion and ownership of humans by arguing that slavery was sanctioned by God. Jones's reading of the Bible assured him that God demanded of the slaveowner only that he treat his slaves well. Paternalistic care included exposure of bondsmen to the promises of the Gospel, as one discovers in the reading below, drawn from Jones's *The Religious Instruction of the Negroes in the United States.* In this work Jones made the following connection between slavery and religion.

It hath pleased the Almighty, in his sovereignty, to bestow the Gospel upon but a portion of the human race. He has, however, chosen to employ human agency in extending the knowledge, and the consequent blessings of this glorious gift, to all mankind, in fulfillment of his expressed designs, and his own most precious promises. He has made it the *duty* under the most solemn commands of all who *possess* the Gospel *to impart it to those who are destitute of it.* The possession of the gift implies the obligation to impart it. No man may question this position who allows himself to be guided by the conviction, of reason, the dictates of conscience, or the declarations of the word of God.

In attempting to fulfill this duty, the general and the just rule of action is, that we impart the Gospel to those of our fellow-men who are *most dependent* upon us for it—who are *most needy and most accessible.*

These three peculiarities meet in the case of the Negroes; and consequently they stand *first* in their claims upon our benevolent attention. . . .

We are prepared now to take up the *obligation of the church of Christ in the slave-holding States to impart the Gospel of Salvation to the Negroes within those States.*

1.   That obligation is imposed upon us in the first instance *by the providence of God.*

This follows undeniably from all our previous statements in the history of their religious instruction, and in the sketch of their moral and religious condition. But it may be of some service to be particular under this head. It was by the permission of Almighty God, in his inscrutable providence over the affairs of men, that the Negroes were taken from Africa and transported to these shores. The inhabitants of the Colonies at their first introduction had nothing to do with the infamous traffic, and were, we may say, universally opposed to it. The iniquity of the traffic and of their first introduction, rests upon the Mother Country.

Being brought here they were brought as *slaves*; in the providence of God we were constituted *masters*; superiors; and constituted their *guardians.* And all the laws in relation to them, civilly, socially, and religiously considered, were framed by ourselves. They thus were placed under our control, and not exclusively for our benefit but for theirs also.

We could not overlook the fact that they were men; holding the same relations to God as ourselves—whose *religious interests* were certainly their *highest and best* and that our *first and fundamental duty* was to provide to the extent of our ability, for the perpetual security of those interests. Our relations to them and their relations to us, continue the same to the present hour, and the providence of God still binds upon us the great duty of imparting to them the Gospel of eternal life. . . .

But we advance a step further. The *word of God recognizes the relation of master and servant, and addresses express commands to us as masters.*

In the constitution of his visible church on earth Almighty God included the *servants of families;* commanded the sign of his everlasting and gracious covenant to be made in their flesh, and thereby secured to them, as well as *to children* the privileges and blessings of the same. He would have them trained up in the knowledge of his most holy name and for his service: nor must they be neglected, nor excluded. Gen. 17:12–13. "And he that is eight days old shall be circumcised among you, every man child in your generations, he that is *born in the house or bought with money* of any stranger, which is not of thy seed"; and the command is *repeated,* to show his tender regard for the poor, and that his covenant embraces them. "He that is born in thy house and he that is bought with thy money must needs be circumcised; and my covenant shall be in your flesh for an everlasting covenant." In obedience to this command Abraham "in the selfsame day circumcised his son Ishmael and all that were *born in his house,* and *all that were bought with his money."* v. 23. He apprehended the will of God as expressed in the covenant, and received the divine approbation: "for I know him that he will command his children and his household after him, and they shall keep the way of the Lord to do justice and judgment, that the Lord may bring upon Abraham that which he hath spoken of him." Gen. 18:19.

The rest of the Sabbath was secured to servants in the Decalogue: "in it thou shalt not do any work, thou nor thy son, nor thy daughter, thy *man-servant* nor thy *maid-servant."* Exod. 20:8–11. The *sacred festivals* were opened to them, and along with their masters they were to rejoice before the Lord: they were also to present *sacrifices* and *offerings* to the Lord, in the appointed place and eat of them "before the Lord," with their masters. "Thou mayest not eat, within thy gates, the tithe of thy corn, or of thy wine, or of thy oil, or the firstlings of thy herds, or of thy flocks, nor any of thy vows which thou vowest, nor thy free will offerings, or heave offering of thine hand: but thou must eat them before the

Lord, in the place which the Lord thy God shall choose, thou and thy son and thy daughter, and thy *man-servant,* and thy *maid-servant,*" Deut. 12:17,18. "And thou shalt keep the *feast of weeks:* and thou shalt rejoice before the Lord thy God, thou, and thy son, and thy daughter, and thy *man-servant,* and thy *maid-servant.*" So also "the feast of *tabernacles.*" Deut. 16:1–16.

Thus in the *Old Testament,* the law of God, and the Sanctuary and all its privileges, were opened to servants and secured to them by the declared will of God: and it was the duty of masters to command their households after them, that they should keep the way of the Lord to do justice and judgment: otherwise the Lord would not bring upon them the promised blessings.

The *New Testament* is, if possible, more explicit.

In several epistles, the relation of master and servant is recognized, and the mutual duties of each arising out of that relation mutually insisted upon. Masters and servants are addressed as *belonging to the same churches* and heirs of the *same grace of life:* 1 Tim. 6:1–5. Eph. Col.

What kind of servants are intended? *Slaves:* the original teaches us so, while the very duties enjoined upon servants and the observations made upon their condition (1 Cor. 7:20–22) confirms the fact that they were *literally Slaves.* And the kind of slavery that existed among the Jews was that allowed in the Old Testament; which may be considered identical with that which prevails amongst us at the present time; and no one will deny that the slavery which existed among the Greeks and Romans and Gentile nations, was identical with our own. All authentic history, and the codification of the Roman laws made in the reign of Justinian, prove it. The slaves were more heterogeneous in their national origin than ours. Among them however existed *Negroes:* and in no small numbers. Indeed a traffic in Negro slaves had been carried on for centuries before Isabella gave permission for their transportation to these western shores; and they were sold and scattered over all the east.

When therefore the New Testament addresses commands to *Masters,* we are the *identical persons* intended. We are Masters in the New Testament sense. We are addressed as directly and as identically, as when we are *Fathers,* and it is said "*Fathers* provoke not your children to wrath."

And what are these commands? "And ye *Masters,* do the same things unto them, forbearing threatening: knowing that your Master also is in Heaven: neither is there respect of persons with him." Eph. 6:9.

As servants are exhorted to fulfill their duties to their masters, "as the servants of Christ, doing the will of God from the heart": having respect to their accountability to God; so also masters are exhorted to do the same things, to fulfill their duties to their servants, from the same principle of obedience to God and respect to future accountability.

"Masters give unto your servants that which is just and equal: knowing that ye also have a Master in Heaven." Col. 4:1. Masters are here required to treat their servants justly and equitably, in respect, of course, to all their interests, both for time and eternity; for they shall account to God for the same.

Thus doth God put his finger upon us as *Masters*. He holds up before our faces our servants and our duties to them. He commands us to fulfill those duties under the pain of his displeasure. He tells us that in the performance of duty he does not respect us more than he respects *them*.[3]

🏴 🏴 🏴

A Former Slave's View of Southern Preachers

Among the sources used by historians of slavery are the oral histories of erstwhile bondsmen gathered during the Great Depression by the Federal Writers' Project, a division of the WPA. The interviews must be used with caution. The subjects recalled events that happened at least seventy years before, when most were still children. The interviewers were sometimes patronizing and condescending, and their questions occasionally broadcast the answer they hoped to hear. Collectively, however, these firsthand accounts give an excellent description of the complexities of slave life and of master-servant relationships.[4] Below is the account of an ex-slave from Richmond County named Leah Garrett.

Leah Garrett, an old Negress with snow-white hair leaned back in her rocker and recalled customs and manners of slavery days. Mistreatment at the hands of her master is outstanding in her memory.

"I know so many things 'bout slavery time 'til I never will be able to tell 'em all," she declared. "In dem days, preachers wuz just as bad and mean as anybody else. Dere wuz a man who folks called a good preacher, but he wuz one of de meanest mens I ever seed. When I wuz in slavery under him he done so many bad things 'til God soon kilt him. His wife or chillun could git mad wid you, and if dey told him anything he always beat you. Most times he beat his slaves when dey hadn't done nothin' a t'all. One Sunday mornin' his wife told him deir cook wouldn't never fix nothin' she told her to fix. Time she said it he jumped up from de table, went in de kitchen, and made de cook go under de porch whar he always whupped his slaves. She begged and prayed but he didn't pay no 'tention to dat. He put her up in what us called de swing, and beat her 'til she couldn't holler. De pore thing already had heart trouble; dat's why he put her in de kitchen, but he left her swingin' dar and went to church, preached, and called hisself servin' God. When he got back home she wuz dead. Whenever your marster had you swingin' up, nobody wouldn't take you down. Sometimes a man would help his wife, but most times he wuz beat afterwards.

"Another marster I had kept a hogshead to whup you on. Dis hogshead had two or three hoops 'round it. He buckled you face down on de hogshead and whupped you 'til you bled. Everybody always stripped you in dem days to whup you, 'cause dey didn't keer who seed you naked. Some folks' chillun took sticks and jobbed (jabbed) you all while you wuz bein' beat. Sometimes dese children would beat you all 'cross your head, and dey Mas and Pas didn't know what stop wuz.

"Another way marster had to whup us wuz in a stock dat he had in de stables. Dis wuz whar he whupped you when he wuz real mad. He had logs fixed together wid holes for your feet, hands, and head. He had a way to open dese logs and fasten you in. Den he had his coachman give you so many lashes, and he would let you stay in de stock for so many days and nights. Dat's why he had it in the stable so it wouldn't rain on you. Everyday you got dat same number of lashes. You never come out able to sit down.

"I had a cousin wid two chillun. De oldest one had to nuss one of marster's grandchildren. De front steps wuz real high, and one day dis pore chile fell down dese steps wid de baby. His wife and daughter hollered and went on turrible, and when our marster come home dey wuz still hollerin' just lak de baby was dead or dyin'. When dey told him 'bout it, he picked up a board and hit dis pore little chile 'cross de head and kilt her right dar. Den he told his slaves to take her and throw her in de river. Her ma begged and prayed, but he didn't pay her no 'tention; he made 'em throw de chile in.

"One of de slaves married a young gal, and dey put her in de 'Big House' to wuk. One day Mistess jumped on her 'bout something and de gal hit her back. Mistess said she wuz goin' to have Marster put her in de stock and beat her when he come home. When de gal went to de field and told her husband 'bout it, he told her whar to go and stay 'til he got dar. Dat night he took his supper to her. He carried her to a cave and hauled pine straw and put in dar for her to sleep on. He fixed dat cave up just lak a house for her, put a stove in dar and run de pipe out through de ground into a swamp. Everybody always wondered how he fixed dat pipe, course dey didn't cook on it 'til night when nobody could see de smoke.

He ceiled de house wid pine logs, made beds and tables out of pine poles, and dey lived in dis cave seven years. Durin' dis time, dey had three chillun. Nobody wuz wid her when dese chillun wuz born but her husband. He waited on her wid each chile. De chillun didn't wear no clothes 'cept a piece tied 'round deir waists. Dey wuz just as hairy as wild people, and dey wuz wild. When dey come out of dat cave dey would run everytime dey seed a pusson.

"De seven years she lived in de cave, diffunt folks helped keep 'em in food. Her husband would take it to a certain place and she would go and git it. People had passed over dis cave ever so many times, but nobody knowed dese folks wuz livin' dar. Our Marster didn't know whar she wuz, and it wuz freedom 'fore she come out of dat cave for good.

"Us lived in a long house dat had a flat top and little rooms made like mule stalls, just big enough for you to git in and sleep. Dey warn't no floors in dese rooms and neither no beds. Us made beds out of dry grass, but us had cover 'cause de real old people, who couldn't do nothin' else, made plenty of it. Nobody warn't 'lowed to have fires, and if dey wuz caught wid any dat meant a beatin'. Some would burn charcoal and take de coals to deir rooms to help warm 'em. Every pusson had a tin pan, tin cup, and a spoon. Everybody couldn't eat at one time, us had 'bout four different sets. Nobody had a stove to cook on, everybody cooked on fire places and used skillets and pots. To boil us hung pots on racks over de fire and baked bread and meats in de skillets.

"Marster had a big room right side his house whar his vittals wuz cooked. Den de cook had to carry 'em upstairs in a tray to be served. When de somethin' t'eat wuz carried to de dinin' room it wuz put on a table and served from dis table. De food warn't put on de eatin' table.

"De slaves went to church wid dey marsters. De preachers always preached to de white folks first, den dey would preach to de slaves. Dey never said nothin' but you must be good, don't steal, don't talk back at your marsters, don't run away, don't do dis and don't do dat. Dey let de colored preachers preach but dey give 'em almanacs to preach out of. Dey didn't 'low us to sing such songs as 'We Shall Be Free' and 'O For A Thousand Tongues to Sing.' Dey always had somebody to follow de slaves to church when de colored preacher was preachin' to hear what wuz said and done. Dey wuz 'fraid us would try to say something 'gainst 'em."[5]

Servant of a Great Man

A final account of slavery is that of Georgia Baker, who once was owned by Alexander H. Stephens, the statesman whose public career included several terms in Congress and four years as vice president of the Confederate States of America. When he died in 1883, he was governor of Georgia. An outspoken opponent of secession, he nonetheless went along with his state after the fateful decision was made. While Stephens disagreed sharply with the policies of Confederate president Jefferson Davis, he seemed to share with Davis an indulgent attitude toward slaves. Both his concern for his dependents and the limits of paternalism are apparent in the passage below.

"Whar was I born? Why I was born on de plantation of a great man. It was Marse Alec Stephens' plantation 'bout a mile and a half from Crawfordville, in Taliaferro County. Mary and Grandison Tilly was my Ma and Pa. Ma was cook up at de big house and she died when I was jus' a little gal. Pa was a field hand, and he belonged to Marse Britt Tilly. . . .

"De long, log houses what us lived in was called 'shotgun' houses, 'cause dey had three rooms, one behind de other in a row lak de barrel of a shotgun. All de chillun slept in one end room and de grown folkses slept in de other end room. De kitchen whar us cooked and et was de middle room. Beds was made out of pine poles put together wid cords. Dem wheat-straw mattresses was for grown folkses mostly 'cause nigh all de chillun slept on pallets. Howsome-ever, dere was some few slave chillun what had beds to sleep on. Pillows! Dem days us never knowed what pillows was. Gals slept on one side of de room and boys on de other in de chilluns room. Uncle Jim, he was de bed-maker, and he made up a heap of little beds lak what dey calls cots now. . . .

"Oh, yessum! Marse Alec, had plenty for his slaves to eat. Dere was meat, bread, collard greens, snap beans, 'taters, peas, all sorts of dried fruit, and just lots of milk and butter. Marse Alec had 12 cows and dat's wher I learned to love milk so good. De same Uncle Jim what made our beds made our wooden bowls what dey kept filled wid bread and milk for de chillun all day. You might want to call dat place whar Marse Alec had our veg'tables raised a garden, but it looked lak a big field to me, it was so big. You jus' ought to have seed dat dere fireplace whar dey cooked all us had to eat. It was one sho 'nough big somepin, all full of pots, skillets, and ovens. Dey warn't never 'lowed to get full of smut neither. Dey had to be cleant and shined up atter evvy meal, and dey sho was pretty hangin' der in dat big old fireplace. . . .

"Us went bar'foots in summer, but bless your sweet life us had good shoes in winter and wore good stockin's too. It tuk three shoemakers for our plantation. Dey was Uncle Isom, Uncle Jim, and Uncle Stafford. Dey made up hole-stock shoes for de 'omans and gals and brass-toed brogans for de mens and boys.

"Us had pretty white dresses for Sunday. Marse Alec wanted everybody on his place dressed up dat day. He sent his houseboy, Uncle Harris, down to de cabins evvy Sunday mornin' to tell evvy slave to clean hisself up. Dey warn't never give no chance to forgit. Dere was a big old room set aside for a wash-room. Folkses laughs at me now 'cause I ain't never stopped takin' a bath evvy Sunday mornin'.

"Marse Lordnorth Stephens was de boss on Marse Alec's plantation. Course Marse Alec owned us and he was our sho 'nough Marster. Neither one of 'em ever married. Marse Lordnorth was a good man, but he didn't have no use for 'omans—he was a sissy. Dere warn't no Marster no whar no better dan our Marse Alec Stephens, but he never stayed home enough to tend to things hisself much 'cause he was all de time too busy on de outside. He was de President or somepin of our side durin' de war.

"Uncle Pierce went wid Marse Alec evvy whar he went. His dog, Rio, had more sense dan most folkses. Marse Alec, he was all de time havin' big mens visit him up at de big house. One time, out in de yard, him and one of dem 'portant mens got in a argument 'bout somepin. Us chillun snuck up close to hear what dey was makin' such a rukus 'bout. I heard Marse Alec say: 'I got more sense in my big toe dan you is got in your whole body.' And he was right—he did have more sense dan most folkses. Ain't I been a tellin' you he was de President or somepin lake dat, dem days?"

"Ma, she was Marse Alec's cook and looked atter de house. . . .

"No Lord! Marse Lordnorth never needed no overseer or no carriage driver neither. Uncle Jim was de head man what got de Niggers up evvy mornin' and started 'em off to wuk right. De big house sho was a pretty place, a-settin' up on a high hill. De squirrels was so tame dar dey jus' played all 'round de yard. Marse Alec's dog is buried in dat yard.

"No Mam, I never knowed how many acres dere was in de plantation us lived on, and Marse Alec had other places, too. He had land scattered evvywhar. Lord, dere was a heap of Niggers on dat place, and all of us was kin to one another. Grandma Becky and Grandpa Stafford was de fust slaves Marse Alec ever had, and dey sho had a passel of chillun. One thing sho Marse Lordnorth wouldn't keep no bright-colored Nigger on dat plantation if he could help it. Aunt Mary was a bright-colored Nigger and dey said dat Marse John, Marse Lordnorth's brother, was her Pa, but anyhow Marse Lordnorth never had no use for her 'cause she was a bright-colored Nigger.

"Marse Lordnorth never had no certain early time for his slaves to git up nor no special late time for 'em to quit wuk. De hours dey wuked was 'cordin' to how much wuk was ahead to be done. Folks in Crawfordville called us 'Stephens' Free Niggers.'

"Us minded Marse Lordnorth—us had to do dat—but he let us do pretty much as us pleased. Us never had no sorry piece of a Marster. He was a good man and he made a sho 'nough good Marster. I never seed no Nigger git a beatin', and what's more I never heared of nothin' lake dat on our place. Dere was a jail in Crawfordville, but none of us Niggers on Marse Alec's place warn't never put in it.

"No Lord! None of us Niggers never knowed nothin' 'bout readin' and writin'. Dere warn't no school for Niggers den, and I ain't never been to school a day in my life. Niggers was more skeered of newspapers dan dey is of snakes now, and us never knowed what a Bible was dem days.

"Niggers never had no churches of deir own den. Dey went to de white fokses' churches and sot in the gallery. One Sunday when me and my sister Frances went to church, I found 50 cents in Confederate money and showed it to her. She tuk it away from me. Dat's de onliest money I seed durin' slavery time. Course you knows dey throwed Confederate money away for trash atter de war was over. Den us young chaps used to play wid it.

"I never went to no baptizin's nor no funerals neither den. Funerals warn't de style. When a Nigger died dem days, dey jus' put his body in a box and buried it. I 'members very well when Aunt Sallie and Aunt Catherine died, but I was little den, and I didn't take it in what dey done 'bout buryin' 'em.

"None of Marse Alec's slaves never run away to no North, 'cause he was so good to 'em dey never wanted to leave him. De onliest Nigger what left Marse Alec's place was Uncle Dave, and he wouldn't have left 'cept he got in trouble wid a white 'oman. You needn't ax me her name 'cause I ain't gwine to tell it, but I knows it well as I does my own name. Anyhow Marse Alec give Uncle Dave some money and told him to leave, and nobody seed him no more atter dat. . . .

"Did I tell you . . . dat de man what looked after Marse Alec's business was his fust cousin? He was de Marse Lordnorth I'se all time talkin' 'bout, and Marse John was Marse Lordnorth's brother. Dere warn't no cook or house gal up at de big house but Ma 'til atter she died, and den when Miss Mary Berry tuk charge of de house dey made Uncle Harry and his wife, Aunt 'Liza, house boy and cook. . . .

"Marse Alec warn't home much of de time, but when he was dar he used to walk down to de cabins and laugh and talk to his Niggers. He used to sing a song for de slave chillun dat ran somepin lak dis:

> 'Walk light ladies
> De cake's all dough,
> You needn't mind de weather,
> If de wind don't blow.'

". . . Us didn't know when he was a-singin' dat tune to us chillun dat when us growed up us would be cake walkin' to de same song.

"On Sundays, whenever Marse Alec was home, he done lots of readin' out of a great, big, old book. I didn't know what it was, but he was pow'ful busy wid it. He never had no parties or dancin' dat I knows 'bout, but he was all time havin' dem big 'portant mens at his house talkin' bout de business what tuk him off from home so much. I used to see Lawyer Toombs dere heaps of times. He was a big, fine lookin' man. Another big lawyer was all time comin' der too, but I done lost his name. Marse Alec had so awful much sense in his haid dat folkses said it stunted his growin'. Anyhow, long as he lived he warn't no bigger dan a boy. . . .

"Whilst Marse Alec was President or somepin, he got sick and had to come back home, and it wern't long atter dat 'fore de surrender. Allen was 'pinted to watch for de blue coats. When dey come to take Marse Alec off, dey was all over the place wid deir guns. Us Niggers hollered and cried and tuk on pow'ful 'cause us sho thought dey was gwine to kill him on account of his bein' such a high up man on de side what dey was fightin'. All de Niggers followed 'em to de depot when dey tuk Marse Alec and Uncle Pierce away. Dey kept Marse Alec in prison off somewhar a long time but dey sent Pierce back home 'fore long. . . .

"I seed Uncle Pierce 'fore he died and us sot and talked and cried 'bout Marse Alec. Yessum, us sho did have de best Marster in de world. If ever a man went to Heaven, Marse Alec did. I sho does wish our good old Marster was livin' now. Now, Miss, I done told you all I can ricollec' 'bout dem days. I thanks you a lot for dat purty yaller dress, and I hopes you comes back to see me again sometime."[6]

NOTES

1. According to F. N. Boney, John Brown was born in Southampton County, Virginia, on the estate of Betty Moore. When Brown was sold, he was living in Northampton County, North Carolina, on the plantation of James Davis, the son-in-law of Betty Moore. The Moore and Davis plantations were about forty-five miles apart. The excerpt below is from F. N. Boney, ed., *Slave Life in Georgia: A Narrative of*

the *Life, Sufferings, and Escape of John Brown, a Fugitive Slave* (Savannah: Beehive Press, 1972), 15–17.

2. John Brown misspelled Finney's first name. Boney identifies Sterling Finney as a large slaveowner from Morgan County, Georgia, who later would serve a term in the Georgia legislature.

3. Charles Colcock Jones, *The Religious Instruction of the Negroes in the United States* (Savannah: Thomas Purse, 1842; reprint, New York: Negro Universities Press, 1969), 156, 159–64.

4. For an insightful analysis of the WPA interviews and the potential pitfalls of oral history, see James West Davidson and Mark Hamilton Lytle, "The View from the Bottom Rail," *After The Fact: The Art of Historical Detection*, 2d ed. (New York: Alfred A Knopf, 1986), 177–212.

5. Leah Garrett, interview by Louise Oliphant, edited by John N. Booth, *The American Slave: A Composite Autobiography*, gen. ed. George P. Rawick, vol. 12, *Georgia Narratives*, part 2 (Westport, Conn.: Greenwood Publishing Company, 1972), 11–16.

6. Georgia Baker, interview by Sadie B. Hornsby, ed. Sarah H. Hall and John N. Booth, *The American Slave*, vol. 12, *Georgia Narratives*, part 1, 37–57.

7

Secessionists and Cooperationists:

The Decision to Leave the Union

For at least thirty years before the Civil War, Georgia and the nation engaged in controversy over slavery vs. freedom and states' rights vs. federal power. While Georgia politicians defended slavery and states' rights, they generally advocated moderation. During the nullification crisis of the 1830s, for instance, a Georgia convention expressed disapproval of tariffs but failed to join South Carolina in declaring them null and void. Another state convention supported the Compromise of 1850, establishing a strong fugitive slave law, permitting California to enter the Union as a free state, and allowing the remaining Southwest territories to decide the question of slavery for themselves.

This 1850 assemblage also adopted the Georgia Platform, warning the nation that southerners had been pushed far enough. Arguing that the North must do its part in maintaining the compact between the states, the Georgia delegates insisted that the fugitive slave law be enforced fairly and that the North not interfere further with the westward movement of slavery. As the years passed, however, southerners increasingly concluded that the North would not keep its part of the bargain. The fugitive slave law was effectively nullified by the northern states, and in 1854 the Republican Party emerged as a regional organization pledged to stop the expansion of slavery. In 1860, the nation elected a Republican President, Abraham Lincoln, despite the fact that ten southern states failed to cast a single ballot for him. Immediately, South Carolina left the Union.

On November 7, 1860, Governor Joseph E. Brown of Georgia sent a special message to the legislature, calling passionately for secession. The Georgia House at this time was perhaps the most inexperienced ever, with the vast majority in their first term, so uncertain legislators, before taking action, decided to invite senior statesmen to come and advise them. From November 12 to November 19, members of the General Assembly and the public gathered in the evenings to hear their leaders debate. Then, on November 20, the legislature chose not to decide the question itself, but to let the people participate in this momentous decision. An election was called for January 2, 1861, to choose delegates to a convention, which would meet two weeks later to determine Georgia's course of action. On a rainy January day, the towns and richer counties turned out for secession and the areas with fewer slaveholders for continued cooperation with the Union. The election was quite close, but the secessionists won and a few weeks later controlled the convention that took Georgia out of the Union.[1]

The Secessionist Argument: Joseph E. Brown

As judge of the Blue Ridge Circuit in north Georgia, Joseph E. Brown had been relatively unknown before he emerged as the Democrats' compromise gubernatorial candidate in 1857. A remarkably good administrator, he was elected governor four times, holding the post until Georgia's surrender in 1865. The first speech below is Brown's special message.

Message of Governor Joseph E. Brown on Federal Relations, November 7, 1860

... In my opinion, the constitutional rights of the people of Georgia, and of the other slaveholding States, have been violated by some of the non-slaveholding States to an extent which would justify them, in the judgment of all civilized nations, in adopting any measures against such offending States, which, in their judgment, may be necessary for the restoration and future protection of all their rights.

At the time of the formation of the Constitution of the United States, the rights of the slaveholder were recognized in all the States. No political demagogue in the Northern States had then been able to ride into power by denouncing the people and the institutions of the Southern States; nor had the Northern pulpit been desecrated by abolition harangues. Since the passage of the law of Congress inhibiting the traffic, most of the illegal importations of Slaves have been made by Northern men, in Northern ships. And it is a well-known fact that the people of the Northern States before the traffic was inhibited by Congress, imported a large proportion of the slaves brought from Africa, and sold them to the people of the Southern States, and received their money for them, which, with its proceeds, was, no doubt, invested in shipping, manufacturing, etc. This fact was fresh in the recollection of the Northern patriots who united with our fathers in forming the Constitution; and they did not hesitate to bind themselves and their posterity to respect our rights in slave property. I regret to say, however, that the conduct of many of their descendants has not been characterized by a like spirit of justice; since many, whose ancestors grew rich by the sale of slaves to the Southern people, are now ready to denounce the traffic by which the fortunes they enjoy were made, as immoral and inhuman, and the Southern people as little better than demons in human shape, because we continue to hold, as property, the offspring of the slaves purchased from their fathers. Numbers of them advocate the doctrine that our slaves should be set free among us, intermarry with our children, amalgamate with us, and be placed, in all respects, upon a basis of perfect equality with our free white population. For the purpose of promoting this object, and producing a general revolt of our slaves, a portion of their number, with fire and sword, have invaded Virginia, one of our Southern sister States, and slaughtered, in cold blood, some of her quiet, law-abiding citizens. It is true, these guilty criminals have suffered the penalty of the law upon the scaffold; but the justice of their punishment has been denied, and their names have been canonized by the abolition masses in the Northern States; and, even in the pulpit, they are frequently referred to as martyrs to the cause of liberty.

Should our citizens invade their territory, and burn down their factories built with money or the proceeds of money paid them by Virginia, Georgia, and Carolina planters for slaves, and butcher their citizens who hold property acquired by the sale of slaves or by the use of the productions of slave labor, how differently they would view the question of criminality! But the invader who should slay the Northern citizen who holds his fortune acquired by the proceeds of slave labor and the sale of slaves, would be no more guilty than those who invaded a slave State and slaughtered her citizens because they held slaves; nor would his moral guilt be greater than that of the political leaders, who, by their doctrines and teachings, prompted and encouraged, the invasion of Virginia. While the abolitionists deny our right to hold the slaves we purchased from them, they do not permit any one to question their right to their property purchased with the money we paid them for slaves. They claim the right to hold their property thus acquired but deny our right to hold the slaves they sold us for it. They claim the right to carry the property which they received from us for slaves into the Territories, but deny our right to carry the slaves they gave us for it, into the same Territories.

This is not the spirit of the Northern patriots of 1776, with whom our fathers united in the Declaration of Independence; nor of those of 1787, with whom they entered into the compact of the Constitution. They were brave, noble, generous men; who required justice from all men, and were ready, in return, to render even-handed justice to all. At that time, Georgia and Massachusetts were alike sovereign and independent States. Each entered the family of States with her faith solemnly pledged to the other to perform all her Constitutional obligations, and to respect all the Constitutional rights of the other.

The Constitution of the United States is a compact in the nature of a treaty, between the sovereign States of this Union; by which each State made concessions to the other, for the sake of the Union, and each bound her faith solemnly to the others, to do, or to permit Congress to do, certain acts which it was agreed would promote the interest of the others, and to omit to do certain other acts which might be to the injury of the others. Each delegated to the General Government, under the qualifications contained in the Constitution of the United States, the exercise of a portion of its sovereign powers, for the good of the whole. Georgia, when she entered the compact with Massachusetts, conceded important commercial and other rights; which concessions, under the operation of our tariff laws, navigation laws, and otherwise, have inured greatly to the benefit of Massachusetts. In return for these concessions, Massachusetts solemnly contracted and agreed with Georgia, that she would, on her part, (among other things) "deliver up" to Georgia her fugitive slaves escaping and going into Massachusetts, on claim of the party to whom the service or labor may be due. No one pretends that Georgia and the other Southern States would have entered into the compact and formed the Union, had Massachusetts and the other Northern States refused to give this express guaranty. . . .

. . . The Black Republican party, organized upon a sectional issue, and standing upon a platform of avowed hostility to our constitutional rights, have probably triumphed over us, by the election of their candidates for the Presidency and Vice-Presidency. Should such be the case, this dominant party in the Northern section of the Union, among whose fanaticism rules the hour, and mob law too often maintains its ascendancy, will consider themselves as victors, and the people of the South as vanquished. In that event, the adoption of other safeguards, may become necessary to the maintenance of the rights and honor of the slave-holding States; as degradation, insult and injury, will probably be the only reward, which Georgia and the other slave States, can then expect to receive, for continued association with them in the Union, and subjection to their foul domination.

So soon as the Government shall have passed into Black Republican hands, a portion of our citizens, must if possible be bribed into treachery to their own section, by the allurements of office; or a hungry swarm of abolition emissaries must be imported among us as office-holders, to eat out our substance, insult us with their arrogance, corrupt our slaves, and engender discontent among them; while they flood the country with inflammatory abolition documents, and do all in their power, to create in the South, a state of things which must ultimately terminate in a war of extermination between the white and the black races.

Whether eight millions of freemen in the Southern States will consent to permit this state of things to exist among them, and will bow the neck in willing subjection to the yoke, is a question to be determined by them in their sovereign capacity.

Whether the sovereign will of the people of the Southern States, shall, in this crisis, be ascertained by a general Convention of all the States, hereafter to be called, and all shall act together in concert, or whether each State shall decide for herself, without conference with the others, are questions upon which a diversity of opinion may exist.

I entertain no doubt of the right of each State, to decide and act for herself. The Union is a compact between the sovereign States of which it is composed. Each State in the Union is in point of sovereignty the equal of every other; and neither is dependent upon another for any of the attributes of sovereignty. So long as all the States abide in good faith by their Constitutional engagement to each other, and the compact is not violated, no State can withdraw from the Union without being guilty of bad faith to the others. If, however, the compact is violated by the refusal of part of the contracting parties to abide by it, and submit to its burdens, while they receive the benefits arising from it, the other parties are no longer bound by it, but may declare it a nullity, and refuse to abide by it on their part. It is an essential part of the law of contracts, that both parties are bound, or neither is bound, and if one violates the contract, the other is no longer bound.

But I may be asked who is to judge of the violation of the contract? I answer that each sovereign State, from the very nature of the case, must judge and decide for herself. There is no common arbitor between them. Each being sovereign, acknowledges no higher power on earth. The Federal Government is but the limited agent of all the States, and has no right to assume to dictate to the principals, from which it derives all the power it possesses, nor to sit in judgment upon the conduct of the creator, whose creature it is, and by whose consent alone, it exists for a single day. It is not to be presumed that a State will secede from the Union without just cause. Of the sufficiency of the cause each sovereign State must judge for herself. When her decision is made, no one has a right to reverse the judgment, because no higher power exists to which an appeal can be taken. The right of a State peaceably to secede from the Union, when, in the judgment of her people, the compacts of the Constitution have been violated, can only be denied by those who deny the sovereignty of the States. . . .

The sentiment, no doubt, prevails in the Northern States, that the people of the South would be in great danger from their slaves, in case we should attempt to separate from the Northern States, and to form an independent Government. Insurrection and revolt are already attempted to be held in terror over us. I do not pretend to deny that Northern spies among us, might be able occasionally, to incite small numbers of slaves in different localities to revolt, and murder families of innocent women and children; which would oblige us promptly to execute the slaves who should have departed from the path of duty, under the deceptive influence of abolition incendiaries. These instances would, however, be rare. Our slaves are usually under the eye of their masters or overseers. Few of them can read or write. They are not permitted to travel on our Railroads, or other public conveyances, without the consent of those having the control of them. They have no mail facilities, except such as their owners allow them to have, and have no means of communication with each other at a distance. They are entirely unarmed, and unskilled in the use of arms. A general revolt would therefore be impossible. But the more important fact, which is well known in Southern society is, that nine-tenths of them are truly and devotedly attached to their masters and mistresses, and would shed in their defence, the last drop of their blood. They feel and recognize their inferiority as a race, and their dependence upon their owners for their protection and support, whose smile of approbation constitutes their highest enjoyment. They have not been accustomed to claim or exercise political rights, and few of them have any ambition beyond their present comfort and enjoyment. In case of a plot or conspiracy, the secret could be communicated to but few, till some would learn it, who would immediately communicate it to their masters, and put them upon their guard. This would lead to an immediate seizure and execution of a few of their leaders. We have therefore but little cause of apprehension from a rebellion of our slaves.

Let us for a moment contrast our difficulties with *our laborers*, in case of division, with the difficulties which the Northern people would have with *their laborers*.

Many of the Northern masters, or employers, if they prefer the term, are now in possession of large fortunes, which they have accumulated by the use of the strong arms of white laborers among them, who have labored and toiled and dropped the briny sweat, for weeks, and months, and years, in their service, and have received from them in return a meagre compensation, which in health, has barely enabled them to support themselves, in a simple style, denying to their families most of the comforts of life; and in sickness has often left them in destitution, and actual want of the necessities of life.

While those who receive the benefits of labor of others, are living in stately mansions, amid ease and luxury, and faring sumptuously every day, many of the laborers whose toil brought these comforts, must spend their days in unpleasant dwellings, doomed to perpetual obscurity, and denied even in sickness, the comforts of life, produced by their own hard labor.

But who are these honest, sturdy laborers, who are kept in a position of inferiority, to those who assume control over them? They are *white men*. They belong to no inferior race. They are the sons of freemen, and they have a right to be free; many of them are descended from revolutionary sires, who shed their blood to secure *liberty* to their posterity. These men have political rights inherited from their ancestors, which are inalienable. They have the right to bear arms, and thousands of them know how to use them. They can read and write and correspond with each other about the wrongs inflicted upon them.

Should a separation take place, and the Northern States take up arms against the people of the South, and attempt to incite our slaves to insurrection, thousands of these Northern *white* laborers, who have suffered so much injustice at the hands of those, who have wrung from them the hard earnings of the sweat of their brows, might feel at liberty to require satisfaction for past injustice, and to assert the principle recognized in the South, that the true aristocracy is not an aristocracy of wealth, but of *color* and of *conduct*. While their sense of justice might prompt them to assist the South against the aggressions of those in the North, who have denied equality to them, as well as to the people of the South.

Among us the poor white laborer is respected as an equal. His family is treated with kindness, consideration and respect. He does not belong to the menial class. The negro is in no sense of the term equal. He feels and knows this. He belongs to the only true aristocracy, the race of *white men*. He blacks no masters' boots, and bows the knee to no one save God alone. He receives higher wages for his labor, than does the laborer of any other portion of the world, and he raises up his children, with the knowledge, that they belong to no inferior cast; but that the highest members of the society in which he lives, will, if their conduct is good, respect and treat them as equals.

These men know, that in the event of the abolition of slavery, they would be greater sufferers than the rich, who would be able to protect themselves. They will, therefore, never permit the slaves of the South to be set free among them, come in competition with their labor, associate with them, and their children as equals—be allowed to testify in our Courts against them—sit on juries with them, march to the ballot box by their sides, and participate in the choice of rulers—claim social equality with them—and ask the hand of their children in marriage. That the ultimate design of the Black Republican party, is, to bring about this state of things, in the Southern States, and that its triumphs, if submitted to by us, will at no very distant period, lead to the consummation of these results, is, I think, quite evident, to the mind of every cool, dispassionate thinker, who has examined this question, in the light of all the surrounding circumstances.

If the madness and folly of the people of the Northern States shall drive us of the South to a separation from them, we have within ourselves, all the elements of wealth, power and national greatness, to an extent possessed probably by no other people on the face of the earth. With a vast and fertile territory, possessed of every natural advantage, bestowed by a kind Providence upon the most favored land, and with almost monopoly of the cotton culture of the world, if we were true to ourselves, our power would be invincible, and our prosperity unbounded.

If it is ascertained that the Black Republicans have triumphed over us, I recommend the call of a Convention of the people of the State at an early day; and I will cordially unite with the General Assembly in any action, which, in their judgment, may be necessary to the protection of the rights and the preservation of the liberties of the people of Georgia, against the future aggressions of an enemy, which, when flushed with victory, will be insolent in the hour of triumph.

For the purpose of putting this State in a defensive condition as fast as possible, and prepare for an emergency, which must be met sooner or later, I recommend that the sum of one million dollars be immediately appropriated, as a military fund for the ensuing year; and that prompt provision be made for raising such portion of the money as may not be in the Treasury, as fast as the public necessities may require its expenditure. "Millions for defence, but not a cent for tribute," should be the future motto of the Southern States.

To every demand for further concessions, or compromise of our rights, we should reply, "The argument is exhausted," and we now "stand by our arms."[2]

🐦 🐦 🐦

The Case for Cooperation:
Alexander H. Stephens

In the previous chapter the reader was presented a portrait of Alexander H. Stephens, paternalistic slaveowner. As a Whig politician of the 1840s, he worked diligently to find a common ground with the party's northern branch. In 1846, the young congressman went along with his party in opposing the U.S.–Mexico War, even though the conflict was popular in the South. Next, he supported the Compromise of 1850 and the Georgia Platform, helping to preserve the Union an extra decade. The squire of Crawfordville joined the Democrats only after the Whigs became hopelessly divided over the slave question.

Stephens has been criticized for his lack of effort in campaigning against secession, prior to the January 2, 1861, election. Nonetheless, he made an eloquent speech to the legislature, urging Georgians to give Lincoln a chance before they acted rashly. After the Unionists failed in their attempt to hold the country together, Stephens elected to stick with his state. He was chosen Confederate vice president and championed the new nation's cause as eloquently as he once supported the Union. In fact, he sometimes advocated the Southern position so vigorously that he embarrassed the Confederate government. The Confederacy wanted the world to think that secession resulted not from the planters' desire to preserve slavery but from Northern violations of states' rights. In his infamous "Cornerstone Speech," however, Stephens became caught up in his rhetoric and said the opposite. After arguing that Republicanism was based on racial equality, he went on to say: "Our new government is founded upon exactly the opposite idea; its foundations are laid, its cornerstone rests upon the great truth, that the negro is not equal to the white man; that slavery—subordination to the superior race—is his natural and normal condition."[3]

The address below reflects Stephens's views before a decision had been made and while the preservation of the Union was still possible.

Union Speech of November 14, 1860

The first question that presents itself is, shall the people of Georgia secede from the Union in consequence of the election of Mr. Lincoln to the Presidency of the United States? My countrymen, I tell you frankly, candidly, and earnestly, that I do not think that they ought. In my judgment, the election of no man, constitutionally chosen to that high office, is sufficient cause to justify any State to separate from the Union. It ought to stand by and aid still in maintaining the Constitution of the country. To make a point of resistance to the Government, to withdraw from it because any man has been elected, would put us in the wrong. We are pledged to maintain the Constitution. Many of us have sworn to support it. Can we, therefore, for the mere election of any man to the Presidency, and that, too, in accordance with the prescribed forms of the Constitution, make a point of resistance to the Government, without becoming the breakers of that sacred instrument ourselves, by withdrawing ourselves from it? Would we not be in the wrong? Whatever fate is to befall this country, let it never be laid to the charge of the people of the South, and especially to the people of Georgia, that we were untrue to our national engagements. Let the fault and the wrong rest upon others. If all our hopes are to be blasted, if the Republic is to go down, let us be found to the last moment standing on the deck with the Constitution of the United States waving over our heads. (Applause.) Let the fanatics of the North break the Constitution, if such is their fell purpose. Let the responsibility be upon them. I shall speak presently more of their acts; but let not the South, let us not be the ones to commit the aggression. We went into the election with this people. The result was different from what we wished; but the election has been constitutionally held. Were we to make a point of resistance to the Government and go out of the Union merely on that account, the record would be made up hereafter against us.

But it is said Mr. Lincoln's policy and principles are against the Constitution, and that, if he carries them out, it will be destructive of our rights. Let us not anticipate a threatened evil. If he violates the Constitution, then will come our time to act. Do not let us break it because, forsooth, he may. If he does, that is the time for us to act. (Applause.) I think it would be injudicious and unwise to do this sooner. I do not anticipate that Mr. Lincoln will do anything, to jeopardize our safety or security, whatever may be his spirit to do it; for he is bound by the constitutional checks which are thrown around him, which at this time render him powerless to do any great mischief. This shows the wisdom of our system.

The President of the United States is no Emperor, no Dictator—he is clothed with no absolute power. He can do nothing, unless he is backed by power in Congress. The House of Representatives is largely in a majority against him. In the very face and teeth of the majority of Electoral votes, which he has obtained in the Northern States, there have been large gains in the House of Representatives, to the Conservative Constitutional Party of the country, which I here will call the National Democratic Party, because that is the cognomen it has at the North. There are twelve of this Party elected from New York, to the next Congress, I believe. In the present House, there are but four, I think. In Pennsylvania, New Jersey, Ohio, and Indiana, there have been gains. In the present Congress, there were one hundred and thirteen Republicans, when it takes one hundred and seventeen to make a majority. The gains in the Democratic Party in Pennsylvania, Ohio, New Jersey, New York, Indiana, and other States, notwithstanding its distractions, have been enough to make a majority of near thirty, in the next House, against Mr. Lincoln. Even in Boston, Mr. Burlingame, one of the noted leaders of the fanatics of that section, has been defeated, and a Conservative man returned in his stead. Is this the time, then, to apprehend that Mr. Lincoln, with this large majority of the House of Representatives against him, can carry out any of his unconstitutional principles in that body?

In the Senate, he will also be powerless. There will be a majority of four against him. This, after the loss of Bigler, Fitch, and others, by the unfortunate dissensions of the National Democratic Party in their States. Mr. Lincoln cannot appoint an officer without the consent of the Senate—he can not form a Cabinet without the same consent. He will be in the condition of George the Third (the embodiment of Toryism), who had to ask the Whigs to appoint his ministers, and was compelled to receive a Cabinet utterly opposed to his views; and so Mr. Lincoln will be compelled to ask of the Senate to choose for him a Cabinet, if the Democracy or that Party choose to put him on such terms. He will be compelled to do this, or let the Government stop, if the National Democratic Senators (for that is their name at the North), the Conservative men in the Senate, should so determine. Then how can Mr. Lincoln obtain a Cabinet which would aid him, or allow him to violate the Constitution? Why, then, I say, should we disrupt the ties of this Union, when his hands are tied—when he can do nothing against us?

I have heard it mooted, that no man in the State of Georgia, who is true to her interests, could hold office under Mr. Lincoln. But I ask, who appoints to office? Not the President alone; the Senate has to concur. No man can be appointed without the consent of the Senate. Should any man, then, refuse to hold office that was given him by a Democratic Senate?

Mr. Toombs interrupted, and said, if the Senate was Democratic, it was for Breckenridge.

Well, then, continued Mr. Stephens, I apprehend that no man could be justly considered untrue to the interests of Georgia, or incur any disgrace, if the interests of Georgia required it, to hold an office which a Breckenridge Senate had given him, even though Mr. Lincoln should be President. (Prolonged applause, mingled with interruptions.) . . .

My honorable friend who addressed you last night (Mr. Toombs), and to whom I listened with the profoundest attention, asks if we would submit to Black Republican rule? I say to you and to him, as a Georgian, I never would submit to any Black Republican aggression upon our Constitutional rights.

I will never consent myself, as much as I admire this Union, for the glories of the past or the blessings of the present; as much as it has done for civilization; as much as the hopes of the world hang upon it; I would never submit to aggression upon it; I would never submit to aggression upon my rights to maintain it longer; and if they can not be maintained in the Union standing on the Georgia Platform, where I have stood from the time of its adoption, I would be in favor of disrupting every tie which binds the States together. I will have equality for Georgia, and for the citizens of Georgia, in this Union, or I will look for new safeguards elsewhere. This is my position. The only question now is, can this be secured in the Union? That is what I am counseling with you tonight about. Can it be secured? In my judgment it may be, yet it may not be; but let us do all we can, so that in the future, if the worst comes, it may never be said we were negligent in doing our duty to the last. . . .

There are defects in our Government, errors in our administration, and shortcomings of many kinds, but in spite of these defects and errors, Georgia has grown to be a great State. Let us pause here a moment. In 1850 there was a great crisis, but not so fearful as this, for of all I have ever passed through, this is the most perilous, and requires to be met with the greatest calmness and deliberation.

There were many amongst us in 1850 zealous to go at once out of the Union—to disrupt every tie that binds us together. Now do you believe, had that policy been carried out at that time, we would have been the same great people we are today? It may be that we would, but have you any assurance of that fact? Would we have made the same advancement, improvement, and progress, in all that constitutes material wealth and prosperity, that we have?

I notice in the Comptroller-General's report, that the taxable property of Georgia is six hundred and seventy million dollars, and upwards—an amount not far from double what it was in 1850. I think I may venture to say that for the last ten years the material wealth of the people of Georgia has been nearly, if not quite, doubled. The same may be said of our advance in education, and everything that marks our civilization. Have we any assurance that had we regarded the earnest but misguided patriotic advice, as I think, of some of that day, and disrupted the ties which bind us to the Union, we would have advanced as we have? I think not. Well, then, let us be careful now, before we attempt any rash experiment of this sort. I know that there are friends whose patriotism I do not intend to question, who think this Union a curse, and that we would be better off without it. I do not so think; if we can bring about a correction of these evils which threaten—and I am not without hope that this may yet be done. This appeal to go out, with all the promises for good that accompany it, I look upon as a great, and I fear, a fatal temptation.

When I look around and see our prosperity in everything—agriculture, commerce, art, science, and every department of progress, physical, mental and moral—certainly in the face of such an exhibition, if we can, without the loss of power, or any essential right or interest, remain in the Union, it is our duty to ourselves and to posterity to do so. Let us not unwisely yield to this temptation. Our first parents, the great progenitors of the human race, were not without a like temptation when in the garden of Eden. They were led to believe that their condition would be bettered—that their eyes would be opened—and that they would become as Gods. They, in an evil hour, yielded—instead of becoming Gods, they only saw their own nakedness.

I look upon this country, with our institutions, as the Eden of the World, the Paradise of the Universe. It may be that out of it we may become greater and more prosperous, but I am candid and sincere in telling you that I fear if we yield to passion, and without sufficient cause shall take that step, that instead of becoming greater or more peaceful, prosperous and happy—instead of becoming Gods, we will become demons, and at no distant day commence cutting one another's throats. This is my apprehension. Let us, therefore, whatever we do, meet these difficulties, great as they are, like wise and sensible men, and consider them in the light of all the consequences which may attend our action. Let us see, first clearly, where the path of duty leads, and then we may not fear to trade therein. . . .

Now, then, my recommendation to you would be this: In view of all these questions of difficulty, let a convention of the people of Georgia be called, to which they may all be referred. Let the sovereignty of the people speak. Some think that the election of Mr. Lincoln is cause sufficient to dissolve the Union.

Some think those other grievances are sufficient to justify the same; and that the Legislature has the power thus to act, and ought thus to act. I have no hesitancy in saying that the Legislature is not the proper body to sever our Federal relations, if that necessity should arise.

I say to you, you have no power so to act. You must refer this question to the people, and you must wait to hear from the men at the cross-roads, and even the groceries; for the people of this country, whether at the cross-roads or groceries, whether in cottages or palaces, are all equal, and they are the Sovereigns in this country. Sovereignty is not in the Legislature. We, the people, are sovereign. I am one of them, and have a right to be heard; and so has every other citizen of the State. You Legislators—I speak it respectfully—are but our servants. You are the servants of the people, and not their masters. Power resides with the people in this country. The great difference between our country and most others, is, that here there is popular sovereignty, while there sovereignty is exercised by kings or favored classes. This principle of popular sovereignty, however much derided lately, is the foundation of our institutions. Constitutions are but the channels through which the popular will may be expressed. Our Constitutions, State and Federal, came from the people. They made both, and they alone can rightfully unmake either.

Should Georgia determine to go out of the Union, I speak for one, though my views might not agree with them, whatever the result may be. I shall bow to the will of her people. Their cause is my cause, and their destiny is my destiny; and I trust this will be the ultimate course of all. The greatest curse that can befall a free people, is civil war. . . .[4]

NOTES

1. Governor Brown's special message and the comments of several of the debaters were published in Allen D. Chandler, ed., *The Confederate Records of the State of Georgia*, (Atlanta: Charles P. Byrd, State Printer, 1909), 1:19–205. Georgia's decision to secede has attracted a considerable amount of scholarly attention. See, especially, Michael P. Johnson, *Toward a Patriarchal Republic: The Secession of Georgia* (Baton Rouge: Louisiana State University Press, 1977); William W. Freehling and Craig M. Simpson, eds., *Secession Debated: Georgia's Showdown in 1860* (New York: Oxford University Press, 1992); and William L. Barney, "Resisting the Republicans: Georgia's Secession Debate," *Georgia Historical Quarterly* 77 (Spring 1993): 71–85.

2. Chandler, *Confederate Records*, 1:20–23, 47–49, 52–57.

3. Savannah, March 21, 1861. For the full text of this speech, see pp. 42–46 of

Edwin C. Rozwenc, ed., *Slavery As a Cause of the Civil War*, revised ed., Problems in American Civilization Series (Lexington, Mass.: D.C. Heath and Company, 1963). The speech is also discussed in Thomas E. Schott, *Alexander H. Stephens of Georgia: A Biography* (Baton Rouge: Louisiana State University Press, 1988), 334.

4. Chandler, *Confederate Records*, 1:184–89, 197–99, 201–2.

8

The Federal Occupation of Georgia, 1864: Perspectives of North Georgia Women

A Deep South state, Georgia was fortunate to avoid invasion during the early years of the war. Except for action along the coastline, the Union army and navy devoted its attention to theaters further north or west. By 1863, however, Chattanooga and the Tennessee River were in Federal hands, and nothing stood between Georgia and a large Northern army.

In the spring of 1864, General William T. Sherman led a force of over one hundred thousand men down the lines of the state-owned Western and Atlantic Railroad. The destination was Atlanta, a small town of strategic significance as the railroad center of the Southeast. Sherman was opposed by General Joseph E. Johnston, a capable officer, who commanded roughly half as many troops.

Johnston attempted a defensive strategy, entrenching his forces on the numerous mountain locations of North Georgia. Battles were quite bloody, with the invaders suffering numerous casualties at places such as Pickett's Mill and Kennesaw Mountain. Nonetheless, the Union time and again outflanked the defenders, forcing them to fall back from their positions. By September 2, Sherman was in Atlanta.

Leaving the city in flames, the Northern commander in mid-November began a month long "scorched-earth" invasion of central Georgia, destroying what little morale the native population had left. He reached Savannah just before Christmas 1864, completing his conquest of Georgia. In a few more months the fighting was over everywhere.

Military history is generally not told from the perspective of women, yet numerous Georgia females stayed home while battles raged around their dwellings and the invaders occupied their neighborhoods and towns. Many of these women kept journals of their experiences, as the four accounts below indicate.

At least since Anne Firor Scott wrote *The Southern Lady* in 1970, scholars of the war have known that plantation mistresses were far more involved in running family enterprises than the stereotype of the fragile Southern belle would imply. Idealized in the literature of the day for their softness and purity, they reared numerous children, ran households, supervised all aspects of food production from cooking to hog butchering, served as the plantation doctor and midwife, taught the children, and sometimes kept the account books. With the men at war, they assumed the management of plantations, frequently with great skill.[1]

The stories that follow relate the experiences of four independent women during the critical period when Northern troops occupied northwest Georgia. All but one of the four were living on farms with no adult men around. These three were devoted to the Southern cause, and sometimes put themselves at great risk because of their loyalties. The fourth, Louisa Fletcher, experienced another type of danger. Born in Massachusetts, she supported the Union, despite being ostracized by some of her neighbors.

☙ ☙ ☙

Invasion of North Georgia

The first document is from a book by Frances Thomas Howard, entitled *In and Out of the Lines*. It was written in 1870 but not published until 1905. She was the daughter of Charles Wallace Howard, editor of several progressive agricultural publications and a planter in Bartow County. The Howards were neighbors of

Godfrey Barnsley, an Englishman who built a magnificent manor house and gardens in the northern part of the county.

Included are excerpts from two parts of the book, first a description of Northern occupation of the countryside around the Howard house, then a description of the hardship of life in north Georgia in the aftermath of the Northern invasion.

There was such a continual knocking at the door that my mother said some one must remain downstairs, so Janet went to the dining-room and I to the parlor. This room had two large glass doors opposite each other and opening on the two verandas. The heavy winter curtains still overhung them, and I dropped them so as to conceal myself from the many soldiers who filled the piazzas.

Picking up a book, I sat for a few moments trying to fix my mind on the words before me. Some disturbance attracted the attention of the men and they left the house, and in the silence that followed I read understandingly. The only light in the room came through one pane of glass which I had left bare, but suddenly this was darkened, and, glancing at the window, I saw a hideous, grinning face flattened against the pane. As I looked the creature nodded and opened its disgusting mouth. I threw down my book and fled from the room.

My sisters were with my mother in her bedroom, where I joined them, and was telling of my late adventure when we were startled by the crash of a falling door.

"They are in the kitchen," said my mother.

We heard the tramp of many feet running across the laundry floor and the next moment the pantry door went down, and they were hammering at my mother's dressing-room. We fled into the dining-room, locking the door behind us. Door after door came rattling down, while we stood with white faces silently looking at one another. Finally some one said: "Let us go upstairs." Hardly had we reached the hall when the mob entered the dining-room, and we raced upstairs and locked ourselves in one of the bedrooms.

There was an awful sound below: not a word uttered, only the tramp of heavy feet and a hoarse, indistinct, growling murmur. I put my fingers on my pulse and found it was beating steadily. I remember I thought I was quite calm. My sisters were deadly pale, though perfectly composed, but my mother cried bitterly. No one spoke. Each was nerving herself for the coming storm.

The Yankees thundered up the stairs. Our door was locked, but the others were open, and we heard them throwing down heavy articles of furniture. At last there came a pause, followed by a tremendous blow upon our door, which instantly flew open. The entry and rooms beyond were full of Yankees, many of them half nude. They looked silently at us for a few moments, then a sergeant, followed by a private, motioned back the others and entered the room. He walked to the bureau, leaned upon it with both elbows, looked at himself in the glass, and began to caress his moustache. Smiling complacently at his reflected image, he turned to us.

"Ladies," he said, "these fellows are annoying you, are they not?" No one replied to the question.

"What are you doing here, sir? Report instantly to your command!" said a voice at the door.

To our great delight we saw a lieutenant walk in, and it was he who had spoken.

"Did you hear, sir?" said the officer, sternly.

"I am aware that I have to report to my command," replied the man sullenly, but still motionless.

Without another word the officer, a powerfully built young man, advanced, and seizing him by the collar dragged him to the head of the stairs, then, with a well applied kick from a foot encased in a heavy cavalry boot, sent him flying in the attitude of a diver down-stairs. . . .

[It still took a while to remove the poorly disciplined soldiers, but two Union officers were soon able to do so. The Howards were protected by a guard until Federal troops moved further south. Frances Howard then went on a journey through Northern lines to be reunited with her father at Savannah. After a dangerous return trip, she describes the difficulties of daily life in the South in the aftermath of the Northern invasion:]

I will now return to the time when I reached Mr. Burton's [Godfrey Barnsley's] house on the 24th of December, 1864. The next four days were spent in hunting up a team strong enough to carry a few of our belongings to our own home, and on the 30th of December we left the house of our kind friend, with many thanks for the shelter he had afforded us in our time of need.

We took with us two mattresses, and just enough household ware to meet our needs, also a shot gun, powder and shot. To save our horses from the thieves, who constantly passed in armed gangs, we put them in the smoke house, a strong log building, with only one heavy door, across which we laced chains with cow-bells attached, so that if the door were tampered with in the night the ringing of the bells would wake us.

The parlor served as a kitchen, dining-room, bedroom and parlor all in one, and from the back window the smoke-house door was visible, and as my pallet was laid under this window, I kept my little seven-shooter and the gun, the latter heavily loaded with buck-shot, close at hand, intending to kneel and shoot through the glass in case the chain was meddled with.

As Maria and I had to provide the wood we kept but one fire, which was really all that was needed, for our cooking consisted of one loaf of bread a day, which was baked in the oven on the hearth, our yeast being made from "Life everlasting," the wild immortelle, a very bitter plant.

Our provisions were flour, salt and yeast, absolutely nothing else—yet we were never stronger or in better health. Jane Miller, who lived with her parents in one of the out-houses, had two dogs that hunted rabbits very well, and she suggested that we try them some night for a possum, Jane saying that "Mrs. Smith had made pies with possum lard and they was powerful nice."

I was delighted with the idea of any break in our monotonous life, and eagerly consented to her proposal. Maria would not go, so the party consisted of Jane Miller, Nancy Morris and myself. It was a dark night, and the ground was frozen as hard as a rock. We wrapped up warmly and at eight o'clock, after calling the dogs we set out, Jane a little in advance with the torch, Nancy following with a bundle of lightwood, split fine, and I with the axe and matches. . . . After this we hunted often at night and occasionally got a possum, which made an agreeable addition to our diet.

In the latter part of January my father came home. I thought he did not at all like our mode of living. Three rolls a day to which, in his case, was added morning and evening a cup of rye coffee without milk or sugar, was not a very strengthening diet, and he had come home on sick furlough to recruit.

Soon after his return he had a visit from one of his men who was also at home on furlough. The soldier had heard that the captain was living on dry bread, and as he had two sides of meat the captain must have one; so saying, he produced a small pig's side from a bag and gave it to my father. We were truly grateful for this act of generosity.

One day, my father, who had been to Mr. McDonald's, returned with a large piece of meat, carefully tied up in a bag. Mr. McDonald had been to Haralson county, had brought back a load of beef, and had given my father a joint which lasted a long time, for we each ate but one small slice a day. During this time my brother stopped to see us, but he staid only three days, for we could barely feed him, and there was nothing but grass for his horse. . . .

I cannot tell you how we felt when the news of the surrender of Johnston's and Lee's armies came. Added to the humiliation of being conquered was the horrible idea of living under the government of a people who, in the past twelve months, had taught us so many bitter lessons. We wished to leave America but, as my father said, "our property now was in land alone,—there was no money,— it was impossible, and we must summon up our fortitude to make the best of it."

No man, not even a Confederate, can appreciate why submission was easier for the men than for the women of the Confederacy. They had fought a good fight, and when the end came, they could look back on duty well done; but we had simply to suffer. We saw deeds of cold-blooded, deliberate cruelty done either to ourselves, our families, or our friends, and there was no help. Previous to the war there did not exist a race of women so tenderly cared for as the women of the South. That chivalry—the derision of those who could not comprehend it—was our guard and protection. It stood between us and all harm; it taught that the strong should protect the weak; the brave, the timid.

By the fortune of war we experienced the tender mercies of men who scorned these doctrines and who shamed not to battle with women; fighting, it is true, not often with blows—which perhaps would have been more merciful—but with starvation and the torch. By the light of their burning homes, Southern women saw their children die of cold and hunger, and they heard the incendiaries laugh as they quoted the words of one of their leaders: "The seed of the serpent must be crushed from the land." Are these things easily forgotten?[2]

🔰 🔰 🔰

The Capture of Cassville

Lizzie Gaines was almost thirty-four years old and living in the village of Cassville, Bartow County, at the time of the Northern occupation. The account below demonstrates Miss Gaines's spunk as well as the problems which Southern civilians had to overcome while under military rule.

The Yankees killed every living thing they could find: cows, calves, sheep, hogs, turkeys, chickens, etc., not because they were in need of it themselves, but to deprive us of the necessaries of life. A few cows, however, escaped with their lives, and these they penned up for their own use.

The morning after the Federals took possession of Cassville, they set Mr. J. Terrill's (or Terrel's) house on fire. We were almost ready to give up in despair, for we felt sure the town would soon be in ashes. But the Yankees were not all entirely destitute of feeling for us poor rebels. We must give them credit for their perseverance in quenching the destroying element before much damage was done to any other buildings. Col. Warren Akin's house was burned the next day (May 19). We now succeeded in getting guards around our houses from the 5th Connecticut. We were well treated by them and felt comparatively secure while they remained. In a few days, we went to several houses to see the destruction. It was heartrending to look upon, and we turned off in disgust at the sight. While looking around, we met some Yankees who were very impertinent and insulting. These we treated with silent contempt. Others again were more civil, asked us if our soldiers did not tell us they would kill us? We told them no indeed. They advised us to remain at home and we would not be molested. We also told them that we had often heard reports of how defenseless females had been treated by them, and could scarcely believe it, but our experiences had removed all skepticism, and we would doubt nothing hereafter. . . .

One day about noon a party consisting of eighteen or twenty horsemen came along driving several cows. I saw them tear the lot fence down and knew they intended to drive ours off also. I ran to the lot and told them they should not have my cow. I stood in the gap and drove her back, as they would drive her out. The commander of the squad was very angry, and told the men to drive the cows over me if I did not get out of the way. So they pierced them with their bayonets, and forced me to fall back. My mother was an invalid, and it was on her account I remained in the Federal lines. She went to the door and said, "Gentlemen, please don't take our cow." They only laughed at her and drove on. They took at the same time a cow belonging to a lady friend of mine. She and I had an old poor horse some of our soldiers had given us. We called him Bragg. He had been a fine spirited animal but was now a mere frame of bones, and very docile and easily managed. So we borrowed an old buggy and hitched Bragg to it, and followed them to Cartersville, a distance of nine or ten miles. It was raining a little, and the roads were muddy and slippery, and as we were not able to afford shoes for Bragg, he could scarcely go up hill at all. When about half way the horse gave out, and we spent the night with Mr. Guyton's family, the father of Cobe, Bill Arp's friend.

The next morning Bragg was all right, and the sun shining brightly, we went on to Cartersville, passed the picket-lines without any trouble, found after inquiring around that we must first go to the Provost Marshall and undergo an examination as to our loyalty before we could do anything towards getting the cows.

When we arrived we found four other ladies on the same errand. We were seated before the judge, whose decision was law, and interrogated as follows:

The first was an old lady. He asked her if she had protection papers, or had taken the oath. She with an air of exultation replied that she had, and drew from her pocket, concealed under her dress, the precious document, which he examined. He asked her no more questions. He then proceeded to the next, with the same result, until he came to me, I happening to be the last in order. This was all new to me. I did not know that this was required of the women, and of course did not expect any favors from them, as I had no proof of my loyalty.

It was now my turn to be questioned. He said, "Have you any protection papers?" "No, sir," said I. "Have you ever been asked to take the oath?" "I have not." "Have you any objection to taking it?" "I have, sir, very serious objections." "What are your objections?" "I am a Southerner by birth and principle, and would not take the oath for all cows in the United States." "You are not loyal, Madam," said he, "and cannot get your cow." "I am as loyal as you are," said I. "Yes, I see you are truly loyal to the Southern Confederacy, and I respect you for it." "We do not take up arms against you," said I. "My tongue is my only weapon, and I wield it when occasion requires." "Yes," said he, "I would rather have one-hundred armed men, than one woman's tongue turned loose on me." He seemed very angry when I first refused to swear allegiance to the United States, but when our conversation ended he was smiling very pleasantly. He made out his report of us, and sent us under guard to Captain Garfield. I do not know whether he was any relation to the President or not, but I am inclined to believe he was, for he was the cleverest Yankee I ever saw. I did not expect to get my cow, but thought I would go on and help any loyal friends to drive theirs home.

The old lady first named chided me severely for talking as I did. Was afraid none of them would get their cows on account of my conduct. Capt. Garfield, who had charge of the slaughter pen, was a fine portly-looking man, with a pleasant good natured face.

I was watching his countenance, saw a smile flit over his face as he looked up and asked, "Which one is Miss Gaines?" "I am the one," said I. "I know I am accused of disloyalty there, but I want my cow." "Well, you shall have her," said he. He asked us to eat dinner, which I told him I would thankfully accept for I was very hungry.

He first told me I could get the cow, but it was contrary to orders for him to let me have the calf. I told him I would be very thankful for the cow, but we had intended to make beef of the calf, and were very much in need of the meat at that time. He then told me I could take it if I would promise to kill it as soon as I reached home. I promised, and had the calf killed, got a man who was subject to fits to kill it, and assisted in skinning it myself. Sent most of it around to the poor. . . .[3]

The Occupation of Marietta

Minerva Leah Rowles McClatchey was born about 1820 in Maryland. Most of her married life was spent in east Tennessee, before the family moved to a farm a mile south of Marietta in 1862. The relocation to Cobb County was an attempt to get away from Union sympathizers and to bring the family close to the Georgia Military Institute in Marietta, where the two oldest sons had been students and where the youngest would enroll during the war.

McClatchey was a writer, having published a number of articles while living in Tennessee. Her husband was a slaveowner and farmer. Suffering from a broken hip, he was unable to join the Confederate army. In 1864, he fled with his slaves and silver to middle Georgia, leaving behind his wife, a disabled son, and a niece. The strong-willed Minerva McClatchey was determined not to abandon her plantation, regardless of the consequences. Her nineteen-year-old son, Devereaux, was exempt from military duty, having lost three fingers in an accident. The narrative starts just after a skirmish at the McClatchey farm where Southern troops were forced to retreat.

July the 3rd. . . . Firing ceased after a while—two were killed and buried near the house and several wounded and carried to the rear. Their limbs were amputated in Mr. Goodman's yard. Genl. Hooker and his staff came up and by this time the whole face of the earth, as far as could be seen in the road, yard, garden and lot—everywhere was crowded with soldiers. The officers, many of them came into the house and behaved gentlemanly towards us. They asked us thousands of questions about the army, the roads, and the way the army would go. Genl. Hooker came in and shook hands cordially as an old friend—saying he was glad to see a citizen at home, that all the houses he had yet passed were deserted and why was it that the inhabitants would run away from their friends. He supposed I did not believe all the tales I had heard about yankee cruelty, etc. I told him that this was my home—I had none other—and had stayed with the hope that all gentlemen and true soldiers would recognize a woman's right to stay at home. "You are right Madam—you have acted wisely and will be protected. We did not come to war with inoffensive citizens, but to preserve the Union and establish the authority of the Government. Let the rebels lay down their arms, and we give them the hand of friendship," and much more in the same strain. Finally the Genl. left giving orders to some Captn. to place guards and have the premises protected. I felt somewhat relieved supposing that General Hooker meant what he said. But the guard only stayed while the Corps was passing—when they left followed by a succession of others, negroes, waggons, men on foot and horse, a continual stream. Many officers still lingered, as they said "glad to see ladies at home." One jumped up saying "I'll go in the parlor—havn't been in a parlor in six months." He seemed to know the way. "Oh, here's a piano"—and threw it open and played quite well. Several of them went in and danced for dear life. I said to one who was standing near me in the hall, "This is Sunday, I never encourage nor permit dancing in my own house—and I think it is particularly wrong on the holy Sabboth day." "Is this Sunday? Well, we never know when Sunday comes in the Army. I'll stop that." And so he did. They all behaved very well after that and soon left—only a few surgeons remaining, who were powerless, or pretended to be so to prevent the men who were prowling about everywhere outdoors, stealing everything they fancied. They did not come in the house, but took everything we had in the storeroom and kitchen. Killed all my fowls but one or two that escaped somehow, took the mothers from little chicks a few days old—and left them chirping. They took all our corn, flour, meal, honey, molasses and meat they found, and left us with a very small supply that we happened to have in the house. Took cooking vessels—flatirons, crocks, pans—pitchers—everything that was outside the house. Took all the children's books—and valuable files of newspapers—pictures, slates, everything out of the office, went to the carriage house and cut the carriage all to pieces—tore the green grapes from the vines, and the green apples were beaten from the trees. The garden was tramped all over and everything destroyed. A field of fine corn near the house, that was cut down in 15 minutes, and fed to their horses. That tho was done first thing in the morning—and even General Hooker's horse notwithstanding his master's loud professions, shared a part of that. Evening was drawing on and I thought if this is the way they do in daytime, what may we expect tonight. My feelings of loneliness, helplessness and dread cannot be described. Hearing that General Thomas was camped at the [Georgia Military] Institute, I sent Devereaux with a note to him, asking for a guard. He sent me two soldiers and I felt quite relieved. They were a great protection and satisfaction to us, but quite an eyesore to other soldiers when they came about on evil business. I have no doubt that the house would have been ransacked from top to bottom if they had not been here. An officer came one day and cursed them bitterly. O, such wicked oaths—said "You are volunteer guards, and if you are not gone in an hour—you will be arrested and punished." I went out and spoke to him politely—told him that I had applied to General Thomas for a guard, and he had sent me those men—I supposed they knew their duty, I had nothing to do with it, but would rather they would stay. He seemed pacified and went off.

In a few days the Provost Marshall sent two other men to relieve them and they very reluctantly went to their command. . . .

August 5th. I was half asleep, half awake this morning—and thought I was up, and out on the porch—giving the men drinks of buttermilk, as I often did, there was a crowd around, each waiting his turn, when my son John came up from the gate—he looked as pale as death and emaciated till no one but his mother would have known him. I thought I was awake and it was really my dear boy I saw. The surprise awoke me—and it was only a dream—but oh what a sad one. It fills me with fear and anxiety. What does it portend? I am cut off from them and can hear nothing. O my God preserve—comfort, save my poor boy, for Thou only canst be of service to him in his perils and privations.

Oct. 18th. O sad terrible heart sickening news has reached me. A friend from Tenn. writes me—he has heard from below from our friends there, that my poor boy was wounded on the 11th of June and died on the 11th of July. Can it be? My God, my God must I believe it—I did not know what it was to have a child cruelly wounded, and to die away from me—I did not know all this time that I have been suffering so much, that this last most severe drop was to be added to my already full, and bitter cup. The Lord has been good to me, I must not question his doings. . . .

Nov. 15th. Now they are all gone, I can but think of the terrors of last night. The Institute was on fire, a sick lad was here to stay with Mary—the officers were upstairs, so I knew the house was safe. Mr. Underwood said he would watch the door so Devereaux and I and a couple of the officers concluded we would go up on the hill and see the wretches at their work—at least that was my motive. Every house was in flames, it was as light as day. The houses in town were burning, many of them. Kinesaw mountain was in flames and as far as the eye could see the railroad was burning too and looked like a fiery serpent stretched through the darkness. Not a man was to be seen for sometime. We went all round the buildings, and finally saw about a half dozen very young soldiers, mere lads, who were doing the horrible work. I asked them if they liked to burn houses, they said "No matter whether we like it or not we have to obey orders. . . ."[4]

A Unionist Viewpoint

Louisa Warren Patch Fletcher was sixty-one years old when Marietta was occupied in 1864 by Union troops. Born in New Salem, Massachusetts, she came to Savannah as a young wife with her husband Dix Fletcher. The Fletchers moved to Marietta in 1849, where Dix managed a hotel. In the mid-1850s, he became proprietor of the four-story Fletcher House (later the Kennesaw House), near the depot for the Western and Atlantic Railroad. In those days Marietta was a resort community, with numerous planters from the Georgia and Carolina coast spending the summer months in the hills of North Georgia. The tourist dollars helped make Marietta more prosperous and aristocratic than one would anticipate in an upper Piedmont town, surrounded primarily by self-sufficient small farmers. The Fletchers were Unionists and Republicans, as was their son-in-law, Henry Greene Cole, who had come to Marietta to help build the W & A Railroad. As the section below reveals, Cole was arrested by the Confederate forces when Union troops moved close to the town. With habeas corpus rights suspended during wartime, the Union sympathizer was detained for about nine months to prevent any possibility that he might pass secrets to Sherman's army. During Reconstruction both Dix Fletcher and H. G. Cole would be actively involved in Republican politics in Georgia. Mrs. Fletcher's diary is important because it is a rare example of a friend of the Union who lived in Georgia for many years before, during, and after the war. It begins just before the battle of Kennesaw Mountain.

June 10, 1864   Have heard indirectly of Porta's [her sister, Sarah Hastings Caldwell] arrival in N.Y. after a fatiguing and perilous journey. Poor Cara [her daughter, Georgia Caroline Fletcher Cole] has been sorely afflicted by the arrest and imprisonment of her husband [Henry Greene Cole] on charge of communication with the enemy—he has always been free to express his Union sentiments but farther than that I believe him to be innocent of the crime (if so it can be called) with which he is charged—my dear Cara has never before known what trouble was—anxiety for his fate, the loss of his society and the great additional care which devolves upon her in consequence of his absence weighs upon her mind heavily—she hardly looks like her former self—so thin and care worn— she has shewn herself a true wife—so devoted to his comfort, so anxious to carry out all his plans and to look after his interests. . . .

July 25   A month of anxiety and trouble has passed since I last wrote—we are once more under the Federal flag but under military rule—Marietta was taken possession of by the Federals on the 3rd and 4th of this month, during which time we have been subject to many annoyances and some losses—stragglers from the army rove about and commit many depredations upon peaceable unoffending citizens which is very much to be regretted as it of course gives them an unfavourable impression of the Federals although some of them have been very kind and gentlemanly—many families have been provided with a guard whose presence secures them from the aggressions of lawless soldiers. . . .

Aug. 8   Since I last wrote have been to see Cara once—on that day she heard that Mr. C. had been removed to Charleston—this intelligence renewed her grief afresh—the thought of his being taken to a climate he was wholly unaccustomed to at this season of the year with no one near to look after and care for him and carry him food and clean clothing—O! How agonizing to her poor lacerated heart! The war is still raging near Atlanta—many sanguinary battles have been fought in the last two or three weeks. . . .

Nov. 20   . . . On the 10th of this month the Federals commenced their work of destruction in this town by firing buildings—this continued till the 15th when they abandoned the city—nearly all the public buildings and some twenty or more private residences have been destroyed—those were days of terror—every one in dread for fear their turn would come next—but not many houses were burned which were occupied. The army has gone South but no one knows their destination. Gen. Sherman passed through the place and remained one or two nights. Mari [her husband, Dix Fletcher] and Cara called to see him respecting Mr. C..e. Mari's Hotel and Stores are burned—we have now only our homes and what they contain—since the evacuation by the Federal Army we have been in constant dread of guerillas, thieves and plunderers. . . .

Feb. 12, 1865   Much has transpired since I last wrote in my journal—one of the most joyful events I ever had the pleasure of recording is the return of Cara with her husband which occurred two weeks ago—I never was more taken by surprise than when they entered the house having rec'd very discouraging letters from her previously—but through her unceasing efforts aided by some friends, his release was at length procured even unexpectedly to her as she had met with no encouragement from the military authorities—after keeping him nearly nine months in confinement they at length release him without a trial. This is one among the many acts of cruelty resulting from this unrighteous war. . . .

May 14   Sabbath after Sabbath rolls round and now it is a year since I have been inside a church—there is preaching in Marietta but under present circumstances and with the present feelings of the Ministers and their congregations I do not feel that it would be right or profitable for me to attend—the ministers still praying for the success of their Pres. and the women feeling so bitter they can hardly find language strong enough to denounce the *Yankees* in, as they always term them. I feel that we are now living in a state of chaos or confusion without any government either civil or military.

July 22, 1866   My dear Cara suffers much in her feelings from the bitterness and hostility of Southerners toward Union people her husband being one of the strongest kind—he recently proffered a very eligible site to the citizens of Marietta for a cemetery for Federal and confederate soldiers which was rejected with scorn because they could not bury *their* dead with the Federal. He afterwards offered it to the government for a national cemetery and it has been accepted, he having been appointed superintendent and has given employment to Mari wh. I hope will relieve him some by giving him some income. . . .[5]

NOTES

1. A fairly extensive literature exists on Georgia women during the Civil War. A few of the more accessible primary sources are Virginia Ingraham Burr, ed., *The Secret Eye: The Journal of Ella Gertrude Clanton Thomas, 1848–1889* (Chapel Hill: University of North Carolina Press, 1990); John Rozier, ed., *The Granite Farm Letters: The Civil War Correspondence of Edgeworth and Sallie Bird* (Athens: University of Georgia Press, 1988); and Robert Manson Myers, ed., *The Children of Pride: A True Story of Georgia and the Civil War* (New Haven: Yale University Press, 1972). Thomas was from Augusta; the Granite Farm was in Hancock County; and *Children of Pride* consists of letters of the Liberty County family of Charles Colcock Jones, the evangelist to the slaves quoted in Chapter 6. For background material one might turn to Anne Firor Scott, *The Southern Lady: From Pedestal to Politics, 1830–1930* (Chicago: University of Chicago Press, 1970); Catherine Clinton and Nina Silber, *Divided Houses: Gender and the Civil War* (New York: Oxford University Press, 1992); or Elizabeth Fox-Genovese, *Within the Plantation Household: Black and White Women of the Old South* (Chapel Hill: University of North Carolina Press, 1988).

2. Frances Thomas Howard, *In and Out of the Lines: An Accurate Account of Incidents during the Occupation of Georgia by Federal Troops in 1864–65* (New York: Neale Publishing Company, 1905), 14–16, 142–44, 148–49, 155–56.

3. Frances Elizabeth Gaines, "We Begged to Hearts of Stone," ed. Frances Josephine Black, *Northwest Georgia Historical and Genealogical Quarterly* 20 (Winter, 1988): 1–6.

4. T. Conn Bryan, ed., "A Georgia Woman's Civil War Diary: The Journal of Minerva Leah Rowles McClatchey, 1864–65," *Georgia Historical Quarterly* 51 (June 1967): 197–216.

5. Louisa Warren Patch Fletcher, "My Journal: Written with Occasional Inter-missions, 1857–1883," Louisa Warren Patch Fletcher Papers, Georgia Department of Archives and History, Atlanta; a transcript of the original by Henry E. Higgins and Connie M. Cox, entitled *The Journal of a Landlady,* can be found in the Georgia Room, Cobb County Public Library System, Marietta.

9

Reconstruction in Georgia

Between 1861 and 1865 Georgia and ten other Confederate states waged an unsuccessful war against the Union. The defeated rebels, however, were soon relieved to find that President Andrew Johnson expected few fundamental changes. He demanded new state constitutions that eliminated wartime debts, the right of secession, and slavery; otherwise, the conventions were permitted to treat former bondsmen as they pleased. Throughout the region, strict limits were placed on black freedom.

By 1867 Congress rebelled against Johnson's lenient plan. Over the president's veto Republican lawmakers required southern states again to revise their constitutions, this time giving black men the right to vote. In Georgia the 1865 constitution was replaced by that of 1868, written by a Republican convention in which about one-sixth of the delegates were black. To some the 1868 constitution seemed a horrible document that allowed into power people unfit to govern. Others praised the instrument for extending new freedoms to African-Americans. Below the two constitutions are compared in their treatment of slavery, civil liberties, and voting.[1]

The 1865 and 1868 Constitutions

A. Slavery

1865: The Government of the United States having, as a war measure, proclaimed all slaves held or owned in this State, emancipated from slavery, and having carried that proclamation into full practical effect, there shall henceforth be, within the State of Georgia, neither slavery nor involuntary servitude, save as a punishment for crime, after legal conviction thereof; provided this acquiescence in the action of the Government of the United States is not intended to operate as a relinquishment, waiver, or estoppel of such claim for compensation of loss sustained by reason of the emancipation of his slaves, as any citizen of Georgia may hereafter make upon the justice and magnanimity of that Government. (Art. 1, sec. 20)

1868: There shall be within the State of Georgia neither slavery nor involuntary servitude, save as a punishment for crime after legal conviction thereof. (Art. 1, sec. 4)

B. Legal Status of Erstwhile Slaves

1865: It shall be the duty of the General Assembly at its next session, and there-after as the public welfare may require, to provide by law for the government of free persons of color, or the protection and security of their persons and property, guarding them and the State against any evil that may arise from their sudden emancipation, and prescribing in what cases their testimony shall be admitted in the Courts; for the regulation of their transactions with citizens; for the legalizing of their existing, and the contracting and solemnization of their future marital relations, and connected therewith their rights of inheritance and testamentary capacity; and for the regulation or prohibition of their immigration into this State from other States of the Union, or elsewhere. And further, it shall be the duty of the General Assembly to confer jurisdiction in criminal cases excepted from the exclusive jurisdiction of the Superior Court, and in civil cases whereto free persons of color may be parties. (Art. 2, sec. 5, par. 5)

1868: All persons born or naturalized in the United States, and resident in this State, are hereby declared citizens of this state, and no laws shall be made or enforced which shall abridge the privileges or immunities of citizens of the United

States, or of this State, or deny to any person within its jurisdiction the equal protection of its laws. And it shall be the duty of the General Assembly, by appropriate legislation, to protect every person in the due enjoyment of the rights, privileges and immunities guaranteed in this section. (Art. 1, sec. 2)

C. Voting

1865: The electors of members of the General Assembly shall be free white male citizens of this State . . . . (Art. 5, sec. 1, par. 1)

1868: Every male person born in the United States and every male person who has been naturalized, or who has legally declared his intention to become a citizen of the United States . . . shall be deemed an elector. . . . (Art. 2, sec. 2)

🚩 🚩 🚩

Resistance to Reconstruction

In April 1868 a coalition of blacks, mountain-county whites, and others elected a Republican governor, Rufus B. Bullock. The new governor was interested in more than equal rights for blacks. Republican rule meant debt relief for small farmers and government-assisted economic development, primarily through aid to railroads. Nonetheless, this southern variety of liberal capitalism started unraveling when Democrats and "moderate" Republicans joined in September to expel three black senators and twenty-five black representatives. By that time the Ku Klux Klan had become an underground arm of the Democratic Party. Through murder and intimidation, terrorists drove from the polls many black and white Republicans.

In 1870 federal troops under General Alfred H. Terry restored the black legislators and purged a number of Democratic officeholders. The army, however, failed to eliminate violence in the countryside. Following new elections, the General Assembly by late 1871 was solidly back in Democratic hands. Just before the new legislature convened, Governor Bullock fled the state, thus ending Georgia's experiment at reconstruction.

Perhaps the worst single example of terrorist violence took place on September 19, 1868, in the southwest Georgia town of Camilla, in Mitchell County. On that day the Republican candidate for Congress, William P. Pierce, was scheduled to speak from the courthouse steps. A white "carpetbagger" from Kentucky,

Pierce had been a captain in the Union army. As a large crowd of mostly black Republicans approached this little town, the white residents became panicky, fearing invasion by an armed mob. The results were tragic. When the Republican entourage neared the courthouse, it was fired upon by surrounding whites. According to historian Lee Formwalt, a minimum of nine African-Americans were murdered.[2]

The closest office of the Freedmen's Bureau was in nearby Albany, from which Major O. H. Howard supervised a fifteen-county district. This federal agency was responsible for relief, education, and the protection of the rights of erstwhile slaves. Major Howard took numerous depositions from survivors, along with statements from the sheriff and a few other Mitchell County whites. The following is the account of a young black man named Daniel Howard.

Before me, O. H. Howard . . . personally came Daniel Howard, freedman, who being duly sworn deposes and says that he is 20 years old, that he is by occupation a laborer in the employ of Col. S. Montgomery in Dougherty County, Ga., that on the morning of Saturday, Sept. 19, 1868, a party of about 20 freedmen, came along the road, and told him that there was to be a speaking at Camilla (Mitchell Co., Ga.) on that day, and that he joined them, that at about 5 miles from Camilla at Tinsley's Mill, they, the freedmen, were joined by Capt. W. P. Pierce, Mr. [Francis Flagg] Putney, Mr. [John] Murphy and Philipp Joiner (colored) in buggies, that about 3 miles from Camilla, the freedmen were met by one James Johns (white) on horse back, with a double barrelled shot gun in his hands, that Johns said "by God, I am courier on this road; and you can't go into Camilla with that music"[3] and added "but you can go in, just as you d——m please, you'll get hurt anyhow." That said John [sic] then rode off in the direction of Camilla, that they were next met by the Sheriff of the County, who said to Mr. Murphy (white)[4] "I don't think you have a right to come down to Camilla with an army of men to take the place" (or words to that effect), that Mr. Murphy replied, "I did not come down for that, but to make a public speech, the same as I have been doing all over the country," that deponent then went on, and heard no more. That when the band-wagon entered the "square" this man Johns went up to it, and said, "stop that music, God damn you, or I'll shoot you" (or words to that effect), that as the music did not stop, Johns said "by God I have been your ruler many years and expect to be for many more" and then raised a double-barrelled gun that he held and taking aim at musicians, fired, that deponent was about 15 steps from Johns when the shot was fired, that this shot was followed by a volley from the whites and that the firing became general from the whites.

Deponent further states that he had his gun with him, but that it was not loaded, that most of the freedmen "broke and run," that the deponent, fearing to be killed, did not run until most of the whites had scattered in pursuit of the fugitives and then took to the woods, but was soon driven to a ditch and forced to surrender, that the deponent was seized and struck over the head with the butt of a gun and forced back to Camilla. Deponent further swears that he was forced to attend a party of whites, with a small wagon picking up wounded men, that other parties were gathering up and burying the dead, that he saw one woman on the public square dead, who was taken up in the wagon, and heard some white men talk about throwing her in an old well. He himself assisted in taking up one colored wounded man in town, who was shot through the bowels and in the head, one who was shot through the thigh who was taken off to a house in the county, another one was taken up in a field close to town, he was shot through the knee and breast, was taken to a mill, where he was working, another wounded man was found in a corn crib close by Dr. Dashers plantation; deponent further states that he and other freedmen were told by a party of whites, who rode into Camilla, to take their wagon out to a pond, back of Dr. Dashers house and see if any negroes were alive there, that they had shot twelve (12) at this pond and if any of them were still alive to bring them into town, that it was nearly dark, and before they reached the pond, the deponent took advantage of the darkness and escaped.

Deponent further states that while with these white men the whites said repeatedly that "if the G——d d——d niggers, had only come without arms, as we tried to have them, we could have surrounded them and killed the last d——d one of them."[5]

Congressional Investigation

In 1871 the U.S. Congress investigated Klan activities in the South. Over twelve hundred pages of testimony were gathered from Georgians alone. The documents below reveal the conflicting views of black Republicans and white Democrats.

Alfred Richardson

Washington, D.C., July 7, 1871

ALFRED RICHARDSON (colored) sworn and examined.

By the Chairman (Mr. Poland):[6]

Question. Where do you live?

Answer. In Clarke County, Georgia.

Question. What is your age?

Answer. About thirty-four years.

Question. Were you born in that county?

Answer. No sir; in Walton County, the adjoining county to Clarke.

Question. Were you born a freeman or a slave?

Answer. I was born a slave.

Question. Did you remain a slave until the general emancipation?

Answer. Yes sir. . . .

Question. Since you became a freeman what have you been doing?

Answer. I have been house-carpentering.

Question. Have you a family?

Answer. Yes, sir.

Question. Of how many does your family consist?

Answer. My wife and three children.

Question. Since you became a freeman have you voted?

Answer. Yes, sir.

Question. With what party have you voted?

Answer. The republican party.

Question. State to the committee whether you have been attacked in any way by anybody; if so, when and how. Tell us the whole story about it.

Answer. Yes, sir. I was attacked twice. The first time was just before last Christmas; I cannot recollect exactly what day.

Question. Tell us all the particulars.

Answer. There was a set of men came down to about a quarter of a mile of where I lived. They were all disguised. They had taken out an old man by the name of Charles Watson. They commenced beating him. His wife and children all ran out, and screamed and hallooed for help to stop the men from beating him to death. We, who were in town, came out to see what was the matter.

Question. You heard the outcry?

Answer. Yes, sir, and came out to see what was the matter. We went up the street a piece, out on the edge of the town, and heard a great parcel of men talking beside the fence. It was the Ku-Klux, who had this old man down in the corner of the fence, knocking him and telling him he had to tell where Alfred Richardson was, and had to go with them to his house and show how he was fixed up. The old man seemed to be sort of dilatory in telling them, and they rapped him over the head again and told him he had to go.

Question. They wanted him to tell where you were?

Answer. Yes, sir; they wanted him to tell where I was, and how I was fixed up; they said he had to go and get me out. In the mean time, while they were telling him this, a crowd of boys came on behind me, and we all ran up, after we heard what they were up to. They all broke and ran, and carried this old man with them. We followed them to the forks of the road, about three hundred yards from where we met them. They all stopped and got over into the field, taking the old man with them. I ran up, and looked first up one road and then the other, to see which way they had gone. I could not see anybody for a long time; a cloud had gone over the moon. After a while I saw one fellow slipping alongside the fence. He had a pistol in his hand, as if to shoot me. When I saw him doing that, I took my pistol, and shot at him. When I shot at him there were three or four men who shot me from through the fence. I did not see them. They shot about twenty shots into my leg and hip. I went off home, and went to the doctor's office. The doctor examined me, and fixed my wounds up. In three or four days I got so that I could travel very well. Things went on till after Christmas. On the 18th of January a man by the name of John O. Thrasher came to me—

Question. Was he a white man?

Answer. Yes, sir; a very wealthy white man. He came to me. My brother was keeping a family grocery; and I was in with him. I did not stay in the store; I worked at my trade.

Question. Were you a partner in the concern?

Answer. Yes, sir. This man told me, "There are some men about here that have something against you; and they intend to kill you or break you up. They say you are making too much money; that they do not allow any nigger to rise that way; that you can control all the colored votes; and they intend to break you up, and then they can rule the balance of the niggers when they get you off." He said, "They said they wanted me to join their party, but I told them I did not want to do it; I never knew you to do anything wrong, and these are a parcel of low-down men, and I don't want to join any such business; but I tell you, you had better keep your eyes open, for they are after you." He talked to me about it that evening for three or four hours. I told him I didn't know why they had anything against me. I talked to the ordinary, and the clerk of the court, and several other citizens. They said they didn't see why anybody wanted to interrupt me; that I had always kept the peace between the colored and the white people; that when there was a fuss I was the only man that could break it up and make the colored people behave themselves; that they hated to let me go away. I talked with all the citizens, and they told me they did not see why anybody had anything against me. I said, "I am told that some men are coming to kill me or run me off, and I think I had better go away. I don't know whether I can stay safely." They told me, "No, don't move away; they are just talking that way to scare you, I reckon." The same night this man was telling me that, I went to bed about 9 o'clock. Between 12 and 1 o'clock these men came; there were about twenty or twenty-five of them, I reckon. About eight or ten of them got abreast and ran against my door. I sort of expected them, and had my door barred very tight; I had long staples at the side, and scantling across the door. They ran against the door and tried to burst it in. They could not do it. One fellow had a new patent ax with him; and he commenced cutting down the door. One lit a candle and put it down in the piazza; the other man cut the door till he cut it down. I stood and looked at him until he cut it spang through. Then I thought I had better go upstairs. I did so. I thought I would stand at the head of the stair-steps and shoot them as they came up. But they broke in the lower door and came up-stairs firing in every direction. I could not stand in the stairway to shoot at them. I had some small arms back in the garret. There was a door up there about large enough for one man to creep in. I thought I had better go in there, and maybe they would not find me—probably they would miss me, and I could make my escape. They all came up-stairs. My wife opened the window to call out for help, and a fellow shot at her some twelve or fifteen times through that window while she was hallooing. A whole crowd came up, and when they saw that window open, they said, "He has jumped out of the window," and they hallooed to the fellows on the ground to shoot on top of the house. Thinking I had gone out the window, they all went down-stairs except one man. He went and looked in the cuddy-hole where I was, and saw me there. He hallooed to the rest of the fellows that he had found me; but they had got down-stairs, and some of them were on the piazza. Then he commenced firing, and shot me three times. He lodged two balls in my side, and one in the right arm. That weakened me pretty smartly. After he had shot his loads all out, he said to the rest of them, "Come back up here; I have got him; and I have shot him, but he is not quite dead; let us go up and finish him." I crept from the door of the little room where I was to the stairway; they came up-stairs with their pistols in their hands, and a man behind with a light. I shot one of them as he got on the top step. They gathered him up by the legs; and then they all ran and left me.

I never saw any more of them that night; and I have not seen them since. I have heard talk of them; and they say they will have me, they don't care where I go. . . .

Augustus R. Wright

Before the Civil War, Augustus R. Wright held public office first as a judge, then as a member of the U.S. Congress. He opposed secession, but served in the Confederate Congress. Just before the war's end, he joined an attempt by several leading Georgians to end hostilities. General William T. Sherman afforded him safe conduct to Washington, where he met with President Lincoln. Wright left the national capital believing he would have been provisional governor of Georgia had Lincoln lived. His last public service was as a member of the 1877 constitutional convention. The following is his testimony.

Washington, D.C., July 13, 1871

Hon. AUGUSTUS R. WRIGHT sworn and examined.

The Chairman (Mr. Poland.) As this witness has been called at your instance, Mr. Blair, you will please commence his examination.

By Mr. Blair:[7]

Question. Where do you live?

Answer. I live in the northwestern part of the State of Georgia, in the city of Rome, and the county of Floyd.

Question. How long have you lived there?

Answer. I have lived, not in the city of Rome, but in that and the adjoining county, since 1836. I went there before the Indians were removed. . . .

Question. You opposed the act of secession, did you not?

Answer. I opposed it with all the power I had on earth. There was no man in the Union, North or South, more utterly hostile to the act of secession than I was. . . .

By the Chairman, (Mr. Poland:)

Question. . . . We are directed to inquire whether the laws were properly enforced, especially the criminal laws; whether special or unusual crimes are committed by bands of disguised men, and, if so, how they are punished, if punished at all. We are directed to ascertain the present condition of the country.

Answer. Upon that subject permit me to say to you that we must first under-stand terms. Ku-Kluxism is a word used to mean different things. As a lawyer, you know that words are the signs of ideas, and you must be particular in their use. If you mean by the Ku-Klux Klan that there are any organized secret clubs, having correspondence with one another throughout the State, having their signs and pass-words and all that sort of thing, like the Free Masons and other secret soci-eties, my candid conviction is that there is no such organization; I have no idea there is any such—none in the world. That there is violence in that country occasionally, everybody knows to be true; no man who has any self-respect would deny that there is violence by men in disguise, and by men having local orga-nizations. I am satisfied that there is one in the adjoining county to the one in which I reside. But I must say to you, so far as my observation has gone, I do not think that its purposes are evil. . . .

By Mr. Blair:

Question. Some of the witnesses from your State have testified that certain men in Georgia, naming them, could by a word put down all this Ku-Kluxing, or all these unlawful proceedings; and among others they have named Mr. [Robert] Toombs, Mr. Alexander H. Stephens, and I believe your own name has been given also. The inference was that you had not exerted any influence to put down this thing, and that if you would exert your influence, it could be done.

Answer. I do not believe that is the truth. In the first place I do not believe we could prevent these outbreaks of violence occasionally, because while there are some things done that are wrong . . . yet, as a rule, I tell you that the purposes of these men are not bad; however wrong their actions may be their purposes are not bad; it is to conserve what they take to be the life of society. I do not think there is any power in the world to prevent that; where they think the life of society is seriously endangered, they will help themselves the best way they can; I do not think a million of troops would prevent it. . . .

I do not believe there is any people on the face of the globe, and I know I am saying it under oath, that is capable of self-government but the white race; and I believe very few nationalities of them are capable of self-government. I have no idea that the people of France are; I do not believe the republic of France will live ninety days. If there is any people on earth that could maintain a republi-can government, besides ours, in my opinion it would be the Germans. . . . But the idea that the black man is capable of self-government—how can I believe it? The history of his race for thousands of years, and his type of civilization now— I do not know, it seems to me so, I may be wrong—but look at him now, just out of slavery. Congress gives its judgment in favor of him, for it gives him the ballot; and it cannot require a higher type of civilization when he receives the ballot;

that is the privilege of the highest type of civilization. I want it to go out to the country, under oath, that I opposed that because I believe the negro is incapable of self-government, not on account of any prejudice against the race.

🖅 🖅 🖅

John B. Gordon

A lawyer and businessman, John B. Gordon rose in the Confederate army to the rank of lieutenant general. Running as a Democrat, he lost to Bullock in the 1868 gubernatorial election. At that time Gordon allegedly was the leader of the Georgia Klan. Following Reconstruction, he represented Georgia as a U.S. senator (1873–80), governor (1886–90), and senator again (1891–97). In testifying before the joint committee, Gordon made the following observations.

Washington, D.C., July 27, 1871

JOHN B. GORDON sworn and examined.

The Chairman, (Mr. Pool.)[8] Mr. Beck, as this witness has been called at your request, you will please open his examination.

By Mr. Beck:[9]

Question. State your place of residence.

Answer. Atlanta, Georgia.

Question. How long have you resided in Georgia?

Answer. I was born and raised there. . . .

Question. You ran for governor once?

Answer. I was a candidate for governor in the spring of 1868.

Question. Where did you reside immediately after the close of the war?

Answer. I removed to Brunswick, which is on the coast, a little south of Savannah; it is one of the most important seaports in our State.

Question. You lived there several years?

Answer. Yes, sir; I lived there about two years — until the latter part of 1867.

Question. And then you returned to Atlanta?

Answer. Yes, sir; I returned to my home in Atlanta; I was down at Brunswick, engaged in the lumber business; I had some saw-mills, &c., there, and was looking after my interests down there.

Question. The object we had in calling you as a witness was to get from you, if possible, a general view of the condition of the State of Georgia, to ascertain whether property and life are protected there, whether any crimes have been committed by disguised men. From your general knowledge of affairs in that State, we desire you to tell us whatever will enable the committee to understand fully the condition of affairs in Georgia, with reference to these matters. In answering the question, you are not limited to your own personal knowledge, but you have a right to tell anything you may have heard from such sources as you believe.

Answer. If it is worth anything to the committee I will give a statement as to the condition of affairs on the coast. Directly after the war I went with my family to Brunswick to engage in the lumber business. On my arrival there I found the place occupied, as were a number of places along the coast, by negro troops. In that portion of Georgia, all along the belt of sea-coast, for probably a hundred miles from the coast and up nearly to the middle portion of the State, the negroes, as a rule, largely outnumber the whites in every county. That is particularly so in the belt of country bordering on the Atlantic, embracing the Sea Islands. I suppose that in the county in which Brunswick is situated—Glynn County—the negroes must out number the whites, at a guess, eight or ten to one. I would say that without knowing the precise statistics. The disproportion of population between the blacks and whites is very great. When I reached Brunswick I found there was a very bad state of feeling between those negro troops and the citizens. I paid very little attention to the matter, but in walking the streets at times I found that these troops were insulting toward those whom they had heard were in the army. In passing by them in the street you would hear such remarks as this: "There is a damned rebel." Meeting you on the side-walk they would, without being absolutely violent, get you off the side-walk; they would refuse to divide it with you. These things attracted my attention. I was acquainted with some citizens there, and, on one occasion, soon after my arrival, some of them came to me and said that an old gentleman, living just out of the city, had been robbed. On inquiry I found that this old gentleman had been stopped on the road and robbed by these troops, and had been treated very badly; had not been personally injured, but very grossly insulted. He had been told that if he dared to oppose them they would take his life—"pin him up to a pine tree," or something of that sort was the language. They had also, directly after my arrival, taken a young man from the town, carried him into the woods, and laid him down, with a negro on each side, and had drawn a knife across his throat three or four times, telling him that they intended to take his life. After tantalizing him in that way for some time they turned him loose.

Such things of course created a good deal of feeling in the little town of Brunswick, which is now called a city; and especially did they excite the population very much, because of the immense number of negroes in the immediate vicinity of Brunswick on the islands around. The negro population generally became very obnoxious. They obtruded themselves everywhere they could. There was not only apprehension but decided alarm among the people. . . . There was a great deal of disturbance on different plantations, and a good deal of plundering; so much so that even the agents of the Freedmen's Bureau had to interfere. I would particularly mention a case which occurred on my own plantation, (I was planting rice at the time,) when the negroes drove the overseer away, threatening his life, on account of some orders he had given about the particular way the rice was to be cultivated. They wanted to cultivate it in their own style. There was no violence at all on his part. There were some fifty-odd negroes on this place, and their violence was so great (they threatened with hoes and implements of that sort, as well as guns) that the Freedmen's Bureau agent had to interfere, and the commander of the troops there had to take soldiers out to quell this difficulty. That was about the state of things when I left the coast. . . .

Question. What do you know of any combinations in Georgia, known as Ku-Klux, or by any other name, who have been violating law?

Answer. I do not know anything about any Ku-Klux organization, as the papers talk about it. I have never heard of anything of that sort except in the papers and by general report; but I do know that an organization did exist in Georgia at one time. I know that in 1868—I think that was the time—I was approached by some of the very best citizens of the State—some of the most peaceable, law-abiding men, men of large property, who had large interests in the State. The object of this organization was explained to me at the time by these parties; and I want to say that I approved of it most heartily. I would approve again of a similar organization, under the same state of circumstances.

Question. Tell us all about what that organization was.

Answer. The organization was simply this—nothing more and nothing less; it was an organization, a brotherhood of the property-holders, the peaceable, law-abiding citizens of the State, for self-protection. . . . We knew that the "carpet-baggers," as the people of Georgia called these men who came from a distance and had no interest at all with us; who were unknown to us entirely; who from all we could learn about them did not have any very exalted position at their homes—these men were organizing the colored people. We knew that beyond all question. We knew of certain instances where great crime had been committed; where overseers had been driven from plantations, and the negroes had asserted their right to hold the property for their own benefit. Apprehension took possession of the entire public mind of the State. Men were in many instances afraid to go away from their homes and leave their wives and children, for fear of outrage. Rapes were already being committed in the country. There was this general organization of the black race on the one hand, and an entire disorganization of the white race on the other hand. We were afraid to have a public organization; because we supposed it would be construed at once, by the authorities at Washington, as an organization antagonistic to the Government of the United States. It was therefore necessary, in order to protect our families from outrage and preserve our own lives, to have something that we could regard as a brotherhood—a combination of the best men of the country, to act purely in self-defense, to repel the attack in case we should be attacked by these people. That was the whole object of this organization. . . .[10]

NOTES

1. The complete text of the constitutions may be found in Walter McElreath, *A Treatise on the Constitution of Georgia* (Atlanta: The Harrison Company, 1912).

2. An Albany State College professor, Lee W. Formwalt gives an excellent account of the Camilla tragedy in "The Camilla Massacre of 1868: Racial Violence as Political Propaganda," *Georgia Historical Quarterly* 71 (Summer 1987): 399–426.

3. A bandwagon accompanied the procession. It was customary to have drum and fife bands at political rallies.

4. A Republican candidate for presidential elector, John Murphy often campaigned with congressional contender Pierce.

5. Daniel Howard deposition, September 25, 1868, Records of the Assistant Commissioner for Georgia, Bureau of Refugees, Freedmen, and Abandoned Lands, 1865–1870, National Archives microfilm publication M798, roll 22.

6. Judge Luke P. Poland (Republican, Vermont); U.S. senator, 1865–67; U.S. congressman, 1867–75 and 1883–85.

7. Francis Preston Blair Jr. (Democrat, Missouri); U.S. congressman as member of Free Soil Party, 1857–59; switched to Republican Party; supported Lincoln; served part of several wartime terms in Congress; also served as U.S. Army officer on General Sherman's staff; in postwar era supported Andrew Johnson and switched to Democratic Party; U.S. senator, 1871–73.

8. John Pool (Republican, North Carolina); U.S. senator, 1868–73.

9. James B. Beck (Democrat, Kentucky); U.S. congressman, 1867–75; U.S. senator, 1877–90.

10. U.S. Congress, Joint Select Committee on the Condition of Affairs in the Late Insurrectionary States, *Report of the Joint Select Committee to Inquire into the Con-*

dition of Affairs in the Late Insurrectionary States, 13 vols. (Washington, D.C.: Government Printing Office, 1872). Volumes 6 and 7 contain testimony from Georgians. The complete transcript of Alfred Richardson's account can be found in 6:1–19. That of Augustus R. Wright is contained in 6:88–149; and that of John B. Gordon, 6:304–49.

10

Postwar Poverty: Fault of the North or the South?

Reconstruction has been described by historian Numan Bartley as the "revolution that failed."[1] He suggests that the Republicans challenged planter domination and tried to empower classes who had little influence before the war. Along with civil rights for blacks, Republicans championed economic development through energetic government support of business. Defeat meant the return of the old social order. Back in control, the Democrats wrote the 1877 constitution, which insured rural domination, severely limited the size of the state debt, curtailed government support for education, and prohibited government from endorsing railroad construction bonds.

Once among the top ten states in per capita wealth, Georgia after the war dropped near the bottom. Following Reconstruction, urban-based "New South" Democrats championed many Republican economic goals and tried to attract northern capital to stimulate industrial growth. *Atlanta Constitution* editor Henry W. Grady became nationally famous for a speech in 1886 to a group of prominent Northerners in which he described Atlanta as a "brave and beautiful city" that had risen from the ashes because the people had caught the work ethic and put the Civil War behind them.[2] According to Bartley, however, the "New South" crusade was defeated before it began. Wedded to one political party and white supremacy, Georgians were stuck with a system fundamentally hostile to urban, industrial interests.

While the state did little to assist economic growth, the U.S. government did less. National power resided with northern businessmen and politicians, who often promoted their region at the expense of everyone else. For example, northern-owned railroads charged much higher rates for hauling freight from southern terminals than from northern. Wall Street banks had ultimate control of investment capital and seemed reluctant to finance ventures that competed with northern interests. Moreover, federal tariff policy placed stiff taxes on foreign imports, favoring American industry (largely northern) over farmers and consumers.

Practically all Georgia leaders were aware of the disabilities their region faced. They differed sharply in what to do about them. The documents below offer descriptions of life among Georgia's poorest workers and examine the paths to prosperity plotted by two prominent Georgians, Joseph E. Brown and Thomas E. Watson.

⚑ ⚑ ⚑

A Business Perspective
on the Southern Problem

The most fascinating opportunist in nineteenth-century Georgia politics undoubtedly was Joseph E. Brown. The Civil War governor, Brown converted to the Republican Party early in the Reconstruction era. He was rewarded in 1868 when Republican Governor Bullock made the erstwhile secessionist the chief justice of the Georgia Supreme Court. Two years later he resigned from the court to form a company that received a twenty-year lease on the state-owned Western and Atlantic Railroad. With the collapse of Republican rule, Brown again switched parties, and quickly moved back into the inner circle of the Democratic Party. In the 1870s he received a lucrative contract to lease state prisoners to work in his north Georgia coal mines. In 1880 he replaced John B. Gordon in the U.S. Senate and held that seat until his retirement a decade later. The following is an 1881 article in the *Atlanta Constitution* that presents succinctly the "New South" philosophy of men such as Henry W. Grady and Brown.

A "Progressive" Democrat: Senator Brown on the New South—Business First, Politics Second

The New York Herald prints a long interview on political questions and the future of the south with Senator Brown, of Georgia. Mr. Brown said that he regarded it to be the first duty of the south to make political agitation subordinate to practical matters. It would be better for it to have nothing to do with politics for the next eight or ten years. The principles of the democracy would not suffer from abeyance, for the party is based on essential principles and they will live without perpetual agitation. Notwithstanding that the south lost $4,000,000,000 by the war, including the value of the slaves, the people are almost out of debt. The immense incomes from cotton and other crops that have been for the past ten or twelve years devoted to rehabilitation and settling up old scores, will, for the next ten years, seek new investment, and it is the highest duty of statesmanship to encourage measures that will lead to a legitimate investment of this money. With this done, the south will, in a few years, be wealthy and independent, and this is the shortest road she can take to power and respect. The course of the representative should be to argue matters quietly and without intemperance, to discourage all sectional feeling, to live on good terms with the representatives of all sections, and move in solid phalanx with them in any movement that promises to aid our common country in working out its great destiny.

Senator Brown then added: "I am very well satisfied that there is no chance for the success of the democratic party of the union until we of the south have convinced the people of the north and west that we have accepted the constitutional amendments which are the results of the war,[3] not only in platforms and on papers, but that we are in practice living up to them and carrying them out in good faith. When we have done this sectional hate will die, and the bloody shirt,[4] which will no longer serve the purposes of the party in power, will be buried to be raised no more. Then it will be no longer in the power of a few imprudent bourbons in the south, who assume to be leaders, to defeat the democracy and bring disaster upon us by their indiscreet utterances, nor will it longer be necessary for the democracy of the south to cringe to the dictation of a few incompetent northern leaders. As there will then be no further cause for the sectional strife, there will be as much reason why the democracy shall subserve the best interests of the south, as there will why the south shall subserve the interests of the democracy of the union. When sectional strife and hate no longer exist and we have one united country, the reason for a solid south and a solid north will cease. Parties will then no longer exist on sectional issues or race lines, but they will be formed upon the great living, practical issues of the day, such as tariffs, bank currency, etc. While this may not be better for the class of politicians who live by keeping sectional issues alive, I am sure it will be better for the south, better for the north, and better for the whole country. The great laboring masses of the south are tired of sectional strife. They want peace; they want a faithful execution of the laws; they want a full restoration of property; they want the union of our fathers, upon the constitution as it is. With this restoration, and the vast resources of the south properly understood and appreciated by the men of means—the substantial business men of the north and west, many of whom would then come south—there is no limit to the future prosperity and wealth of the south. It is destined to be the richest section of the union, because Providence has been more lavish of His gifts there than in any other section."

He further said that although he was an original secessionist, he had abandoned all those old ideas not in harmony with the new era. He advocated the protection of the colored race in all its rights and in educating the colored people, so that they can vote with intelligence and honesty. The south was now anxious to welcome immigrants, and he spoke more particularly of the advantages which Georgia offers. The state wanted a large importation of yankee energy, yankee enterprise, yankee education and yankee business sense.[5]

Mill Workers ✓

In Georgia's depressed economy of the post–Civil War era, little opportunity existed for those at the bottom, white or black. Agriculture was depressed, and Southern industry provided no escape from grinding poverty. Poor whites tended to drift from sharecropping to the mills and back again. Labor in the Georgia cotton mill often included entire families. Indeed, the men sometimes had greater difficulty finding work than the women and children.

Written in 1891, the article below provides a window into the lives of lower-class Georgians. The author, Clare de Graffenried, came from a prominent Macon, Georgia, family. Following Reconstruction, she moved to Washington, D.C., where she eventually became an investigator for the U.S. Bureau of Labor. Her job was to study the treatment of working women and children. By providing a realistic portrayal of labor conditions, she hoped to shock the public into reform.

The Georgia Cracker in the Cotton Mills

Flung as if by chance beside a red clay road that winds between snake fences, a settlement appears. Rows of loosely built, weather-stained frame houses, all of the same ugly pattern and buttressed by clumsy chimneys, are set close to the highway. No porch, no doorstep even, admits to these barrack-like quarters; only an unhewn log or a convenient stone. To the occupants suspicion, fear, and robbery are unknown, for board shutters, stretched swagging back leave the paneless windows great gaping squares. Hospitably widespread doors reveal interiors original and fantastic enough for a Teniers or a Frère to paint. The big, sooty fireplace is decked with an old-time crane and pots and kettles, or with a stove in the last stages of rust and decrepitude. A shacklin bed, tricked out in gaudy patchwork, a few defunct "split-bottom" chairs, a rickety table, and a jumble of battered crockery keep company with the collapsed bellows and fat pine knots by the hearth. The unplastered walls are tattooed with broken mirrors, strips of bacon, bunches of turkey feathers, strings of red peppers, and gourds, green, yellow, and brown. The bare floors are begrimed with the tread of animals; and the muddy outline of splayed toes of all shapes and sizes betoken inmates unused to shoes and stockings. The back door looks upon an old-fashioned moss-covered well with its long pole and a bucket at the end hung high in the air. Yard there is none, nor plant, nor paling, nor outhouse, in the whole community. On the nearest limbs a few patched garments flap ghostlike in the breeze. Forest trees shade the black-lichened roof, and the dogwood, azalea, and laurel riot on the hillside. Surmounting the crest is a little squat, frame building that only irredeemable ugliness proclaims to be a church. The path that leads to it is almost untrodden.

Over the scene broods the stillness of virgin woods. The peacefulness that flees from busy marts inwraps the smokeless chimneys and silent hearths. It is a deserted village. The homes are but the shells of human presence. Not even the ticking of a clock answers the lonely cricket in the mantel. The wood fire is half burned out, the embers dead; a simple breakfast has been partly consumed; great hollows formed by recent occupation punctuate the unmade feather beds. What sprite, what fiend, has snatched up the inmates in the midst of work and hurry? What mysterious power suspended in a moment all the functions of life, and swept away its representatives?

A steady, throbbing pulsation, a singular persistent whir not caused by bird or

wants reform
Breakdown of family — no education

beast or wind, unnoticed at first, frets the ear at last into consciousness. A turn in the road; the swish, splash of falling waters is accented by a stronger pulse-beat, and around a farther bend comes into view an ancient wheel, wheezy and dilapidated, picturesquely dipping into a turbid stream and scattering rainbows of dazzling yellow drops. A low, straggling brick mill gives forth the sound of flying spindles and the measured jar of many looms.

Herein are gathered the missing denizens of the settlement, of both sexes and of all ages and conditions. Grandsires feebly totter about the cotton-house; grandames, mothers, sons, and daughters tend the whirling machinery; while children too young to work play along the walls under the maternal eye. Of one class only there is lack. Has war in the land claimed all the able-bodied male adults. . . .

The genius for evading labor is most marked in the men. Like Indians in their dislike of household work, they refuse to chop wood or bring water and often subsist entirely upon the earnings of meek wives or fond daughters, whose excuses for this shameless vagabondism are both pathetic and exasperating. One young wife claims that her stalwart husband has "been er-cuttin' wood"; yet when closely questioned she is obliged to admit his worthlessness: "For mos' two years now he hain't er-binner." The father of two little children in the mill does no work at all "'cep'in' hit's haulin' light wood." A straggling potato row, a scant corn patch on the hillside, an attenuated cow, a few chickens, one pig, and woods full of pine knots for fires bound the Georgia countryman's earthly aspirations except as to clothing, tobacco, and whisky, which the spouse's wages supply. She it is who must feed the poultry and milk the cow. His lordship descends to no duties so menial. . . .

[The women's clothing is topped] by that homeliest head-gear, the slat sunbonnet, universal badge of the female cracker. From the end of the tunnel formed by the uncompromising pasteboard slats a shrewd, hard, yellow, cadaverous face peers out. When the covering is removed, the scant hair is revealed caught straight back from the brow and skewered into an untidy knot. . . .

The men wear baggy jeans trousers, often home-made, strapped up almost under the armpits, or else without suspenders and dragging about the hips. The shirt is of unbleached homespun without collar or cuffs. A low battered, soft felt hat, or a third-hand beaver, completes the costume, except when for grandeur a vest is added. The favorite occupation of the men is to spit, stare, and whittle sticks. In the mills the boys are dressed in trousers a world too big, father's or grandfather's lopped off at the knees and all in tatters. Girls are clad in cotton gowns through whose rifts the skin is visible, and few have ever disported even a cast-off hat or an outgrown wool dress. Shoes and stockings, though a luxury, are possessed by all except the most miserable and abandoned women. They are, however, put away "for Sunday," and so carefully economized that the simple owners walk barefooted four or five miles to church or camp-meeting with the precious articles wrapped in a handkerchief. Within sight of their goal they sit down in a bend of the snake fence, dust off their tired feet, and, donning the prized hosiery and shoes, march with pride into the assembled congregation. . . .

The inevitable hardships everywhere so disastrous to the workers in textile fabrics fail to account for the feeble constitutions and wrecked health of so many of these Southern toilers. Other causes are manifestly active. The malaria lurking about water-courses ravages the mills on the streams and invades the houses of the employees, usually close to the bank. Drainage is neglected and epidemics stalk relentless. The use of snuff is a withering curse. . . . Unmarried women of thirty are withered, bent, and haggard. Mothers who, despite maternal cares, ought to look as fresh as their daughters, seem to carry the weight of a century on their bowed backs. Twenty years of vitality, sapped by summer heat, eaten out by ague, stolen by dyspeptic miseries! Sickly faces, stooping shoulders, shriveled flesh, suggest that normal girlhood never existed, that youth had never rounded out the lanky figure, nor glowed the sallow cheek. A slouching gait; a drooping chest, lacking muscular power to expand; a dull, heavy eye; yellow, blotched complexion; dead-looking hair; stained lips, destitute of color and revealing broken teeth—these are the dower of girlhood in the mills. Take a little maid whose face is buried in her sunbonnet, and who, when asked her age, responds, "I'm er-gwine on ten." Push back her bonnet, hoping to find the personification of that grace, vigor, and joy which some demon has stamped out of the saturnine faces of the elders. A sad spectacle reveals itself. Out of a shock of unkempt hair look glassy eyes ringed with black circles reaching far down her yellow cheeks. Her nose is pinched, the features aborted, the yellow lips furrowed with snuff stains. The skin is ghastly, cadaverous, the flesh flabby, the frame weak and loose-jointed. The dirty legs and feet are bare. A tattered cotton slip clings to the formless limbs.

"When do you go to school, my child?"

"Hain't never been thar," the waif responds when shyness has yielded to cajoleries. . . .

"How long have you been working?"

"Ev'ry sence I was mighty nigh er kitten."

Importuned to state at what age the delights of kittenhood ceased and toil began, she vouchsafes:

"Seven year."

"What do you do in the mill?"

"Pieces ainds." Then, with sudden recollection, "But I hain't been nowhar 'cep'n' in mill he'pen' maw sence I was five year ole. . . ."

The nearly and the quite illiterate comprise all grades of character and manner. Even among confirmed snuff devotees, however, illiteracy is not always synonymous with unworthiness or vulgarity. Rather it is often a misfortune, sealing a beautiful nature from higher possibilities. The normal Georgia cracker under all her nicotine stains overflows in simplicity and unperverted goodness. The dust of the mill makes a halo about lovely, unselfish lives. Roughness of speech and manners covers a gentle, loyal heart and unswerving integrity. . . .

In bearing the crackers are not surly and forbidding, but friendly and naive; not brazen or dogmatic, but shy and deprecating; not dull and hidebound, but alert and responsive; not subtle or introversive; not overreaching and selfish, but full of sympathy and gentle tact. Their shrewdness, loyalty, quaint simplicity, frank, open-mouthed wonder, their transparent mentality and unexpected moral obliquities, make a fascinating study.[6]

Farm Laborers

Following the Civil War and Reconstruction the country entered a deflationary era in which prices for farm products steadily dropped. One result was the rise in the percentage of farm operators who could not afford to own the land they worked. In 1880 some 45 percent of all Georgia farmers were tenants; twenty years later the proportion was up to 60 percent and by 1910 to 66 percent. At the last date some 50 percent of all white farmers and 87 percent of blacks had descended into farm tenancy.

Some tenants worked for fixed rents and lived relatively independent lives, free from extensive landlord supervision. Nonetheless, the typical Georgia tenant family labored as sharecroppers, paying the rent with a portion of the production and generally doing what the landlord told them to do. Those at the bottom rented their farm animals and tools as well as their land and paid half the crop in rent. If they were slightly better off, they owned their animals and tools and thus paid a lower rent, usually a third of the corn and a fourth of the cotton.

Regardless of the contractual details, tenants found it virtually impossible to stay out of debt to the merchants who provided them with essential supplies. In exchange for credit purchases, the storekeeper demanded a lien on the farmer's crop. Since tenants rarely had any other collateral, they continued buying on credit from that one merchant until the harvest. Consequently, the businessman was free to raise prices to whatever level he preferred. One study has indicated that Georgia farmers in the 1880s paid on average the equivalent of 59 percent interest per annum on their credit purchases.[7] Needless to say, tenants found it difficult to break the cycle of poverty which encompassed them.

In 1908 an Atlanta University study was published under the editorship of W. E. B. Du Bois entitled the *Negro American Family*. We will encounter Du Bois, the social activist, in the next chapter. This work was a scholarly attempt to document the life of blacks in America in the early twentieth century. The brief excerpt below describes housing conditions in the Albany area for perhaps the lowest group in Georgia's social hierarchy, rural African-American laborers.

The Negro Families of Dougherty County, Georgia

The plantations of Dougherty in slavery days were not as imposing as those of Virginia. The Big House was smaller and one-storied, and the slave cabins set closer to it. Today the laborers' cabins are in form and disposition the same as in the slavery days. They are sprinkled in little groups all over the land clustered about some dilapidated Big House where the head-tenant or agent lives. Out of fifteen hundred homes of Negroes only fifteen have five or more rooms; the mass live in one or two-room homes. The one-room cabin is painfully frequent—now standing in the shadow of the Big House, now staring at the dusty road, now rising dark and sombre amid the green of the cotton fields. Rough-boarded, old and bare, it is neither plastered nor ceilinged, and light and ventilation comes from the single door and perhaps a square hole in the wall. Within is a fireplace, black and smoky, unsteady with age; a bed or two, high, dark and fat; a table, a wooden chest and chairs or stools. On the wall is a stray showbill or a newspaper for decorations.

It is not simply in the tenement abominations of cities like New York that the world's flesh is crowded and jammed together, sometimes twenty-two persons to every ten rooms; here in Dougherty county there are often over twenty-five persons to every ten rooms of house accommodations. To be sure, the rooms are large—fifteen to twenty-five feet square. And there is the fresh air and sunshine of all outdoors to take refuge in. Still I met one family of eleven eating and sleeping in one room, and thirty families of eight or more. Why should there be such wretched tenements in the Black Belt? Timber is rotting in the forest, land is running to waste and labor is literally cheaper than dirt. Over nine-tenths of the cabins belong to the landlords yet nearly all of them let the quarters stand and rot in rude carelessness. Why? First, because long custom, born in slavery days, has assigned this sort of house to Negroes. If the landlord should hire white men he would not hesitate to erect cosy three-room cottages such as cluster around the Carolina cotton-mills. Small wonder that the substitution of white for Negro labor is often profitable, since the white being better paid and better cared for often responds by doing better work. Again, the Negroes themselves, as a mass, do not demand better homes; those who do, buy land and build their own homes, roomy and neat. But the rest can scarcely demand what they have seldom thought of. As their fathers lived so they live; and the standard of the slave still lowers the standard of the quasi-freeman. . . . Lastly, amid such conditions of life there is little to inspire the laborer to become a better farmer. If he is ambitious, he moves to town or tries other kinds of labor; as a tenant-farmer his outlook in the majority of cases is hopeless, and following it as a makeshift or in grim necessity, he takes its returns in shelter, meat and bread, without query or protest. . . .[8]

☙ ☙ ☙

The Populist Revolt

The first serious challenge to the status quo came in the 1890s from the Populist Party. As farmers suffered through several decades of dropping agricultural prices, they came to doubt the basic fairness of the American economic system. They saw giant fortunes being made on Wall Street while their own security was undermined. Economists announced that the problem was simply one of overproduction: too many farmers growing too much of everything. Country folk, however, looked at the alarming increase of poverty in city tenements as well as in rural areas. They asked why, in a land of plenty, did urban masses go without adequate food or clothing. Was it possible, they wondered, that the nation suffered from underconsumption rather than overproduction?

The most important Georgian to answer this question in the affirmative was Thomas E. Watson, a planter-attorney from the town of Thomson, near Augusta. Watson and the Populists told the farmer that poor whites and blacks should join together in a new political party to bring about fundamental alterations in national economic policy. Among other things, they favored the vote for blacks and women, popular election of U.S. senators, the secret ballot, a progressive income tax to replace protective tariffs, government ownership of railroads and other means of communication, and inflation of the currency through the free and unlimited coinage of silver. The last plank would make it easier for debtors to pay back the money they owed.[9]

The leaders of the Democratic Party were quick to respond to the Populist challenge to the status quo. The older party controlled the election machinery and knew how to steal votes. In the absence of secret ballots, ordinary blacks and whites were often intimidated into supporting established Democratic leaders. Recognizing the appeal of the third party's economic objectives, Georgia Democrats appropriated a few Populist ideas, such as free silver, while attacking the Populist commitment to political equality.

The People's Party, therefore, did not remain a threat for long. The organization maintained a shadowy existence into the early twentieth century. As late as 1904 and 1908 Tom Watson ran token campaigns as the Populist candidate for president. After the 1896 election, however, the party was essentially dead. As we shall see in later chapters, the consequences for Georgia were frightening. Watson remained a powerful figure until his death in 1922; but increasingly his radicalism turned to crusades against blacks, Catholics, and Jews.[10]

The following excerpts from Watson speeches reveal the Georgia Populist's analysis of why southerners, farmers, and workers were poor.

Labor-Day Address

. . . How much ought labor to get? No man can be more definite than this: "It should get all that it makes after due allowance for material and the use of the capital."

But we can be perfectly definite on this point. It does not get a fair share now. Eight million bales of cotton flood the markets of the world, and have hammered the price down to zero. Yet millions of laboreres haven't decent clothes to wear!

Corn was made in the West so plentiful that people burned it for winter fires because it would only bring twelve cents per bushel. Yet millions of laborers hunger, and some of them starve.

The earth quivers every second with the falling of the majestic pines as the lumberman seeks rafter, and joist, and sill, and planking, and never before were hurrying cars so laden with lumber, yet thousands of laborers shelter their families in wretched hovels, through whose sunken roof patters the rain, and through whose gaping cracks steal the bitter cold.

They tell us the country is suffering from overproduction of food! Then why do men go hungry through your streets? Overproduction of goods? Then why do shrinking women and feeble children go shivering down the icy sidewalks so scantily clad that suffering speaks in every line of pinched and haggard features? Overproduction? I will tell you where the overproduction is. It is in the cold-hearted and hard-hearted men who will not see any good thing which does not belong to their class! It is in the men who consider the mere getting of gold the gospel of life; it is in the men who have grown proud and cruel because they possess capital (the thing which was labor yesterday), but utterly despise the labor of to-day. . . .[11]

How the Law Controls the Distribution of Wealth

Gentlemen of the Farmers' Union:

It is my purpose to show you that the South, which by the law of nature, should abound in wealth, is comparatively barren, and that this comparative lack of wealth has been brought about, not by nature, not by the fault of the people, but by the fault of the lawmakers who have passed laws against you to enrich the East at the expense of the South and West. (Applause.) I am going to prove to you to-night that the comparative barrenness of the South is the result of hostile legislation, that the fabulous wealth of New England is the work not of nature, but of the legislators who passed laws in favor of New England against the other sections of the Union. . . .

In 1850 the South had half the wealth that there was in the Union. The North had the other half. They labored and competed for ten years. The North has the advantage of a twenty per cent tariff. The North is making the race with wings to her shoulders; the South is making the race with clogs to her feet, and yet in ten years the South had outstripped the North twelve million dollars! But, now, what? Juggle with your tariff, juggle with your money system — change your laws and you change your conditions. To what extent? Between 1880 and 1900, the one little New England State of Massachusetts gained more wealth than nine great agricultural States, made up of four in the West and five in the South. The State of Pennsylvania, aided by this great McKinley and Dingley tariff,[12] had gathered to herself as much wealth as the entire South. In other words, under a twenty per cent tariff, the entire South could beat the entire North in the race of material prosperity. But under a tariff of fifty and one hundred per cent, the one State of Pennsylvania could outstrip the entire South. Is that enough to impress you? Oh! but you may say Southern men and Western men are lazy, they are not business-like, they are not 'cute. Let's go up among the country people of

New England. Let's see how the Yankee farmers have been getting on, as compared with the Yankee manufacturers. Nobody ever accused a Yankee farmer of being anybody's fool. Well, in 1880, the amount of capital the Yankee farmer had invested was the same as that which the Yankee manufacturer had invested. They run along for ten years, to 1890, and then, what do we find? The Yankee manufacturer has doubled his estate, and the Yankee farmer has not only made nothing but he has lost one-fourth of which he had, and he has abandoned four thousand, one hundred and sixty of his farms. (Applause.) We go forward another ten years, to 1900, and the Yankee farmer, after ten years of tremendous struggle, has just about been able to hold his own; he has not made a dollar—not a cent; he's got just what he had ten years before, with ten years of labor thrown in, "free gratis, for nothing." (Applause.)

But sometimes our editors go into ecstasies because a New England cotton mill has come down South—the Northern capitalist has brought his money South and built another cotton mill down here, and, oh, they go into raptures, jubilating! What difference does it make to you whether the Northern manufacturer comes down South to rob you or stays up yonder and robs you? (Laughter and applause.) I believe, if the robbery's got to go on at all, I would prefer for him to stay in the North, where he would grind up his own little children into dividends—(Tremendous applause and cheers of "Go after him Tom")—and not come down here to the South, where our corrupt legislatures allow them to grind up our children into dividends. (Great applause.) . . .[13]

NOTES

1. Numan V. Bartley, *The Creation of Modern Georgia* (Athens: University of Georgia Press, 1983), chaps. 3–4.

2. Mills Lane, ed., *The New South: Writings and Speeches of Henry Grady* (Savannah: Beehive Press, 1971), 7–8.

3. Brown was referring to the Thirteenth Amendment, which abolished slavery; the Fourteenth, which defined citizenship and guaranteed equal protection of the laws; and the Fifteenth, which prohibited states from denying the vote on the basis of race.

4. The "bloody shirt" was a reference to northern Republicans who perpetuated sectional hatred for years after the Civil War by continuing to blame the conflict and its high casualty rate on the Democrats.

5. "A 'Progressive' Democrat: Senator Brown on the New South—Business First, Politics Second," *Atlanta Constitution*, January 25, 1881, p. 4.

6. Clare de Graffenried, "The Georgia Cracker in the Cotton Mills," *The Cen-*

tury Magazine 41 (February 1891): 483–98. Despite her southern roots, De Graffen-ried angered many Georgians with her bleak depiction of the mill villages. Critics believed that she slandered the region by reenforcing a stereotypical view of south-ern backwardness and debasement. Her most articulate and persistent opponent, Rebecca Latimer Felton, saw the mills as an escape from degradation for white women, many of whom had been widowed and left in poverty by the Civil War. From Felton's perspective, the alternative to mill work for widows was agricultural labor, for which their gender was unsuited. The cotton mills allowed them to keep their dignity and a semblance of family values. For a discussion of the controversy see LeeAnn Whites, "The De Graffenried Controversy: Class, Race, and Gender in the New South," *Journal of Southern History* 54 (August 1988): 449–78.

7. Roger L. Ransom and Richard Sutch, *One Kind of Freedom: The Economic Consequences of Emancipation* (Cambridge: Cambridge University Press, 1977), 128–30.

8. W. E. Burghardt Du Bois, "The Negro Families of Dougherty County, Geor-gia," *The Negro American Family* (Atlanta: Atlanta University, 1908; reprint, New York: Negro Universities Press, 1969), 128–30.

9. There were limits to the Populist support of equal rights. Watson, for instance, was typical of his generation in opposing race mixing and in praising the alleged intellectual superiority of Anglo-Saxons. Because he was aware, however, of the ad-vantages of being white, he argued in the 1890s that society need not succumb to the fear tactics of those who railed against "Negro domination." He thought that whites could safely divide their votes, because whites would remain in control regardless of which party was in power. It was also clear to Watson that the Populists needed the blacks if they were to defeat the Democrats. See, for example, Watson's speech, "The Creed of Jefferson, the Founder of Democracy," *The Life and Speeches of Thos. E. Watson*, 2d ed. (Thomson, Ga.: The Jeffersonian Publishing Company, 1911), 128–29.

10. One of the best biographies of any southern politician is C. Vann Woodward, *Tom Watson: Agrarian Rebel* (New York: Macmillan, 1938).

11. From "Labor-Day Address, at Augusta, Georgia, May, 1891," *Life and Speeches of Thos. E. Watson*, 59–70.

12. As a member of Congress, Republican William McKinley was instrumental in the adoption of the McKinley Tariff (1890), which raised rates to about 48.5 per-cent, the highest peacetime duties to that point. In his first year as president (1897), McKinley persuaded Congress to pass the Dingley Tariff, elevating duties even higher, to an average of 57 percent.

13. "How the Law Controls the Distribution of Wealth: Mr. Watson's Speech to Farmers' Union," Atlanta, January 22, 1907, *Life and Speeches of Thos. E. Watson*, 255–75.

11

"Jim Crow" Georgia and
Its Leaders, Black and White

The period of political equality in Georgia politics was extremely brief. As we have seen, the constitution of 1868, written by the Republicans, gave African-Americans the right to vote, but did not prevent the Georgia legislature from expelling the black members. After Reconstruction a few blacks would be elected to office from time to time, but none held much power.

The federal Fifteenth Amendment prohibited any direct disfranchisement of black men. Consequently, Georgia and the other Southern states resorted to tests for voting that ostensibly had nothing to do with race. The post-Reconstruction 1877 constitution permitted a cumulative poll tax, which fell particularly hard on poor people. Georgia had many poor whites, of course, but a larger percentage of poor blacks. In 1900 the Georgia Democrats set up a white primary, arguing that political parties could be as inclusive or exclusive as they wanted in their primaries, as long as all registered voters retained suffrage rights in the general elections.

The final attempt at disfranchisement was a product of the 1906 gubernatorial election, in which the major adversaries in the white Democratic primary were Hoke Smith and Clark Howell. The victor, Smith, raised as a campaign issue the alleged danger of black power. In 1908 the people heeded his warning and ratified an amendment to the 1877 constitution that erected further barricades against black voting, while providing loopholes for whites. The text of that amendment is part of the documents below.

At the same time African-Americans were denied the vote, they lost other rights. Between 1890 and 1910 the Southern states enacted a host of measures referred to as the "Jim Crow" laws, which legislated segregation in most public places where blacks and whites came together. African-Americans responded to these new indignities in a variety of ways, as the documents below reveal.

🏴 🏴 🏴

Henry McNeal Turner and Black Nationalism

Two Georgia clergymen are famous for their contributions to black nationalism. Lucius Henry Holsey was a bishop of the Colored Methodist Episcopal Church. Born into slavery in 1842, Holsey spent most of his career building bridges to the white community. Among his tangible accomplishments was Paine College in Augusta, which he and other black and white Methodists helped to create. In 1903, however, Holsey recommended that "some territory or parts of the public domain . . . be set aside by the Government for the specific purpose of forming a state or states for qualified Negro American citizens."[1]

Henry McNeal Turner also at different times advocated cooperation and separation. While Holsey called for a black territory within the United States, Turner led a back-to-Africa movement. Indeed, in the late nineteenth century he was the movement's chief spokesperson. Turner was born free in South Carolina in 1834. Early in life he experienced a call to the ministry, first in the white-dominated Methodist Church, South, and then in the African Methodist Episcopal Church. During the Civil War he was the U.S. Army's first black chaplain.

Settling in Georgia following the war, Turner was an agent of the Freedmen's Bureau and a circuit-riding AME preacher. He was a delegate to the 1868 constitutional convention and then a representative in the legislature. One of his best speeches came in 1868 in opposition to the expulsion of black members of the assembly. In 1880 he became an AME bishop and increasingly espoused the idea of emigration to Africa. The following excerpts deal with African emigration.

The *Christian Recorder*, January 25, 1883.

Do you know any instance in the world's history where a people shut out from all honorable positions, from being kings and queens, lords, dukes, presidents, governors, mayors, generals and all positions of honor and trust by reason of their race, ever amounted to anything? No sir, I will answer for you. There is no instance on record, except where preceded by revolution. People must have one like them on high to inspire them to go high. Jesus Christ had to take upon himself our very nature before his plan of redemption was a success. It required a God-man on the throne of the universe to awaken the aspiration of a world. And till we have black men in the seat of power, respected, honored, beloved, feared, hated and reverenced, our young men will never rise for the reason they will never look up. . . . Now all I contend for is this, that we must raise a symbol somewhere. We are bitten, we are poisoned, we are sick and we are dying. We need a remedy. Oh for some Moses to lift a brazen serpent, some goal for our ambition, some object to induce us to look up. Have we that object here? Is there any possibility of getting it here? I do not see it. Therefore I maintain that African colonization should be encouraged. Let the brave-hearted men, who are advanced enough to peril land and sea in search of better conditions, alone. Let them give us a respectable civil and Christian negro nation. Let them raise a banner standard that the world will respect and its glory and influence will tell upon the destinies of the race from pole to pole; our children's children can rest securely under the aegis, whether in Africa, Europe, Asia, America or upon the high seas.

The *Christian Recorder*, February 22, 1883.

. . . I will now define my African position:

1st.   I do not believe my race will ever be respected, or ought to be respected who do not show themselves capable of founding and manning a government of their own creation. This has not been done creditably yet by the civilized negro, and till it is done he will be a mere scullion in the eyes of the world. The Colonization Society proposes to aid him in accomplishing that grand result. They are our best friends and greatest benefactors, as the stern and inexorable logic of facts will soon show.

2nd.   I do not believe that American slavery was a divine institution, but I do believe it was a providential institution and that God intends to make it the primal factor in the civilization and Christianization of that dark continent, and that any person whomsoever opposes the return of a sufficient number of her descendants to begin the grand work, which in the near future will be consummated, is fighting the God of the universe face to face.

3rd.   The civilized world is turning its attention to Africa as never before, including all the Christian and semi-Christian nations under heaven except America (for the Colonization Society gives the movement here no national character) and it seems to me as if the time had arrived when America, too, or the United States, at least, should awake to her share of duty in this great movement, as she owes us forty billions of dollars for actual services rendered, estimating one hundred dollars a year for two million of us for two hundred years.

4th.   I am no advocate for wholesale emigration: I know we are not prepared for it, nor is Africa herself prepared for it. Such a course would be madness in the extreme and folly unpardonable. Five or ten thousand a year would be enough. I would like to take yearly those who are sent to the penitentiary, hung or lynched for nothing. With them alone I could establish a government, build a country and raise a national symbol that could give character to our people everywhere. Empty to me your jails and penitentiaries and in ten years I will give you a country before which your theories will pale and disappear.

5th.   To me the nonsensical jargon that the climate of Africa is against us, we can't live there, the tropics are no place for moral and intellectual development, coming from the mouths of so-called intelligent men and would-be leaders, is simply ridiculous. If I were so ignorant, I would hold my tongue and pen and not let the people know it. Such language not only charges God with folly, but contradicts the teachings of both science and philosophy. They have not even learned that man is a cosmopolitan, that his home is everywhere upon the face of the globe. They have not read the history of this country that they pretend to love so well. They appear to be ignorant totally of the fearful mortality that visited the early settlers of this nation at Roanoke, Annapolis, Plymouth Rock, Baltimore, Philadelphia, Charleston, and there is nothing on record, possibly, that equals the fatality of Louisville, Ky. I read it with horror at this late day. Men seem to be ignorant on the philosophy of human existence, yet they plunge into the whirlpool of great questions with intoxicated impunity. God have mercy upon their little heads and smaller hearts, is my prayer. . . .

The Voice of Missions, March, 1899:

Much has been said, and many wild calculations have been made, by men of no education or of no brain, about the hundred millions of dollars that we said, sometime ago, the colored people of this country should ask the general government for, to enable them to leave the United States, the lowest and meanest domain this side of hell, and there have been about as many white fools babbling over it as black, pretending to estimate the limited number that a hundred million would carry over to Africa. We are sure if the necessary ships could be gotten to running between the United States and Africa, the colored people could go as cheaply as the millions of whites have been brought from Europe to this country, averaging from ten to fifteen, eighteen and twenty dollars a head. Suppose we take the middle number and what would be the result, one hundred and five million of dollars would pay for the transportation of seven millions of emigrants to Africa, I mean Liberia being the objective point. If the general government will give us a hundred million dollars and let us charge, as we would, from five to ten dollars each, we will return to Africa the eight millions of colored people said to be in the United States, if they desire to go, and still have a few million left for incidental expenses. . . .[2]

☙ ☙ ☙

W. E. B. Du Bois

In the early twentieth century, Georgia's most distinguished intellectual, white or black, was W. E. B. Du Bois. Born in 1868 in Massachusetts and the holder of a Ph.D. from Harvard, Du Bois taught at Atlanta University from 1897 to 1910 and for another decade beginning in 1934. In between he was the NAACP's director of publicity and research and editor of *The Crisis*. A leader of the Pan-African movement, he spent the last years of his life in the newly independent African country of Ghana, where he died at age ninety-five in 1963.

The great African-American scholar was a prolific writer who published numerous books and articles. For most of his career he advocated full suffrage, with no educational or economic restrictions. Nonetheless, the following is a remarkably moderate petition, submitted by the young Du Bois in 1899 to the Georgia legislature, protesting the Hardwick Bill, an early attempt to impose a literacy test in Georgia.

A Memorial to the Legislature of Georgia on the Hardwick Bill

We, your petitioners, understanding that there lies before your honorable body a bill known as the Hardwick Bill, designed to change radically the basis of suffrage in this Commonwealth, desire respectfully to lay the following considerations before you. . . .

It has come to be the consensus of opinion in civilized Nations that in the long run government must be based on the consent of the governed. This is the verdict of more than three centuries of strife and bloodshed, and it is a verdict not lightly to be set aside. Nevertheless, the Nineteenth century with its broader outlook and deeper experience has added one modifying clause to this, to which the world now assents, namely: That in order to take part in government, the governed must be intelligent enough to recognize and choose their own best good; that consequently in free governments based on universal manhood suffrage, it is fair and right to impose on voters an educational qualification, so long as the State furnishes free school facilities to all children.

To these principles, we, as representatives of the Negroes of Georgia, give full assent. We join heartily with the best conscience of the State, of the Nation, and of the civilized world in demanding a pure intelligent ballot, free from bribery, ignorance, fraud and intimidation. And to secure this, we concur in the movement toward imposing fair and impartial qualifications upon voters, whether based on education, or property, or both.

Nor is this, gentlemen of the Legislature, a light sacrifice on our part. We Negroes are today, in large degree, poor and ignorant through the crime of the Nation. Through no fault of our own, are we here brought into contact with a civilization higher than that of the average of our race. We have not been sparing in our efforts to improve.

Notwithstanding all this, so far as the Hardwick Bill proposes to restrict the right of suffrage to all who, irrespective of race or color, are intelligent enough to vote properly, we heartily endorse it. . . .

We protest against the clause which restricts the right to vote to those who can read and UNDERSTAND a clause in the Constitution: and which allows the local election officers to be the final judge of this "understanding." . . . The "understanding clause" of the proposed bill is an open door to manipulation and dishonesty. In a free and just government no local election officer ought to be clothed with discretionary or judicial function. Wherever this has been done, fraud and chicanery have been the inevitable result. If this clause should become a law the registrars and election managers would virtually have the power of deciding who should vote. The Party in power today which places such a weapon in the hands of its appointees, may in the future, find the very machinery turned against itself by the Party in power tomorrow. In such ways are the foundations of popular government sapped. . . .

We know that there are among our white fellow citizens broad-minded men who realize that the prosperity of Georgia is bound up with the prosperity of the Georgia Negro; that no Nation or State can advance faster than its laboring classes, and that whatever hinders, degrades or discourages the Negroes weakens and injures the State. To such Georgians we appeal in this crisis: Race antagonism and hatred have gone too far in this State; let us stop here; let us insist that we go no further; let us countenance no measure or movement calculated to increase that deep and terrible sense of wrong under which so many labor today. . . .[3]

🏳 🏳 🏳

Hoke Smith, Progressivism, and Race

Hoke Smith is a good example of Georgia's turn-of-the century obsession with race relations. The Atlanta lawyer hardly fit the description of the stereotypical Southern demagogue. As governor he was Georgia's foremost progressive. The son of a professor, he had a sincere interest in education and argued that a state's wealth was directly correlated to the amount of money spent on schools. He greatly increased educational appropriations during his first gubernatorial term, and later, while serving in the U.S. Senate, he sponsored the Smith-Lever Act (1914), which set up the nationwide system of county extension agents to provide scientific advice to farmers.

Smith's governorship was also characterized by legislation to increase the state's regulatory authority over railroads and utilities, to control lobbyists and campaign contributors, and to abolish the convict lease system. Railroad reform was perhaps the premier progressive cause. After 1904 the Atlanta Chamber of Commerce and the *Atlanta Journal* led a crusade against the state railroad commission, after it failed to reduce freight rates. Local businessmen were particularly upset over the high cost of transporting goods to and from Atlanta and the port of Savannah. The *Journal* demanded the resignation of the railroad commission and called for a "Trust-Buster in Georgia." A former owner of the *Journal*, Hoke Smith responded to the challenge by campaigning strenuously for reform. In office he kept his promise by pushing through the General Assembly the Candler-Overstreet Act (1907), a strong regulatory measure modeled after the public utilities law of New York.[4]

Before 1906 Smith was relatively moderate on the race issue and was even praised in 1893 by Henry McNeal Turner. In a letter to President Grover Cleveland, Turner described Smith as a "liberal in everything involving human rights." In 1906, however, Smith needed the support of erstwhile Populist leader Tom Watson, now a rabid race hater. To gain that support the opportunistic Atlanta lawyer agreed to work for disfranchisement.

The 1906 campaign was perhaps the low point of Smith's career. Throughout the state, he equated the denial of black suffrage to the elimination of corruption, arguing that "no more important question can be presented to the people of Georgia than the disfranchisement of the ignorant, purchasable negro vote." The speech that follows, delivered by Smith at Columbus, Georgia, January 10, 1906, combines the race question with charges that his opponent, Clark Howell, was the candidate of big business.

. . . [The Central Railroad and the Southern Railroad] are permitted by the railroad commission to charge 25 per cent in excess of the standard tariff on business inside the State of Georgia. A considerable portion of this increase was made by the Georgia railroad commission during the year 1893 on account of the hard times then prevailing.

A motion is now pending before the railroad commission to bring the charges back to the standard tariff. The commission is to pass upon this motion today.

Forcing The Commission.

I have discussed this question in many places throughout the State during the past six months, and I have shown how unjust it is to the people of Georgia for the Southern and Central railroad companies to be receiving during this period of great prosperity the increased rates allowed them in 1893 on account of the hard times which then existed. Then the amount of traffic was small — now it is immense. Then it was hard to pay operating expenses; now their profits are much more than a reasonable interest upon their investments.

I have stated a number of times that when the people understand their burdens, the railroad commission will yield to the demand of the people and lighten them. . . .

More Powerful Commission.

The powers of the railroad commission should be enlarged. The commissioners should be required to remain at the capitol, constantly at work not less than ten months during the year.

They should investigate every injustice placed by the transportation companies upon the shippers, and the whole power of the State should be used through the office of the Governor to support the commission in doing so.

I have been desirous of meeting Mr. Howell face to face to discuss with him the freight rate problem. In his formal announcement he practically declared "all is well," and urges that we should "let well enough alone. . . ."

Preserve White Supremacy.

I urge the adoption of an amendment to the Constitution of Georgia, which will eliminate by law all possible danger from the use of ignorant, purchasable negro votes at the ballot box.

I am aware of the fact that at present the State at large is not suffering from the use of the ballot by this class of negroes. There are a few counties and localities which are injured by it.

The claim has been made by those who opposed legislation upon this subject that the white primary and the requirement of the payment of poll-tax have disfranchised the negroes. This position can not stand investigation.

Before the existence of the white primary the negroes were PRACTICALLY DRIVEN FROM THE POLLS BY THE MENTAL AND PHYSICAL DETERMINATION OF THE WHITE PEOPLE THAT WHITE SUPREMACY SHOULD EXIST.

The report of our able comptroller-general for the year ending December 31, 1904, shows that over 110,000 negroes paid their poll tax.

It also shows that IN THIRTY-THREE COUNTIES MORE NEGROES THAN WHITE MEN PAY POLL-TAX. In these counties, therefore, neither the white primary nor the payment of poll-tax prevents the negroes from voting. IT IS IN THEIR POWER TO GO TO THE POLLS AND ELECT THE COUNTY OFFICERS.

It is only the mental and physical domination of the white man that protects. THE WHITE MEN WOULD RATHER DIE THAN BE RULED BY IGNORANT, PURCHASABLE NEGROES, AND THIS FACT HAS KEPT THEM IN CONTROL. . . .

Poll Tax Still to Be Paid.

It is not PROPOSED BY THE FRIENDS OF THIS MEASURE TO GIVE UP OUR WHITE PRIMARIES. It is not proposed to give up the PROVISIONS WE NOW HAVE REQUIRING THE PAYMENT OF POLL-TAX.

In each of the six Southern States which have adopted constitutional amendments to protect their people from the ballot in the hand of ignorant and purchasable negroes, provision has been made requiring the payment of poll-tax to BE PAID SIX MONTHS BEFORE THE ELECTION, thereby making it impossible for the excitement of the election or interest in the election to permit designing parties to raise funds and furnish the money necessary to pay the poll tax and give to the purchasable voters a chance to vote.

The petition of the friends of this measure is that we SHOULD KEEP ALL THE SAFEGUARDS WE HAVE, and ADD OTHERS WHICH EXPERIENCE HAS SHOWN ARE HELPFUL. . . .

Glorious Victory Predicted.

THIS IS A CONTEST BY THE PEOPLE OF GEORGIA. IT RISES FAR ABOVE A PERSONAL RACE.

WE ARE DETERMINED TO PRESERVE WHITE SUPREMACY AND TO PROTECT IT WITH EVERY ADDITIONAL LEGAL MEANS FOR THE WELFARE OF THOSE OF TODAY, AND FOR OUR CHILDREN.

WE DESIRE THE INDIVIDUAL VOTER TO TAKE A DEEPER INTEREST IN PUBLIC MATTERS, AND WE CALL EVERY VOTER TO A HIGHER STANDARD OF CIVIC RIGHTEOUSNESS.

WE ARE OPPOSED TO THE CONTROL OF STATE, COUNTY OR MUNICIPAL AFFAIRS BY MEN WHO MAKE POLITICS THEIR BUSINESS, AND WHO SEEK THEIR OWN PROMOTION THROUGH MACHINE OR RING RULE.

WE DESIRE TO MAKE IT IMPOSSIBLE FOR THE BIG CORPORATIONS TO CONTROL THE POLITICS OF GEORGIA BY CONTRIBUTING MONEY TO BE USED IN ELECTIONS. WE ARE DETERMINED TO DESTROY THE REIGN OF THE EMPLOYED POLITICAL AGENT AND TO PUT AN END TO THE THIRD HOUSE.

WE RECOGNIZE THAT WE ARE NOT HAVING A SQUARE DEAL IN MATTERS OF RAILROAD TRANSPORTATION.

WE INTEND TO ENLARGE THE POWERS AND DUTIES OF THE RAILROAD COMMISSION, AND PUT UPON THAT BODY MEN WHO WILL BRING RESULTS. . . .[5]

The 1908 Amendment to the 1877 Constitution

In 1907 Hoke Smith introduced a disfranchisement amendment into the Georgia legislature. With minor changes, the General Assembly approved the proposal and placed it on the ballot in the regular election of 1908. On October 7 the voters adopted it by a vote of 79,968 to 40,260. The amendment categorized as eligible voters those who met all other requirements and at least one of the following:

Paragraph 4:

1. All persons who have honorably served in the land or naval forces of the United States in the Revolutionary War, or in the War of 1812, or in the war with Mexico, or in any war with the Indians, or in the War with Spain, or who honorably served in the land or naval forces of the Confederate States or of the State of Georgia in the War between the States, or

2. All persons lawfully descended from those embraced in the classes enumerated in the subdivision next above, or,

3. All persons who are of good character and understand the duties and obligations of citizenship under a Republican form of government; or,

4. All persons who can correctly read in English language any paragraph of the Constitution of the United States or of this State and correctly write the same in the English language when read to them by any one of the registrars, and all persons who solely because of physical disability are unable to comply with the above requirements but who can understand and give a reasonable interpretation of any paragraph of the United States or of this State, that may be read to them by any one of the registrars; or

5. Any person who is the owner in good faith in his own right of at least forty acres of land situated in this State upon which he resides, or is the owner in good faith in his own right of property situated in this State and assessed for taxation at the value of $500.

Paragraph 5:

The right to register under sub-divisions 1 and 2 . . . shall continue only until January 1st, 1915. . . .[6]

A Northern Journalist's View
of the Jim Crow System

Ray Stannard Baker was one of the leading "muckrakers" of early twentieth-century journalism. Along with fellow writers such as Lincoln Steffens, he devoted his career to investigative reporting, hoping that his efforts would lead to progressive reform. A graduate of Michigan State College, Baker published many of his articles in *McClure's* and the *American Magazine*. His best-known works were on labor relations, discriminatory railroad rates, and Southern race problems. The selection below describes Atlanta's Jim Crow system in the first decade of the 20th century.

Atlanta is a singularly attractive place, as bright and new as any Western city. Sherman left it in ashes at the close of the war; the old buildings and narrow streets were swept away and a new city was built, which is now growing in a manner not short of astonishing. It has 115,000 to 125,000 inhabitants, about a third of whom are Negroes, living in more or less detached quarters in various parts of the city, and giving an individuality to the life interesting enough to the unfamiliar Northerner. A great many of them are always on the streets far better dressed and better-appearing than I had expected to see—having in mind, perhaps, the tattered country specimens of the penny postal cards. . . .

One of the points in which I was especially interested was the "Jim Crow" regulations, that is, the system of separation of the races in street cars and railroad trains. Next to the question of Negro suffrage, I think the people of the North have heard more of the Jim Crow legislation than of anything else connected with the Negro problem. . . . I was curious to see how the system worked out in Atlanta. Over the door of each car, I found this sign:

WHITE PEOPLE WILL SEAT FROM FRONT OF CAR TOWARD
THE BACK AND COLOURED PEOPLE FROM REAR TOWARD FRONT

Sure enough, I found the white people in front and the Negroes behind. As the sign indicates, there is no definite line of division between the white seats and the black seats, as in many other Southern cities. This very absence of a clear demarcation is significant of many relationships in the South. The colour line is drawn, but neither race knows just where it is. Indeed, it can hardly be definitely drawn in many relationships, because it is constantly changing. This uncertainty is a fertile source of friction and bitterness. The very first time I was on a car in Atlanta, I saw the conductor—all conductors are white—ask a Negro woman to get up and take a seat further back in order to make a place for a white man. I have also seen white men requested to leave the Negro section of the car. . . .

I heard innumerable stories from both white people and Negroes of encounters in street cars. Dr. W. F. Penn, one of the foremost Negro physicians of the city, himself partly white, a graduate of Yale College, told me of one occasion in which he entered a car and found there Mrs. Crogman, wife of the coloured president of Clark University. Mrs. Crogman is a mulatto so light of complexion as to be practically undistinguishable from white people. Dr. Penn, who knew her well, sat down beside her and began talking. A white man who occupied a seat in front with his wife turned and said:

"Here, you nigger, get out of that seat. What do you mean by sitting down with a white woman?"

Dr. Penn replied somewhat angrily:

"It's come to a pretty pass when a coloured man cannot sit with a woman of his own race in his own part of the car."

The white man turned to his wife and said:

"Here, take these bundles. I'm going to thrash that nigger."

In half a minute the car was in an uproar, the two men struggling. Fortunately the conductor and motorman were quickly at hand, and Dr. Penn slipped off the car. . . .

After I began to trace the colour line I found evidences of it everywhere—literally in every department of life. In the theaters, Negroes never sit downstairs, but the galleries are black with them. Of course, white hotels and restaurants are entirely barred to Negroes, with the result that coloured people have their own eating and sleeping places, many of them inexpressibly dilapidated and unclean. . . . Going along Decatur Street, one sees the saloons designated by conspicuous signs.[7]

"WHITES ONLY"   "COLOURED ONLY"

And when the Negro suffers the ordinary consequences of a prolonged visit to Decatur Street, and finds himself in the city prison, he is separated there, too, from the whites. And afterwards in court, if he comes to trial, two Bibles are provided; he may take his oath on one; the other is for the white man. When he dies he is buried in a separate cemetery. . . .

Considering the fact that only a few years ago, the Negro did no business at all, and had no professional men, it is really surprising to a Northerner to see what progress he has made. One of the first lines he took up was—not unnaturally—the undertaking business. Some of the most prosperous Negroes in every Southern city are undertakers, doing work exclusively, of course, for coloured people. Other early enterprises, growing naturally out of a history of personal service, were barbering and tailoring. Atlanta has many small Negro tailor and clothes-cleaning shops.

The wealthiest Negro in Atlanta, A. F. Herndon, operates the largest barbershop in the city; he is the president of a Negro insurance company (of which there are four in the city) and he owns and rents some fifty dwelling houses. He is said to be worth $80,000, all made, of course, since slavery.

Another occupation developing naturally from the industrial training of slavery was the business of the building contractor. Several such Negroes, notably Alexander Hamilton, do a considerable business in Atlanta, and have made money. They are employed by white men, and they hire for their jobs both white and Negro workmen. . . .

The appearance of Negro drug-stores was the natural result of the increasing practice of Negro doctors and dentists. Time was when all Negroes preferred to go to white practitioners, but since educated coloured doctors became common, they have taken a very large part—practically all, I am told—of the practice in Atlanta. Several of them have had degrees from Northern universities, two from Yale; and one of them, at least, has some little practice among white people. The doctors are leaders among their people. Naturally they give prescriptions to be filled by druggists of their own race; hence the growth of the drug business among Negroes everywhere in the South. . . .[8]

NOTES

1. For more on Holsey, see Bishop L. H. Holsey, *Autobiography, Sermons, Addresses, and Essays* (Atlanta: Franklin Printing and Publishing, 1899).

2. Edwin S. Redkey, ed., *Respect Black: The Writings and Speeches of Henry McNeal Turner* (New York: Arno Press and the New York Times, 1971), 53–56, 182.

3. Herbert Aptheker, ed., *Pamphlets and Leaflets by W. E. B. Du Bois* (White Plains, N.Y.: Kraus-Thomson, 1986), 13–16.

4. Dewey W. Grantham Jr., *Hoke Smith and the Politics of the New South* (Baton Rouge: Louisiana State University Press, 1958), 132–33, 163–65.

5. Hoke Smith, "Speech of Hoke Smith at Columbus, Georgia, January 10, 1906, in His Debate with Clark Howell," MS 2334, box no. 15:15, Hargrett Rare Book and Manuscript Library/University of Georgia Libraries.

6. An amendment to Art. 2, sec. 1, para. 4–5.

7. Baker indicated in a footnote that since his visit to Atlanta the legislature had passed a statewide prohibition law (1907), closing all the saloons.

8. The material appeared originally in the *American Magazine* in May 1907, then, with a few minor changes, in Ray Stannard Baker, *Following the Color Line: American Negro Citizenship in the Progressive Era* (New York: Doubleday, Page, 1908; reprint, New York: Harper Torchbooks, 1964), 27–41. Baker visited Atlanta in November 1906, less than two months after the infamous Atlanta Riot, in which a dozen or so people were killed. The first chapter of *Following the Color Line* described the riot and its aftermath. Baker blamed the riot on yellow journalism, too many saloons, and the large number of men who carried weapons wherever they went. The riot was provoked by several alleged assaults on white women by black men. Baker described the rioters as lower-class riffraff and argued that the better sort of white people were embarrassed and afterward worked hard to reestablish harmonious race relations. Baker made clear that white business and civic leaders were upset not only for humanitarian reasons but for fear that negative publicity would hurt Atlanta's image. He quoted one spokesman as saying: "Saturday evening at eight o'clock [before the riot started], the credit of Atlanta was good for any number of millions of dollars in New York or Boston or any financial centre; to-day we couldn't borrow fifty cents. The reputation we have been building up so arduously for years has been swept away in two short hours. Not by men who have made and make Atlanta, not by men who represent the character and strength of our city, but by hoodlums, understrappers and white criminals" (18–19).

12

The Leo Frank Case

Georgia's most celebrated case of the early twentieth century began with the murder of a teenage girl at her place of employment on Confederate Memorial Day, 1913. Born in Cobb County, Mary Phagan and her family had moved to Atlanta, where she worked for the National Pencil Company. The factory superintendent was a young Jewish businessman from New York named Leo M. Frank.

On Saturday, April 26, 1913, Mary left home shortly before noon, boarded a trolley, and rode uptown. Only a handful of people were working in the factory on the Confederate holiday, but Mary hoped her boss would be in the office, so she could collect $1.20 in wages owed her for ten hours of work. She never left the building. Later that afternoon her body was found in the basement. She had been assaulted, beaten, and strangled.

The police concluded that Frank, in a deserted back room, had killed the little girl in a crime of passion. The star witness against him was a black custodian named Jim Conley. Originally a suspect himself, the frightened employee told the police a number of conflicting stories. On the witness stand, however, he stuck to a version of the day's activities which Frank's attorneys, through hours of cross examination, were unable to break.

Conley testified in court that he saw Mary enter the factory and go upstairs. Shortly afterward, he heard a scream and commotion coming from the direction of the metal room behind Frank's office. A few minutes later, the superintendent summoned the janitor; and he saw Mary's mangled body. Afraid not to follow the order of his white employer, the terrified black man helped his boss carry the body to the elevator and down to the basement. When Conley was given permission to leave, he went out and got drunk.

Conley further testified that Frank frequently had women in the factory for immoral purposes. His janitorial duty on these occasions was to lock the entrance door until Frank whistled for him to let the women out. The question of Frank's alleged immorality was a major part of the prosecution's case. Several female employees testified that they had been sexually harassed by their young employer, or that they had seen Mary Phagan receiving unwanted sexual advances. On the other hand, the defense produced some two hundred witnesses, including a large number of women from the factory, who testified to Frank's good character.

There was much about the Frank case that was contradictory and confusing at the time, and the trial remains controversial to this day. For instance, even in 1913, one had good reason to question the truthfulness of Jim Conley's testimony. He had a criminal record, changed his story several times, and seemed unable to remember details of anything except what he may have been coached to say. Moreover, it was unlikely that Frank and Conley could have done all the latter said they did in the short time for which Frank lacked an alibi.

It seems improbable that the body was carried to the basement by elevator, as Conley claimed. He admitted that he defecated in the elevator shaft the morning of the murder. Whenever the elevator descended to the basement it always went to the bottom of the shaft, where it should have smashed the stools. Yet that had not happened before the police went down to the basement, by the stairs, to begin their investigation. The obvious conclusion was that the elevator had not been taken to the basement between Mary's arrival and the time that the police entered the building many hours later. Yet somehow the defense attorneys failed to notice this critical detail, and it was not impressed upon the jury. Two years later the fact became significant when Governor John M. Slaton reviewed the evidence while trying to decide whether to commute Frank's death sentence.

Perhaps even more damaging to Conley's testimony today is the revelation of Alonzo Mann in 1982. A fourteen-year-old employee at the time of the murder, young Alonzo had shown up at the factory on the fateful Saturday afternoon and had seen Conley, alone, on the first floor, carrying a body. After the janitor threatened to kill him if he talked, Alonzo fled the factory, confided only in his mother, and never told the police what he knew. Despite a troubled conscience, he remained silent until he was over over eighty years old. Then he was discovered by some newspaper reporters, who made his story public. His account played a major role in persuading the Georgia Board of Pardons and Paroles to issue a posthumous pardon to Frank in 1986.

While we will never know for sure who murdered Mary Phagan, we can reach conclusions about the climate of opinion in Georgia. Long before the Jewish manufacturer was convicted by an Atlanta jury, many Georgians had made up their minds that he was guilty. Large crowds gathered around the courthouse throughout the trial to cheer for the prosecution. The trial judge was so concerned about the safety of Frank and his attorneys that he urged them not to appear in court while the jury's verdict was read. The courtroom atmosphere became a major issue in the defendant's later appeals.

By 1915 Frank had been turned down in his attempts to gain a new trial by both the state and the U.S. Supreme Court. Before the death sentence could be carried out, however, Governor Slaton expressed doubts about the verdict and commuted the sentence to life in prison. Unfortunately, Slaton had a conflict of interest, since he was a former partner of one of Frank's attorneys. Those Georgians who had no doubts about the superintendent's guilt jumped immediately to the conclusion that the governor had been bought off by Frank's rich friends. When a riot broke out near the governor's home, Slaton, whose term was just ending, fled the state and did not return for many years. Meanwhile, the Frank case by 1917 propelled the prosecutor, Hugh M. Dorsey, into the governor's office.

With Frank confined to the state prison in Milledgeville, a group of prominent Mariettans formed themselves into the Knights of Mary Phagan. They traveled to Milledgeville, kidnapped the Jewish convict, and drove him to Cobb County, where Frank, on August 17, 1915, was lynched. None of the lynch party was ever brought to justice. Two months later another group of "knights" gathered on Stone Mountain to revive the Ku Klux Klan.

Described as the worst example of anti-Semitism in American history, the Frank case is one of enduring interest. Historians will probably never be sure who killed Mary Phagan. If Frank was not the murderer, Conley would seem to be the most likely alternative. But perhaps there was an unknown third party. A more important question for students of history is why an apparent majority of Georgians in 1913–15 believed passionately that Frank did it. The documents below, it is hoped, will reveal much about the attitudes and values of the two opposing camps in this tragic case.[1]

Solicitor-General Dorsey's Closing Argument

Proof That He Knew Mary.

Way back yonder in March, as far back as March, little Willie Turner, an ignorant country boy, saw Frank trying to force his attentions on this little girl in the
metal room; he is unimpeached, he is unimpeachable. She backed off and told
him she must go to her work, and Frank said, "I am superintendent of this factory," — a species of coercion — "and I want to talk to you." You tell me that that
little girl that worked up there and upon the same floor with you in the metal department, and you had passed right by her machine, this pretty, attractive, little
girl, twelve months, and a man of your brilliant parts didn't even know her, and
do you tell me that you had made up the pay-roll with Schiff fifty-two times during the year that Mary Phagan was there and still you didn't know her name or
number? You tell me that this little country boy who comes from Oak Grove,
near Sandy Springs in the northern part of this county, was lying when he got
on that stand? I'll tell you no. Do you tell me that little Dewey Hewell, a little
girl now from the Home of the Good Shepherd in Cincinnati, who used to work
at the National Pencil Company, who probably has lost her virtue though she
is of such tender years, was lying when she tells you that she heard him talking
to her frequently, — talked to Mary frequently, placed his hands on her shoulder
and called her Mary?" . . .

I am prepared to believe, knowing this man's character as shown by this evidence, that way back yonder in March, old passion had seized him. Yesterday,
Mr. Rosser quoted from Burns, and said it's human to err; and I quote you from
the same poem, in which old Burns says that "there's no telling what a man will
do when he has the lassie, when convenience snug, and he has a treacherous,
passionate inclination." There's no telling what he will do when he's normal,
there's no telling what he will do when he's like other men, but, oh! gentlemen,
there's no telling what a pervert will do when he's goaded on by the unusual,
extraordinary passion that goaded on this man, Leo M. Frank, when he saw his
opportunity with this little girl in that pencil factory, when she went back to find
out if the metal had come.

Claimed He Didn't Know Her.

. . . I wouldn't be at all surprised if the truth of the business is that this man
coveted that little girl away back yonder in March, I wouldn't be at all surprised,

gentlemen, and indeed, I submit that it's the truth, that every one of these girls has told the truth when they swore to you on the stand that back yonder in March, after this little girl had come down to work on the office floor in the metal department, that they observed this man, Leo M. Frank, making advances towards her and using his position as superintendent to force her to talk with him. I wouldn't be at all surprised if he didn't hang around, I wouldn't be at all surprised if he didn't try to get little Mary to yield. . . .

Laying Snare for Mary.

And you say that you and Schiff made up the pay-roll Friday, and I wouldn't be at all surprised that, after little Mary had gone and while you and Schiff were making up the pay-roll Friday afternoon, you saw little Mary's name and you knew that she hadn't been notified to come there and get her money Friday after-noon at six o'clock, and then, as early as three o'clock—yes, as early as three,— knowing that this little girl would probably come there Saturday at twelve, at the usual hour, to get her pay, you went up and arranged with this man Jim Conley to look out for you,—this man Jim Conley who had looked out for you on other occasions, who had locked the door and unlocked it while you carried on your immoral practices in that factory,—yes, at three o'clock, when you and Schiff were so busy working on the pay-roll, I dare say you went up there and told Jim that you wanted him to come back Saturday but you didn't want Darley to know that he was there. And I wouldn't be at all surprised if it were not true that this little Helen Ferguson, the friend of Mary Phagan, who had often gotten Mary's pay envelope before, when she went in and asked you to let her have that pay envelope, if you didn't refuse because you had already arranged with Jim to be there, and you expected to make the final onslaught on this girl, in order to de-flower and ruin her and make her, this poor little factory girl, subservient to your purposes.

Mary Falls in Trap.

Ah, gentlemen, then Saturday comes, Saturday comes, and it's a reasonable tale that old Jim tells you, and old Jim says "I done it,"—not "I did it," but "I done it" just exactly like this brilliant factory superintendent told him. There's your plot. I'll tell you, you know this thing passion is like fraud,—it's subtle, it moves in mysterious ways; people don't know what lurks in the mind of a libertine, or how anxious they are, or how far ahead they look, and it isn't at all improbable, indeed, I submit to you as honest men seeking to get at the truth, that this man, whose character was put in issue and torn down, who refused to go into specific instances on cross-examination, if he didn't contemplate this little girl's ruin and damnation it was because he was infatuated with her and didn't have the power to control that ungovernable passion. There's your plot. . . .

His Own Acts Prove His Guilt.

Gentlemen, every act of that defendant proclaims him guilty. Gentlemen, every word of that defendant proclaims him responsible for the death of this little factory girl. Gentlemen, every circumstance in this case proves him guilty of this crime. Extraordinary? Yes, but nevertheless true, just as true as Mary Phagan is dead. She died a noble death, not a blot on her name. She died because she wouldn't yield her virtue to the demands of her superintendent. I have no purpose and have never had from the beginning in this case that you ought to have, as an honest, upright citizen of this community. In the language of Daniel Webster, I desire to remind you "that when a jury, through whimsical and unfounded scruples, suffers the guilty, to escape, they make themselves answerable for the augmented danger to the innocent."

Your Honor, I have done my duty. I have no apology to make. Your Honor, so far as the State is concerned, may now charge this jury,—this jury who have sworn that they were impartial and unbiased, this jury who, in this presence, have taken the oath that they would well and truly try the issue formed on this bill of indictment between the State of Georgia and Leo M. Frank, charged with the murder of Mary Phagan; and I predict, may it please your Honor, that under the law that you give in charge and under the honest opinion of the jury of the evidence produced, there can be but one verdict, and that is: We the jury find the defendant, Leo M. Frank, guilty! GUILTY! GUILTY!![2]

🔖 🔖 🔖

Frank's Appeal

As soon as Leo Frank was convicted in 1913, he began petitioning the courts for a new trial. The grounds were that the evidence did not support a conviction, that the jury had been influenced by loud demonstrations outside the courtroom, and that prejudice had condemned an innocent man. To these arguments the prosecutor responded with affidavits from the jurors that they had neither heard nor been intimidated by the crowds. On October 13, 1913, the trial judge, Leonard Roan, denied the defense motion, but issued the following statement, in which he expressed his doubts about the verdict: "I am not certain of the man's guilt. With all the thought I have put on this case, I am not thoroughly convinced that Frank is guilty or innocent. The jury was convinced. There is no room to doubt that."

In 1914 the Georgia Supreme Court twice rejected appeals. Frank's lawyers then took the case to the federal level. The document below is part of the argument presented before the U.S. District Court for the Northern District of Georgia.

. . . My trial in the Superior Court of Fulton County, State of Georgia, before Hon. L. S. Roan and a jury, began on July 28, 1913, in the Court House at Atlanta, Georgia, and continued until August 25, 1913. The court room in which the trial took place was on the ground floor of the Court House. The windows of the court room were open during the progress of the trial, and looked out on Pryor Street, a public street of Atlanta. An open alley ran from Pryor Street along the side of the Court House, and there were windows looking into this alley from the court room. The noises from the street were thus conveyed to the court room, and the proceedings in the court room could be heard in the street and alley. Considerable public excitement prevailed during the trial, and it was apparent to the Court that public sentiment seemed to be greatly against me. The court room was constantly crowded, and considerable crowds gathered in the street and alley, and the noises which emanated from them could be heard in the court room. These crowds were boisterous. Several times during the trial, the crowd in the court room and outside of the Court House applauded, in a manner audible both to the Court and jury, whenever the State scored a point. The crowds outside cheered, shouted and hurrahed, while the crowd within the court room evidenced its feelings by applause and other demonstrations. Practically all of the seats in the court room were occupied, both within and without the bar. The aisles at each end of the court room were packed with spectators. The jury, in going to and from the court room, in the morning, at noon and in the evening, were dependent upon the passageways made for them by the officers of the court. The bar of the court room itself was so crowded as to leave but a small space for occupancy by the counsel. The jury box, which was occupied by the jury, was enclosed by the crowd sitting and standing in such close proximity to it that the whispers of the crowd could be heard during a part of the trial.

On Saturday, August 23, 1913, during the argument of Solicitor General Dorsey to the jury, Reuben R. Arnold, Esq., one of my counsel, made an objection to such argument, and the crowd laughed at him. While Mr. Arnold, my counsel, made a motion for a mistrial, and was engaged in taking evidence in support thereof before the Court, the crowd applauded a witness who testified that he did not believe that the jury heard the applause of the crowd on the previous day, as at that time the jury was in the jury room about twenty feet distant.

On Saturday, August 23, 1913, while the court was considering whether or not the trial should proceed on that evening and to what hour the trial should be extended, the excitement in and without the court room was so apparent as to cause apprehension in the mind of the Court as to whether the trial could be safely continued on that day, and before deciding upon an adjournment, the presiding Judge, Hon L. S. Roan, while upon the bench, and in the presence of the jury, conferred with the Chief of Police of Atlanta and the colonel of the Fifth Georgia Regiment, stationed in Atlanta, who were well known to the jury. The public press of Atlanta, apprehending danger if the trial continued on that day, united in a request to the Court, that the proceedings should not continue on Saturday evening. The trial was thereupon continued until the morning of Monday, August 25, 1913.

It was evident on that morning, that the public excitement had not subsided, and that it was as intense, as it had been on the Saturday previous. Excited crowds were present as before, both within and outside of the court room. When the Solicitor General entered the court room, he was greeted by applause by the large crowd present, who stamped their feet and clapped their hands, the jury being then in its room, about twenty feet distant. . . .

On the morning of Monday, August 25, 1913, shortly before Hon. L. S. Roan, Presiding Judge, began his charge to the jury, he privately conversed with Messrs. L. Z. Rosser and Reuben R. Arnold, two of my counsel, in the jury room of the Court House, and referred to the probable danger of violence that I would incur if I were present when the verdict was rendered and the verdict should be one of acquittal or of disagreement. After he had thus expressed himself, he requested my counsel to agree that I need not be present at the time when the verdict was rendered and the jury polled. In the same conversation the Judge expressed his opinion to counsel, that even they might be in danger of violence should they be present at the reception of the verdict. Under these circumstances they agreed with the Judge, that neither I nor they should be present at the rendition of the verdict.

I knew nothing of this conversation, nor of any agreement made by my said counsel with the Judge, until after the rendition of the verdict and sentence of death had been pronounced.

Pursuant to this conversation, I was not brought into court at the time of the rendition of the verdict, and I was not present when the verdict was received and the jury was discharged, nor was any of my counsel present when the verdict was received and the jury discharged.

I did not give to my counsel nor to any one else, authority to waive my right to be present at the reception of the verdict, or to agree that I should not be present at that time, nor were they in any way authorized or empowered to waive my right so to be present; nor did I authorize my counsel, or any of them, to be absent from the court room at the reception of the verdict, or to agree that they or any of them might be absent at that time. My counsel were induced to make the aforesaid agreement as to my absence and their absence at the reception of the verdict, solely because of the statement made to them by the Presiding Judge, and their belief that if I were present at the time of the reception of the verdict and it should be one of acquittal or of disagreement, it might subject me and them to serious bodily harm, and even to the loss of life. . . .

After the jury had been finally charged by the Court and the case had been submitted to it, when Mr. Dorsey, the Solicitor General, left the court room, a large crowd on the outside of the Court House and in the streets, greeted him with loud and boisterous applause, clapping their hands and yelling "Hurrah for Dorsey," placed him upon their shoulders, and carried him across the street into a building where his office was located. The crowd did not wholly disperse during the interval between the submission of the case to the jury and the return of the jury to the court room with its verdict, but during the entire period a large crowd was gathered in the immediate vicinity of the Court House. When it was announced that the jury had agreed upon a verdict, a signal was given from within the court room to the crowd on the outside to that effect, and the crowd outside raised a mighty shout of approval, and cheered while the polling of the jury proceeded. Before more than one juror had been polled, the applause was so loud and the noise was so great, that the further polling of the jury had to be stopped, so that order might be restored, and the noise and cheering from without was such, that it was difficult for the Presiding Judge to hear the responses of the jurors as they were being polled, although he was only ten feet distant from the jury.

All of this occurred during my involuntary absence from the court room, I being at the time in the custody of the Sheriff of Fulton County and incarcerated in the jail of said County, my absence from the court room, and that of my counsel, having been requested by the Court because of the fear of the Court that violence might be done to me and my counsel had I or my said counsel been in court at the time of the rendition of the verdict.[3]

Tom Watson and Southern Honor

After the U.S. district court failed to overturn the decision, the case was appealed to the U.S. Supreme Court, where Frank again lost. On April 19, 1915, by a 7–2 vote, the nation's highest court sided with the finding of the state supreme court that the allegations of mob influence were largely groundless. Nonetheless, the two dissenters, Oliver Wendell Holmes and Charles Evans Hughes, reached the opposite conclusion, discovering a strong presumption that the jury was influenced by the "passions of the mob."

At this point, Frank had exhausted all judicial remedies, but there was still one avenue open. The Georgia Prison Commission could recommend clemency to the governor. In the late spring of 1915 the prison commission held a public hearing in which both sides repeated their arguments. On June 10 the Prison Commission sided two to one against the unfortunate defendant. Then, eleven days later, after agonizing over the case at length, Governor John M. Slaton announced he was reducing the sentence from death to life in prison.

Slaton claimed to be disturbed by Judge Roan's doubts, by the discrepancies in Jim Conley's testimony and other parts of the government's case, by the circumstantial nature of the evidence, and by the fact that two U.S. Supreme Court justices and one state prison commissioner had reservations. Comparing himself to Pilate, he said that he did not want to wash his hands while another Jew was turned over to a mob. The governor further maintained that if he failed to do his duty he would consider himself "an assassin through cowardice." At 2:00 A.M. on the morning of the announcement Slaton reportedly told his wife, "It may mean my death or worse, but I have ordered the sentence commuted." Mrs. Slaton allegedly replied, "I would rather be the widow of a brave and honorable man than the wife of a coward."

Perhaps no one more clearly tied the Frank case to the Lost Cause than Tom Watson. The former leader of the People's Party is one of the most haunting figures of Georgia history. Once he seemed to be an advocate of tolerance and political equality. Now, he had transformed himself into one of the most vicious bigots of Southern politics.

The following is the conclusion to a long article, written just after the governor had commuted Frank's sentence to life in prison.

Leo Frank is now at the State Farm, an honored guest of the managers, awaiting his triumphant release from even the politely formal fetters of the Law.

His little victim, whose upraised hands—fixed by the *rigor mortis*—proved that she had died fighting for her virtue, lies in Georgia's soil, amid a grief-stricken, and mortified people—a people bowed down by the unutterable humiliation of having been sold out to Jew money.

On the heights from which the immortals look into the lives of human beings, how vast must seem the moral distance between *the little girl*, who died, rather than soil the purity that God gave her, *and the Governor*, who brought this eternal disgrace upon himself and our State!

A *child* died a heroine's death, and sleeps in a heroine's grave: *the man* is pilloried in eternal infamy.

We gave him a clean commission; and he returned it to us, covered with filth.

The Constitution which he swore to respect, he trampled into the mud.

The great Seal of the State went, LIKE A THIEF IN THE NIGHT, *to do for an unscrupulous law firm, a deed of darkness which dared not face the sun.*

We have been betrayed! The breath of some leprous monster has passed over us, and we feel like crying out, in horror and despair,

"Unclean! UNCLEAN!"

When John M. Slaton tosses on a sleepless bed, in the years to come, he will see a vivid picture of that little Georgia girl, decoyed to the metal room by this satyr-faced Jew: he will see her little hands put out, to keep off the lustful beast: he will hear her cry of sudden terror; he will see her face purpling as the cruel cord chokes her to death—and *John M. Slaton will walk the floor, a wretched, conscience-smitten man,* AND HE WILL SWEAT BLOOD! . . .

Are the old lessons lifeless? Are the old glories gone? Are there no feet that tread the old paths?

Once, there were *men* in Georgia—men who were afraid of nothing, save to do wrong; men who sprang to arms, and went to death, on a bare question of *principle*; men who would no more lie than they would steal; men who flamed into passionate indignation when a legislature was believed to have disgraced the State; men who caught the fire from the heavens to burn a law which outraged Georgia's sense of honor and justice.

The sons of these men carried the Grey lines, and the tattered Stars and Bars farthest up the heights of Gettysburg; met the first shock of battle at Manassas; led the last charge at Appomattox.

And the sons of these Georgians are today bowed down with unspeakable grief—for they feel that *our grand old Empire State* HAS BEEN RAPED!

Like the Roman wife of old, we feel that something unutterably loathsome has crept to bed with us, and that, while the morning has come, it can *never* restore our self-respect.

We have been violated, AND WE ARE ASHAMED![4]

The Lynching and the Pardon

Despite Governor Slaton's efforts, and probably in part as a result of Watson's inflammatory rhetoric, Frank died at the hands of a lynch mob less than two months after his sentence was commuted. Other Jewish residents of Georgia became victims of abuse and economic discrimination. In Marietta a Vigilance Committee distributed handbills warning Jewish businessmen to close their establishments and threatening punishment if they did not. Thus, an atmosphere of prejudice and suspicion lingered long after the case came to its unfortunate end.

Altanta's Jewish community and other champions of civil liberties and religious toleration refused to let the case die. For seventy years they worked to clear Leo Frank's name. Finally, in 1986, the Board of Pardons and Paroles decided the time had come to end the matter. While stopping short of declaring Frank innocent, the board decided that he at least deserved a pardon, as its statement below reveals.

On April 26, 1913, Mary Phagan, a thirteen-year-old employee in an Atlanta pencil factory, was murdered. Georgians were shocked and outraged. Charged with the murder was the factory superintendent, Leo M. Frank.

The funeral of Mary Phagan, the police investigation, and the trial of Leo Frank were reported in the overblown newspaper style of the day. Emotions were fanned high.

During the trial a crowd filled the courthouse and surrounded it. While the verdict was read, Frank was kept in jail for protection. He was convicted on August 25, 1913, and subsequently sentenced to death.

After unsuccessful court appeals the case came to Governor John M. Slaton for his consideration. The Governor was under enormous pressure. Many wanted Frank to hang, and the emotions of some were fired by prejudice about Frank being Jewish and a factory superintendent from the North. On June 21, 1915, the Governor, because of doubts about Frank's guilt, commuted the sentence from death to life imprisonment. Thus Frank was saved from the gallows, and his judicial appeals could continue, or so it seemed.

On the night of August 16, 1915, a group of armed men took Frank by force from the State Prison at Milledgeville, transported him to Cobb County, and early the next morning lynched him.

The lynching aborted the legal process, thus foreclosing further efforts to prove Frank's innocence. It resulted from the State of Georgia's failure to protect Frank. Compounding the injustice, the State then failed to prosecute any of the lynchers.

In 1983, the State Board of Pardons and Paroles considered a request for a Pardon implying innocence but did not find "conclusive evidence proving beyond any doubt that Frank was innocent." Such a standard of proof, especially for a 70-year-old case, is almost impossible to satisfy.

Without attempting to address the question of guilt or innocence, and in recognition of the State's failure to protect the person of Leo M. Frank and thereby preserve his opportunity for continued legal appeal of his conviction, and in recognition of the State's failure to bring his killers to justice, and as an effort to heal old wounds, the State Board of Pardons and Paroles, in compliance with its Constitutional and statutory authority, hereby grants to Leo M. Frank a Pardon.

Given under the Hand and Seal of the State Board of Pardons and Paroles, this eleventh day of March, 1986.[5]

NOTES

1. There are many books on the Phagan murder and its aftermath. Perhaps the best is Leonard Dinnerstein, *The Leo Frank Case* (New York: Columbia University Press, 1968; reprint, Athens: University of Georgia Press, 1987).

2. Hugh M. Dorsey, *Argument of Hugh M. Dorsey, Solicitor-General, Atlanta Judicial Circuit, at the Trial of Leo M. Frank, Charged with the Murder of Mary Phagan* (Macon, Ga.: N. Christophulos, 1914), 73–77 and 145–46. The address lasted three days and was Dorsey's closing argument to the jury. The *Atlanta Constitution* claimed at the time that the speech was "worthy of Bob Toombs in the first-flush of vigorous manhood."

3. *Leo M. Frank v. C. Wheeler Mangum, Sheriff of Fulton County, Georgia,* December 17, 1914.

4. "The Celebrated Case of the State of Georgia vs. Leo Frank," *Watson's Magazine* 21 (August 1915): 182–235.

5. *Decision in Response to Application for Posthumous Pardon for Leo M. Frank,* March 11, 1986, Georgia Board of Pardons and Paroles, Atlanta. A copy of the decision may also be found in Ann W. Ellis and Helen S. Ridley, eds., *Federal Court Decisions,* vol. 2, *Historic Cases,* prepared in collaboration with the National Archives — Southeast Region (Marietta: Kennesaw State College, 1989), p. v–39.

13

🏴 🏴 🏴

Georgia's Rejection
of Woman Suffrage

Patriarchal in race and class relations, Georgia had little use for women's rights. Southern ladies were honored for purity, self-sacrifice, and altruism, not for their assertion of individual interests. Viewed as fragile and defenseless, women supposedly needed protection from the harsh realities of the world. Their place was in the home, managing the domestic economy and rearing the children. Since their fathers and husbands represented them in public, women did not need the vote—unless they had views and aspirations different from the rest of the family. And such a thought was too heretical for most Georgians to consider.

Nonetheless, a small suffrage movement emerged in Georgia around 1890, almost a half century after the origins of the cause in the North. The earliest leader was Augusta Howard of Columbus, who organized the Georgia Woman Suffrage Association. Her major achievement was to persuade the National American Woman Suffrage Association, headed by Susan B. Anthony, to hold its 1895 annual convention in Atlanta, the first time the NAWSA had ventured south. Despite the publicity of a national convention, the Georgia Woman Suffrage Association had less than one hundred members and remained small until the second decade of the twentieth century, when the question of the vote for women finally was debated seriously in the state legislature.

🦋 🦋 🦋

Rebecca Latimer Felton

In the early twentieth century two sisters, Rebecca Latimer Felton of Cartersville and Mary Latimer McLendon of Atlanta, played central roles in the Georgia struggle, the latter as president for many years of the Georgia Woman Suffrage Association. Frances Smith Whiteside, principal of an Atlanta school and sister of Hoke Smith, headed another group, the Georgia Woman Suffrage League. By far the most effective spokesperson for the movement was Rebecca Latimer Felton (1835–1930).

A graduate of Madison Female College, Rebecca Latimer in 1853 married William Harrell Felton, a physician who served three terms in Congress during the 1870s as an Independent. While Dr. Felton served in the House, Mrs. Felton served as his secretary and advisor. From time to time she also was active as a school teacher, as the author of three books, and as a columnist for twenty-eight years for the *Atlanta Journal*. In 1912 she was a delegate from Georgia to the Progressive ("Bull Moose") Party convention; and in 1922, at age eighty-seven, she was honored by a brief appointment to the U.S. Senate, following the death of Senator Thomas E. Watson. Although she served for only two days, she became the first woman ever to occupy a senate seat. The article below gives her views on women's rights.

Why I Am a Suffragist?

Former Subjection of Women.

Savage tribes used physical force to manage their women. The club and the lash were their only arguments. Moslem fanatics go a step further in saying women have no souls. According to statistics these Mohammedans comprise about one-third of such religionists at this time. Athenian law allowed a man to sell his wife or sister under certain conditions. Feudal law allowed men to imprison their sisters in convents—while they used the property that was rightfully their sisters'—in riotous living.

English law, in the time of Herbert Spencer, allowed a man to beat his wife, and he could lock her in any room in his house, and keep her imprisoned until her will was subdued to his own. English law was copied by the Colonies of America. Lawyers will tell you now, that English law has been the basic stone of our laws—State and Federal. As late as the year 1857, a man in Georgia was allowed to beat his wife, provided the hickory withe was no larger than his thumb. I wish I knew the Georgian's name who introduced the bill for a married woman's relief in 1857, three years before secession. I would like to contribute to a fund to place a suitable tablet to his memory in our State Capitol.

As late as 1868 a Supreme Court Judge in North Carolina, reiterated the law allowing a man to beat his wife, with a rod no bigger than his thumb. In his verdict (on a wife beating case) he said a man should make his wife behave herself, otherwise it would *"engender insubordination."*

A woman in Georgia could not own her own wages—as late as 1897. Hon. W. H. Fleming introduced the bill to allow a married woman to receive and spend what she earned outside her home. Before that time "her man" could demand them from her employer on pain of compelling him to pay twice, and he could spend them where he pleased, in a dram shop or gambling den, or bawdy house—and she could not recover them to her own use. Before the Civil War, a married woman in Georgia could not own her own clothes. When she went to her new home she might carry a fortune in lands and slaves, but she did not really own a copper cent of their value. Thousands of slaves and lands belonging to ante-bellum women were sold for the husband's security debts. Sometimes her first information was received when the sheriff came to dispossess her. Sometimes a marriage contract was required by anxious parents, but the woman was made to suffer for it. I knew a young woman who declined a marriage contract, because her fiancé told her it would be a reflection on himself and it would "break his heart" to be thus distrusted. Nevertheless, he proved himself faithless—in mind, morals and her estate. A woman cannot practice law in Georgia today, no matter how well prepared by study and genius. There are scores of women doctors—but our legislators draw a line at the law.

Before the war *her only chance lay in her foresight in accepting or finding for herself a good master.* I have known the same privilege extended to favored slaves —who were forced to sale for legal reasons. There were many, I trust, very many men of good character and proper self-respect, who did not push legal rights to the extent of the law, but there were thousands of two-legged brutes who used the lash on short notice. The prevalence of wife beating has had much to do with the coarse manners and insolent behavior of their own male progeny. As I understand the meaning of law, it is to provide against what an evil doer is apt to do, but our ante-bellum Georgia laws furnished the opportunity to brutal men to exercise their right as masters over wives as well as slaves. What is known as chivalry found no expression on the statute books of Georgia until the Civil War made changes. It exploited itself in courting days, in bowing and scraping in public company, and in personal encounters, which were known as duels. An insult called for a challenge, and then pistols. Nevertheless the law of Georgia allowed any sort of a man to beat his wife, provided the switch was no bigger than his thumb. Glance down at your thumb, my dear reader, and then we will proceed a little further.

In the homes where the lash was used the sons either despised the father or concluded it was the proper way to treat women. The daughters, afraid and disgusted, took chances, hoping to do better in selecting kinder masters than their mothers had done.

Those who were fortunate were contented in their ignorance. Those who felt the lash were helpless before the law of the land.

In Georgia before the war, a woman might teach school as a genteel profession—if she was educated. If she was illiterate she could weave or sew, if her rich neighbors gave her such work to do. The school teacher generally married some man with slaves to wait on her. The illiterate woman went to the kitchen and cornfield, like the slave woman of the big plantations. The well-fed negroes made a standing joke on "po-white trash."

Constitutional Convention of 1868.

This convention has been abused without mercy, as a radical body, controlled by scalawags and carpet-baggers, but it was the first state convention in Georgia to secure property rights to women who were married. It was said to be a selfish proposition because the vast majority of our men were hopelessly in debt when the war closed. If the woman could claim the property, then there would be a home, a living, and maintenance. Otherwise the dear good man would be in bondage to his obligations. It has proved to be a popular law for the men as well as the women. "Calico pensioners" are still plentiful. And if the man was mean and cruel he could make his wife turn over the proceeds—and if he was suave and polite, he could borrow and forget to pay back. If she was prosperous, he was more so—and he is still amusing himself by putting all things doubtful in "*his wife's name.*" And the majority of these "calico pensioners" are almost rabid maniacs in opposition to votes for women! . . .

Is the Ballot a Right or a Favor?

It is an erroneous idea that has been actively promulgated for a purpose—that women have no claim to the ballot privilege, because they have no title to its possession. One objector says the ballot is a franchise and a dispensation, without any inherent or moral or legal right, as pertaining to women. I claim that they were born into all the rights that are the property of their brothers, born of the same parents and raised in the same home and educated in the same way. The law of inheritance, where parents die intestate, gives to each child, *regardless of sex*, equal shares in the inherited property, and when the property is divided, dollar for dollar, the daughters own their parts as legally as the sons own their parts, but the law of the land gives to the males liberty to say how and when and by whom, that property shall be taxed, and denies to the females this essential and inherent right. The right to own property is allowed to every person in a republican form of government, regardless of sex, but the right to say how, or when, or by whom that property is to be taxed is denied to one half the citizens of the United States, except in the States which have been franchised by the good sense and common honesty of the men of those States—after due consideration, and with the chivalric instinct that differentiates the coarse brutal male from the gentlemen of our nation. Shall the men of the South be less generous, less chivalrous? They have given the Southern women more praise than the man of the West—but judged by their actions Southern men have been less sincere. Honeyed phrases are pleasant to listen to, but the sensible women of our country would prefer more substantial gifts. . . .

So long as women were denied property rights, denied higher education and kept in bondage by hickory withes no larger than a man's thumb—the women dared not ask for more than liberty to live and to bear their children in quiet homes, but with education and property rights and the ballot conferred on all negro men, who are not idiots or criminals, Southern women are not willing to be disfranchised when a dozen states of this Union have conferred the ballot on the wives, mothers and daughters of that section of our country. . . .

It is said that women are represented by their husbands at the ballot box. This is not true; of the ten millions of unmarried women who have nobody to vote for them, there are between eight and nine millions of unmarried men, who vote for nobody but themselves. *And nobody votes for the drunkard's wife?* There are as many widows in this country as widowers. As a rule they manage well their business affairs and they were forced to learn under difficulties. They deserve the ballot because their property is taxed to the limit and beyond, and they are not allowed to protest. *Women make fine teachers.* A callow youth can vote at

21, while his capable teacher, if *a woman*, is forbidden to vote. Women are the mainstays in public schools. They are not only forbidden the vote, but their pay is reduced because of their sex. They make superior stenographers, but while pay may reach fifty dollars a month the young man in trousers gets from seventy-five to a hundred, with no better work—and according to common report, not so reliable as to fidelity and regular habits. The more I think about these inequalities and this manifest injustice, the more I am tempted to eulogize the heathen, who lived on the Ganges river, and who drowned the girl babies, because they were unfit to live! . . .

New Men as Well as New Women.

The "New Woman" is often criticized. The term is never applied as a compliment, but there also is the "New Man" to be reckoned with. . . . He has had clear vision in the great West. The Star of Empire is turned, and leading to the East. He knows that the elevation of women has given vitality and strength to mankind. "He knows that the standard of mothers is the final standard of all races of men. He knows as the mother's brain weakens, the brain of her son weakens; as her muscles soften, his child's muscles soften; as she decays, the people decay in every station in life. The parasitism of child-bearing women has always weakened the race. The mother of his children must be given the best, that she may do her best. While he knows there are women who are more selfish than patriotic, more indifferent to the duty of child-bearing than to society fribbles, and there are those "who prefer like Helen of Troy to be passed along from man to man, and who will, like Cleopatra, entice great men to their overthrow," yet he also knows that the coming mothers of the United States must be prepared to understand the principles of government, to meet the exigencies that doubtful conditions are forcing upon the country. He knows that he can trust the wife of his bosom with the nearest and dearest interests of his existence. The call of the age is for the wise and capable women, and the New Man understands that his mate must be his comrade and likewise his friend in every emergency.

This woman's movement is a great movement of the sexes toward each other, with common ideals as to government, as well as common ideals in domestic life, where fully developed manhood must seek and find its real mate in the mother of his children, as well as the solace of his home. "The time has long passed since the hard-drinking, fox-hunting, high-playing country squire was excused because of his generosity and hospitality." He was not the equal of his sober mate, whose hand held the distaff, who made good cheer from kitchen to drawing-room. The call of the age is for partnership in the family, in the church, in the State and National affairs, between men and women.

The brothel, the gaming table, the race course and habits of physical excess are still with us, but the hope of this Nation lies in the broad-minded men who boldly acclaim woman's success in every field of literature, science, music, art, in the organized professions, and great national philanthropies. These are the men to whom we look for the early recognition of women everywhere, in the every-day duties, with everyday experience, and mutual acquaintance with the various problems of government.

Cartersville, Ga., May 14, 1915.[1]

🔰 🔰 🔰

Dolly Blount Lamar

Not all women in Georgia wanted the vote. Neither Georgia's Federation of Women's Clubs nor the Georgia Woman's Christian Temperance Union showed much interest. In a meeting at Macon in May, 1914 several women came together to form the Georgia Association Opposed to Woman Suffrage. Its first president was Caroline Patterson, but its chief spokesperson was Dolly Blount (Mrs. Walter D.) Lamar. Active in numerous women's organizations and the eventual author of an autobiography, Mrs. Lamar argued that most Georgia women had a higher calling than politics and were not interested in the vote. Along with most Southern opponents of woman suffrage, she also suggested that votes for women might undermine white supremacy. The following is a speech she delivered to her organization in March 1916.

The Vulnerability of the White Primary

"I will be a voter; nobody shall save me." Thus do those who cry for suffrage answer friends who would warn them against the evils that accompany woman suffrage, and more especially such evils as would result therefrom to the South.

Lest the sophistry of their arguments affect the minds of some who have not studied or who do not know that the question is one which every care-taking citizen should consider, the following facts are cited:

In answer to the proven statement that a national suffrage law would take from the states their right to control in this matter, it is urged, "Well, what if our negroes do vote, there are a great many more white women than of the other race, and we could always outvote any effort of the Republican party to control the South in this way." Alas! for this lack of intelligence and patriotism! Lack of knowledge of the workings of suffrage, which has proven that the women who might be helpful, do not use the vote in any large numbers, and that where the privilege counts for anything at all it counts on the side of vice rather than up-lift, it exploits the vote that is buyable, its drawbacks keep from the polls many a woman who might be a power for good in politics had she not discovered that the alleged slime of politics is really there, and that not enough of her sex com-bine to make the vote of good women an appreciable asset. . . .

Look before You Leap!

The gullibility of the woman who thinks she wants to vote is equalled only by the sophistry of the woman who argues for suffrage. When bitten by the suffrage bug, the victim immediately runs about and tries to bite somebody else that the number, not the quality, be increased. In witness thereto, behold how neither accuracy, nor patriotism, nor any other qualification is required of the exponent of suffrage.

Only let her want the ballot, then fling discretion as to statements to the winds. Notable among her shortcomings is her willingness to accept and present to her immediate following anything she reads in the organs of suffrage. For instance, she assigns the alliance with liquor interests to the woman who does not want to vote, she credits all reforms in suffrage states to the woman vote. She assumes that all women will vote for uplift, she claims that women exercise the voting privilege wherever it is given them. She ignores the fact some women are not good, some men are good.

These are some of the many fallacies presented and believed by some vote seekers.

The errors in these statements is taken ad seriatim.

Eleven states had prohibition with men alone voting before a single state adopted it with women voting. Six states have had woman suffrage from four to forty-six years, yet prior to November 3, 1914, no state having woman's suffrage adopted prohibition. Kansas had prohibition 22 years before it adopted woman suffrage. California, which adopted woman suffrage in 1911, defeated prohibi-tion in 1914 by nearly 200,000 majority. In Springfield, Ill., at the last election 4,800 women voted for a wet city, and only 4,390 for a dry city. The women of Reno, Nevada, voted against reducing the number of saloons from 80 to 40.

Pasadena, Cal., during its whole previous history went wet for the first time when women voted.

Wyoming has had suffrage for more than 40 years, and yet it is the wettest state in the Union. Apparently, the temperance cause has nothing to expect from woman suffrage. . . .

Miss Anna Steese Richardson, formerly a voter of Denver, now residing in New York, renders the following testimony: "When forced by necessity into the wage earning field, even with the ballot in my hand, I had to start at the bottom of the industrial ladder and fight my way up as desperately as if I had lived in a state where women did not vote. Never once did my right to vote affect my working hours, my salary, my opportunities for advancement, or the conditions under which I worked. During more than twenty years of economic independence, sex discrimination has never reared its head, no man ever refused to pay me full value for my work. Every large opportunity has come to me through some man who considered neither sex attraction nor sex antagonism—only the task and the fitness of the individual to perform it. So long as suffrage leaders offer the so-called enslavement of woman as reason for conferring the ballot upon woman, they raise a false issue. The woman who is a slave to man without the ballot will be a slave with the ballot. Let women study the power of the ballot and how to use it, for unless they do this experience has taught me that they will not use it, even were it forced upon them. . . ."

Why Suffrage in the South Can No Longer Be Restricted.

When the law was passed a few years ago requiring the election of senators by the people, there became at the same time, as part of the law and the constitution a proviso whereby the United States government was empowered to supervise elections, appoint registrars at the instance of any two malcontents, and with the additional right to send troops to enforce the decision of the government-appointed registrars and supervisors.

Why has not the government taken hold? Were this right exercised over the South, it is obvious to the most sanguine, that the white primary would be as chaff before the wind, and that those whom we have deemed it wise to prevent voting up to this time would have the countenance and the support of the government wherever that government, in the exigencies of politics, is composed of a party inimical to the South.

By the Women Must the South Be Conquered.

Senator Beveridge said at the "Progressive Convention" in Chicago, when advocating the adoption by his party of a suffrage platform: "We must break the solid South and we can do this through the women only."

O women! can ye not see the tools ye be?

Shall it be said that Southern women are so eager for the vote that they will lend themselves to the undoing of their section?

The White Primary.

The white primary is no permanent bulwark. Would that it were! It is tottering under the assaults of such fanatics as forced the negro into the recent fight by the recallers in Atlanta.

There arise from time to time in our midst, those who signify their unwillingness to abide by the white primary and since the power of the white primary comes by harmony alone, these repeated assaults weaken its strength, and prove its vulnerability.

The undesirable voter that required the institution of the white primary has no back taxes to pay, or rather the female of the species has none, and when the registration of the male is much needed, south-haters will readily supply the funds.

A Leader Is The Only Need.

Evils that are suspended in air have descended and will descend as long as time lasts, and it is idle to ignore the fact that all which is needed to tear down the white primary is a leader against it and for this the Southern suffragette is paving the way.

Look out for the scalawag in our midst or an influx of carpetbaggers from the would-be controllers of the negro vote! There would be no split amongst the negro women. Theirs would be a solid Republican asset — it has been ascertained from good authority that they are keen about suffrage and the imagined social privileges it would bring to them. This last we know to be as much a fallacy as was the forty acres and a mule promised by the carpet-baggers of old, but it serves to show the trend of this movement.

When there was an independent candidate for governor in 1896, he and his spielers made fervent appeals for the negro vote.

So it will be when some man not in line with the Democratic party wants office so bad, that he will appeal for the negro vote, wants it so bad that he, a renegade, will appeal to the government to enforce the new law by which said government may require the bowling over of the state disfranchisement.

And when this law requires Gen. Walter Harris of the National Guard to command Georgia men to fire on other Georgia men to enforce the right the negro has to vote, perhaps Southern suffs will wake up.

Said Senator Bacon concerning the law which gives the federal government control of our elections:

"In time of peace it is hard to believe that there will be war. It is hard to look upon a peaceful ocean and realize the fact that on the day before the storm had lashed it into fury, and still more difficult that on the next day it will be seething in a tempest. With such convulsions as we have been through, such dangers as we have had to face, such troubles as we have had to endure, are we now to neglect all opportunity for precaution on the simple ground that there is peace now?" . . .

An Appeal.

Suffragist of the South, be not the maker of an ungovernable Frankenstein! Bring not this rending of our statehood upon us! Do not have to look back upon a peace and harmony that now exists between the races with the guilty knowledge that you have caused its destruction in a foolish effort to prove what is already known and gracefully acknowledged, namely, a woman's ability to do everything. Do not be responsible for a sigh and a sorrowful retrospect after what you will have destroyed. You are, perhaps, unwittingly trying to relegate to the past the good, the sweet, the natural. Do not make a future of regrets for "what might have been."

"I Did Not Mean to Do It."

Were it at all within the region of the probable for enough Southern women to ask for the vote to secure the necessary legislation for such a disaster in our section, there would follow race antagonism such as was not known even in the days of reconstruction, and the suffragist would cry out, "O, I did not mean to do this to my people!"

Treason is determined by results; not by the intention of the traitor.[2]

A Newspaper Account of the Debate

In 1914 a legislative committee held a public hearing on the suffrage issue before narrowly rejecting the idea. The report in the *Atlanta Constitution* is reprinted below.

"Suffrage Bill Is Lost by One Vote": Vote of Committee Was a Tie and Chairman Myrick Cast His Ballot against the Measure.

The woman's suffrage bill was acted upon adversely by the house committee on constitutional amendments Tuesday afternoon. The vote was a tie and the chairman, Mr. Myrick, of Chatham, voted against the bill. There were nine members of the committee present and the vote stood as follows:

For the bill: Mr. Cheney, of Cobb; Mr. Lesueur, of Crawford; Mr. McCurry, of Hart, and Mr. Edmondson, of Brooks.

Against the bill: Mr. Nunnally, of Floyd; Mr. Stone, of Taliaferro; Mr. Wisdom, of Forsyth; Mr. Ennis, of Baldwin; and Mr. Myrick, of Chatham.

Five members of the committee were absent.

Mr. McCurry gave notice of a minority report.

Two hundred ladies were present, some for the passage of the bill and some against it. There were also present about fifty or sixty men, mostly interested citizens of Atlanta.

Four speeches were made for the bill, and two against it. Mrs. Mary P. McLendon, president of the Georgia Woman's Suffrage Association, introduced the speakers after making a talk herself for the bill.

The chairman announced in the beginning that there should be no applause, but there was applause and plenty of it. Mr. Wisdom said he might ask that the hall be cleared if there was any more applause, but this was also greeted with applause.

Mrs. McLendon Speaks.

Mrs. McLendon said her association had been working for equal suffrage since 1890. "We are adding star after star to our banner," she said. "The negro men, our former slaves, have been given the right to vote and why should not we southern women have the same right? The states that have granted woman suffrage now control 150 votes of the electoral college and 129 more will soon be added. Some of you say that women cannot understand business. There are 9,000,000 women in this country making their own living and they surely know something about business. We only ask you for what belongs to us. . . ."

A Woman In Opposition.

Mrs. Walter B. Lamar, of Macon, president of the Georgia Association Opposed to Woman's Suffrage, was the first speaker against the bill. She said that a majority of the women of Georgia were opposed to equal suffrage. Women, she said, were needed to carry on their vocation of mothers and wives and for educational work. It is best to keep women out of politics, best for her and best for the state. The ignorance and apathy among the women on the suffrage movement is appalling. The bulk of those who are for suffrage form a fungus growth of misguided women, she said.

She spoke of sovereignty and said it was threatened by the woman suffrage movement. She took the position that just as soon as the southern states adopted woman suffrage there would be a national law on the subject that would give the negro women the right to vote. She pleaded with the members of the committee to vote against the bill and help the women and the state. . . .

Miss Rutherford's Argument.

Miss Mildred Rutherford, of Athens, was the next speaker against the bill.[3] She argued that to let all women vote would give the franchise to negro women. She said that when the south had acted, then the nation would act, and that meant a blow at the very foundation of state rights. "The women," she said, "who are working for this measure are striking at the principle for which their fathers fought during the Civil War. Woman's suffrage comes from the north and the west and from among women who do not believe in state rights, and who wish to see negro women using the ballot. I do not believe that the state of Georgia has sunk so low that her good men cannot legislate for the women. If that time ever comes then it will be time enough for women to claim the ballot. . . ."

Mrs. Felton Closes Debate.

Mrs. W. H. Felton closed the debate, speaking in favor of the bill. She is 80 years old and, despite her years, made a most forcible address. She scouted the idea that the enfranchisement of women would result in negro women dominating the ballot in Georgia. She advocated polling places for women in the public schools. "Why should our women not have the right to vote?" she asked. "Why can't they help you make laws the same as they help you run your homes and your churches? I do not want to see a negro man walk to the polls and vote on who shall handle my tax money, while I myself cannot vote at all. Is that fair? A mere accident of sex should take away an inherited right. Taxation without representation brought on the revolution, and it is the very root of this great and grand movement."

At the close of the debate the vote was taken after a motion was made to go into executive session and was voted down.

There promises to be another lively fight on the floor of the house when the bill comes up for final action.[4]

🚩 🚩 🚩

Final Defeat

The issue of woman suffrage continued to come up annually in the Georgia legislature for the rest of the decade. Following the June 1919 adoption of the Anthony amendment by both houses of Congress, the Nineteenth Amendment was submitted to the states for ratification. In most parts of the country the proposal was ratified easily, but not so in the South. In July 1919 Georgia became the first state to reject the suffrage amendment when the House voted it down by the lopsided margin of 118–29 and the Senate by 35–8. (Technically Georgia did not reject it because the resolutions of the two houses differed slightly and neither bothered to approve the other's version, but Georgia's example was copied by other Deep South states who also rejected the proposal.)

By 1920 three-fourths of the states in the Union had ratified, and the Nineteenth Amendment was officially part of the Constitution. Even then, the Georgia legislature dragged its feet and failed until 1921 to amend the state election laws allowing women to vote. Thus, Georgia and Mississippi were the only states depriving women of the vote in the 1920 presidential election. Finally, in 1970, on the fiftieth anniversary of the adoption of the suffrage amendment, the Georgia legislature passed a resolution supporting the issue.

NOTES

1. Rebecca Latimer Felton, "Why I Am a Suffragist," *Country Life in Georgia in the Days of My Youth* (Atlanta: Index Printing Co., 1919; reprint, New York: Arno Press, 1980), 246–60.

2. Mrs. Walter D. Lamar, "The Vulnerability of the White Primary," 8-page pamphlet issued by Georgia Association Opposed to Woman Suffrage, Macon, Georgia, 1916, Noncirculating Book Collection, Georgia Department of Archives and History.

3. For forty years Rutherford was teacher, principal, and president of the Lucy Cobb Institute, a prestigious girls' school in Athens. She also was historian-general of the United Daughters of the Confederacy and president of the Confederated Southern Memorial Association.

4. *Atlanta Constitution*, July 8, 1914, 1–2.

14

Crisis in Agriculture: The Great Migration, Boll Weevil Invasion, and Great Depression

As noted earlier, the collapse of farm prices generated in the 1890s a Populist revolt. In contrast, a stronger economy and more optimistic spirit accompanied the Progressive Era of the next two decades. Prices rose somewhat, and Georgia farmers expanded production. The peak of prosperity came with World War I. That conflict disrupted European agriculture and created a seemingly insatiable demand for cotton and other crops. The year after the war (1919) the cotton price reached an all-time high of about forty cents a pound.

Nonetheless, the good times could not last. During the war, farmers greatly expanded their cultivated acreage. Afterward, the old evil of overproduction returned, with the cotton price dropping in 1920 to seventeen cents. By the end of the war a new problem had also surfaced: the arrival in Georgia of the boll weevil. This insect plagued Texas as early as 1892 and slowly worked its way eastward.

Its larvae hatched in the developing cotton bolls and destroyed them. Greene County, Georgia, offers one example of the impact of the pestilence. In 1919 this lower Piedmont county ginned 20,030 bales of cotton, in 1922 only 333![1] Insecticides ultimately controlled the boll weevil, but Georgia's cotton production never again returned to pre-1920 levels.

During World War I northern defense industries sent agents throughout the south to recruit black workers. Once the first wave of emigrants reported back on life in the north, many others followed. With the rural depression of the 1920s, the movement reached tidal proportions. So many blacks left the farm that their departure was called the Great Migration. Some went to southern cities, but the ultimate destination of most was the industrial centers of the midwest and northeast.

The magnitude of the African-American departure can be seen in these figures: in 1900 blacks made up 47 percent of Georgia's population, but by 1930 the percentage was down to 37 and by 1970 to only 26.[2] Clearly, the central cause of the Great Migration was the dismal state of the southern economy and much more attractive opportunities elsewhere. The denial of civil rights and the reemergence in 1915 of the Ku Klux Klan were contributing factors.[3]

Reflecting back on the 1920s, northerners often used terms such as "Jazz Age" and "Prosperity Decade." These appellations also had some validity for middle- and upper-class Atlantans, who benefited from the Georgia capital's role as a center of transportation and trade. For city dwellers in most parts of the nation the economy seemed unusually vibrant until the stock market crash of 1929. In the southern mill villages of the 1920s, however, life was about as uncertain as it was in the countryside. Facing competition from synthetic fibers, the cotton textile industry experienced the same problem as the farmer: overproduction. So Georgia's leading industry could offer little relief to suffering white agrarians and, of course, none at all to blacks.

If the 1920s were bad, however, the 1930s were worse. As the Great Depression took hold, cotton dropped to five cents a pound, the lowest price since the 1890s. On the federal level, the Hoover Administration (1929–33) made a few attempts to alleviate rural misery; but only with the New Deal's agricultural programs was there much hope of better days, and then primarily for the minority of farm operators who owned their land.[4] Through committees elected by local farmers, the Agricultural Adjustment Act (1933) provided benefits to those who curtailed production, on the assumption that a reduced supply would force up prices. The committees, however, tended to be dominated by the larger, more powerful planters, making it difficult for tenants and marginal owners to receive their fair share of subsidies.

Moreover, crop allotments reduced the need for labor, forcing many poor sharecroppers and farmworkers off the land. With the unemployed in the cities underfed and underclothed, plans that limited farm production and uprooted tenants seemed perverse to many. A further criticism of Franklin Roosevelt's agricultural programs was that they undermined farmers' proverbial independence and accustomed them to look to Washington for assistance. The New Deal created a new form of paternalism in which the president and Congress became the nation's father figures.

On the other hand, Georgia Congressman Carl Vinson believed the South had turned from "rugged individualism" to a "new order where the individual benefits with the group, and not at the expense of the group." [5] To Georgia's landowners the value of government programs could be measured in rising market prices, credit more readily available at reasonable rates, subsidies that encouraged conservation, and through the Rural Electrification Administration, the extension of power lines to the countryside. Funds were also set aside for direct loans to tenants, first through the Georgia Rural Rehabilitation Corporation, then the federal Farm Security Administration.

By the outbreak of World War II rural Georgia had undergone a remarkable change in just two decades. For the first time since the Civil War the percentage of tenant farms was declining, as poor country folk flocked to the cities. Farmers who survived the boll weevil and the Great Depression consolidated their farms into bigger, more profitable businesses. First the insect invasion, then government programs also encouraged diversification. In 1920 some 66 percent of Georgia's crop income came from cotton; in 1940 only 40 percent. Tobacco, peanuts, pecans, and other commodities rivaled King Cotton. A final trend was the tendency of many planters to abandon row crops altogether, for cattle, poultry, or tree farms. Thus, Georgia experienced an agricultural revolution that fundamentally altered the relationship of the people to the land and set the stage for equally revolutionary political and social changes in the post–World War II era. [6]

Exodus from Greene County

The following interview was conducted in 1986, for a radio show, by Atlanta historian Cliff Kuhn. Mrs. Mary Ann Kimbrough Brewer was born on a Greene County farm in 1894. As this account reveals, she had vivid memories of the collapse of the cotton crop in central Georgia and the impact on African-American families.

CRISIS IN AGRICULTURE ☙ 181

Brewer: Well, I married in 1912, me and my husband [Elmo Brewer]; and we were trying to farm and trying to make a decent living and along when the children come along with being able to take care of them. In 1915 me and my husband started to want to rent us a farm. We got us a mule and started to farming, and we moved on right in here into Judge Parks's. J. B. Parks. . . . So we lived on his farm from 1916 to 1924 where most of my children, before I moved them to south Georgia, were born on his farm. He was a nice man to live with. . . . So we stayed on his place 1916, 1917, and in 1918 we made eleven bales of cotton with one plow. In 1919 we fell back to nine. In 1920 we fell back to two. In 1921 we fell back to 35 pounds! That was in the boll weevil time. . . .

Kuhn: That was in 1921. What about 1922?

Brewer: . . . Well, in 1922, we didn't plant no cotton. Just planted corn and had cane syrup, had raised a lot of potatoes and things like that. As a matter of fact, we fared just about as well making no cotton and planting something to eat as we did making cotton. . . .

Kuhn: Then what about the next year? Did you do the same or did you plant cotton?

Brewer: Well, in 1923 we planted some cotton; in 1924 we made two bales of cotton. Still we had corn and potatoes and syrup and killed our own meat and just what money you got you bought that for things that you didn't raise.

Kuhn: What caused you to leave Greene County?

Brewer: Nineteen twenty-five was a dry year like it is now. We planted cotton after the seventh of April. Some of it come up, some of it didn't come up. It got so dry the cotton seed just rotted. We had enough cotton come up to make us a bale of cotton, and that was all. We planted corn about as high as this chair, and it didn't even make stalk. It didn't even make an ear. It got ripe; no ear come. The only time we made any corn he had a bottom down on the creek. He broke that bottom up, and he planted corn, and we made on that bottom land, we made some corn. We made some sweet potatoes; no we didn't because it got so dry we couldn't set out none. It just stayed dry, dry, just like it is this year. It would make up a cloud and come over and look like it was going to rain every minute and rain a drop or two and just done gone. My husband had a brother that lived down in Crisp County, Cordele, writing and telling him about how his crop come out and how much he made, and so he just decided to sell out our farming tools and sell out our stock and went down there and lived down there twenty years before I moved here.

Kuhn: Now, boll weevil—you remember when the boll weevil came?

Brewer: Oh, I remember all about the boll weevils. It come a rain this year 1920. . . . When it started to raining like it is now the cotton got up as tall as that lamp there if not taller. You couldn't see a horse walking in it, it was so tall. Two little bitty bolls down here at the bottom; where the other [ones] come the boll weevils stung them and they fell off and the cotton just got gone. We made two bales of cotton; when we got two bales picked out that was through.

Kuhn: How did he try to get rid of the boll weevil, did you try?

Brewer: . . . Well, I'll tell you about Greene County then. The most of the people what was able to help the farming people, they had died. There just wasn't no money circulation to help them. They had to do the best they could. Well, you see, when I moved down to south Georgia, we moved with a man that was president of the bank, named Joe Williams, and the bank was Exchange Bank. He would furnish the money to farm with. . . . Then when the time come what looked like the boll weevil was started, they would furnish you a machine and then furnish you dust to dust your cotton with. You could make cotton.

Kuhn: Down in Crisp.

Brewer: Down in Crisp County. Then he was a man that—some of them didn't believe in planting peanuts—but he said he did. He said, "If you miss it with the cotton your peanuts will catch you," which that was true, because like would come a rain like this morning, this evening he furnished you dust and you'd get out there and dust your [cotton]. I don't know whether the dust done any good or not or just scared them off; I don't know which. You see, he had a machine with two things sitting like this that you could carry two rows at the time, and that dust would go all up under them leaves. . . .

Kuhn: What kind of price were you getting for a bale during those years, do you remember?

Brewer: Well, in 1916 cotton went up to fifteen cent a pound. [In] 1917 and '18 it was bringing thirty-five and forty cent a pound. I know my husband to sell a bale of cotton weighed over five hundred, the bale of cotton and the seeds brought him two hundred dollars, but that didn't last long when them boll weevils got in there.

Kuhn: So 1919 and '20, what was the price?

Brewer: It was a good price in 1919; it got up to forty cent a pound.

Kuhn: Then in the twenties?

Brewer: In the twenties there wasn't much made. We made two bales of cotton. One we paid for the fertilizer and the other one we let the man have it. But now we didn't have no debt; only that guano [fertilizer] debt. But we had enough food to last. We didn't have no debt for no food at all. Just the guano and the rent. One went for the guano, and the other went to Judge Parks.

Kuhn: So were you on halves with him?

Brewer: No, we were renting.[7]

Kuhn: Before that you had been on halves?

Brewer: Well, me and my husband worked on halves from '13 up until '15, and then we started buying us some stock and renting out our own farm. . . .

Kuhn: What was it you didn't like about being on halves?

Brewer: I didn't like giving half of the corn—that's the one they would get—some people would get half of your syrup, some would get half of your potatoes; but we didn't do that.

Kuhn: How would that work, being on halves?

Brewer: He furnish everything.

Kuhn: The landlord?

Brewer: Yes.

Kuhn: And then in exchange what would he get?

Brewer: Well, he'd get half of your corn and half of your [cotton]. When you sell the cotton . . . what the bale of cotton brought he got half of it and you got half. But now when you're renting you pay so much for renting and then you have possession over your cotton.

Kuhn: So you don't have to give anything to the landlord.

Brewer: No, nothing but just that rent. . . .

Kuhn: Do you remember anything, it just came to my mind, about a fellow in the early part of this century, called Peg Leg Williams?

Brewer: Peg Leg Man, Peg Leg immigration man. Of course, I know a right smart about it to be a child because—that was in 1898 if I'm thinking right. . . . You know, he carried people to different places. He carried some to Louisiana and Mississippi; that was the big place, and it was tough out there. He carried a whole lot of people to Mississippi. . . . My auntie named Mary Kimbrough, she married to a first cousin of papa's. Two sisters married first cousins. They was brought back to Greensboro and stayed a week before Peg Leg got out, and when he got out of jail he never stopped riding people away.

Kuhn: He was put in jail in Greensboro?

Brewer: No, in Madison . . . in Morgan County. But when he got out of jail he didn't stop immigrating people. It looked like it made him worse.

Kuhn: Now why did people want to leave Greene?

Brewer: That's the year when they didn't make nothing. You see, just like it was in the year 1925.

Kuhn: Now tell me about 1925 and then the twenties, because you weren't the only family to leave Greene County around that time.

Brewer: Oh no, I wasn't the only family. They were leaving every day. In 1925 it was a dry year and people's crops—what they had up done all right but it didn't come up. There was people from all around now. I got acquainted with some white people that went from up around Athens, Georgia, named Bill Sax; he lived not far from us and he said his upper land corn didn't get but knee-high. . . .

Kuhn: So the cotton prices dropped, the boll weevil and then the drought, one on top of the other.

Brewer: Yeah. People wasn't making anything. Some left and went to Savannah. I know a fellow used to live not far from me up on the hill not far from the Taylors. . . . This fellow named Walter O'Neal and his family moved to Savannah. We moved to south Georgia and this man named Mr. Bill Sax, he moved from up there around Athens. . . . He went to south Georgia and we lived close neighbors.

Kuhn: And where else did people go that you knew in Greene that left around that time?

Brewer: Around about that time? Just lots and lots of them come here [Atlanta] to live. Lots of people come here during that time to live in Atlanta. Some went to Tennessee. Now I had a sister, she's dead now—she went to Tennessee, Knoxville, Tennessee, to live. Some more people I know in Jackson, they went to Knoxville, Tennessee, to live.

Kuhn: What did the landowners, the landlords, think about all this?

Brewer: Well, there wasn't nothing they could think about because the people wanted to go where they could make a living and there wasn't a thing for them to think about. They didn't try to keep them from going.

Kuhn: Because they tried to keep them when Peg Leg was around.

Brewer: Oh yeah, they tried to keep them when Peg Leg . . . but that didn't do no good. Arrested him and put him in jail and looked like when he got out he got worse immigrating people away from here. Louisiana, Mississippi, Arkansas and Texas. . . .

Kuhn: Now, this fellow I told you about who wrote this history recounting . . . he called all this an exodus.

Brewer: Lots and lots of people left Greene County. Lots of them. . . .

Kuhn: Do you remember how you made that decision to leave Greene?

Brewer: Oh, yes, we just decided we'd go where we could do better on the farm. That's what my husband wanted to do and we did, we done much better while we was down there. As I said, the people, the rich people that could help you, they was dying out and so that was one reason why the people was leaving.

Kuhn: So the whole kind of plantation system was dying out.

Brewer: Yes, that's right.

Kuhn: Did they call it plantation at that time?

Brewer: Yes, plantation.[8]

🖾 🖾 🖾

Relief

Sociologist Arthur F. Raper spent the years 1926–39 working as research secretary for the Atlanta-based Commission on Interracial Cooperation. Between the world wars the CIC existed as the leading biracial organization in the South attempting to promote better understanding between whites and blacks. Raper's efforts for the CIC and, later, the U.S. Department of Agriculture led to a number of landmark studies on Georgia rural poverty and race relations. In 1933 he published *The Tragedy of Lynching*, followed in 1936 by *Preface to Peasantry*, a revision of his University of North Carolina doctoral dissertation. With Ira DeA. Reid he completed in 1941 *Sharecroppers All*; and, finally, in 1943 he wrote *Tenants of the Almighty*.[9] For over two decades after World War II he conducted similar studies in Asia, Africa, and the Middle East. The following is a March 1933 report for the CIC on relief efforts in central Georgia and Alabama at the end of the Hoover administration.

"National Services in the Alabama and Georgia Rural Black Belt"

With the nation-wide depression have come numerous nation-wide forms of relief. The rural Black Belt of the South has shared in two of these national services: The feed, seed, and fertilizer loans and the Red Cross rations and cloth. Some rural counties have also shared in the work relief projects made available through loans from the Reconstruction Finance Corporation.[10]

The Feed, Seed, and Fertilizer Loan

The feed, seed, and fertilizer loans are designed to finance small farmers who otherwise could not plant a crop. In numerous localities, informed local people reported that farm operation would scarcely be possible without these loans; in other communities, it is evident that solvent local planters and bankers put their own tenants on this loan service simply because they did not wish to take the risk involved in present farm operation.

The loans have been variously administered. In some few Black Belt areas tenants got and spent the loans made to them: They bought their feed, seed, and fertilizer at cash prices. This use of these loans afforded the borrowers a chance to keep their debts at a minimum.

The planters, however, usually got control of their tenants' checks through a verbal agreement between the landlord and the tenant. As a matter of fact, the landlord virtually forced the tenant to deliver the check to him. . . .

In some instances, the planter took the money and deposited it in his own account, and issued cash back to the tenant as he thought the tenant needed it. The planter usually charged eight or ten per cent interest. Thus the tenant paid double interest—six per cent to the government for the money and an additional eight or ten per cent to the planter for keeping it for him. This practice is common in the upper part of the Georgia Black Belt. . . .

There are numerous instances of even more flagrant violations of the feed, seed, and fertilizer loan service. Some few planters got the loan money from their tenants and either applied most of it to old debts of their tenants, which is against the stipulations of the loans, or deposited it to their own accounts. Cases in both states have been reported where planters secured money upon the names of Negro tenants who never saw the money. Some of these cases came to light when the tenants received receipts from the government for repaid loans of which they knew nothing. . . .

Red Cross Service

In a number of counties informed local people stated that the Red Cross had virtually kept many people alive during the past winter. Nevertheless, some felt that the Red Cross was having a most unsalutary effect upon the Negro farm laborers—a matter discussed a little later.

The Red Cross service has been variously administered. In nearly all counties the plantation has been the unit of administration. Not infrequently, the plantation trucks carried the flour and cloth from the county seat to the plantation headquarters. Only in a few instances did the Negroes have any effective part in determining which families should receive Red Cross aid. The Negro Red Cross Chapter at Tuskegee, Macon County, Alabama—the only separate and distinct Negro Red Cross chapter in the United States—explains the active part taken by Negroes in that county. . . .

There have been occasional flagrant abuses of the Red Cross service. In some communities flour and cloth have been used to feed and clothe families who had been stripped of their provisions. "Let the Red Cross feed them," was what the planters could readily say after they had virtually "cleaned out" their tenants. In one community the administrator of the Red Cross services is reported to have charged his tenants for the flour and cloth which "he secured" for them. Not uncommonly, the tenants willingly repaired fences or did other occasional work for their landlords who "secured" the flour and cloth for them. It is impossible to estimate the proportion of the Red Cross' rations and cloth virtually "sold" to the tenants of the Black Belt.

Not all the accusations made against the planters are legitimate. Instances were reported of tenants who secured flour and cloth by merely stating that they lived on such and such a planter's land. While these planters correctly pointed out that it was not their fault that these undeserving Negroes were served, it will be borne in mind that the whole Red Cross service, like everything else in these Black Belt counties, is so completely within the control of the few planters that the local Red Cross administrator was usually little more than their agent, and accordingly was quite mindful of any statement from a tenant which had even the semblance of authority. Moreover, many of the local Red Cross administrators were without adequate staff and altogether unmindful of the best methods of relief giving. . . .

Work Relief Through the R.F.C.

But very few rural Black Belt Georgia counties have secured R.F.C. funds. A large number of Alabama counties are using this form of relief. . . . At Macon, Georgia, in the heart of the Georgia Black Belt, the R.F.C. employed whites at 90 cents a day and Negroes at 60 cents—the Negro's lower standard of living was the explanation. As the R.F.C. relief reaches the rural counties, other aspects of standards of living emerge. For example, in a rural Georgia county, when R.F.C. work was made available in the county seat town a number of Negro tenants moved into town: They could make more by being unemployed and work for the R.F.C. than by continuing their employment on the plantations.

In Conclusion

There are some inescapable implications in the planters' dislike for the R.F.C. wage scales and their fear that the Red Cross rations and cloth will disorganize labor conditions. The principle involved here is simply this: A minimum ration, whether from R.F.C. work or Red Cross, can successfully compete with employment only when employment provides but a minimum ration. One tenant expressed it well when he said: "Why work anyway, when I can quit work and get 'on the Cross!' I get more when I'm 'on the Cross' than when I work."

The fact that planters are paying low wages is perchance not due to their avarice so much as to the low economic production of the cotton-plantation worker: Where work is done by hand, as in cotton picking, low prices for produce inevitably means low wages. The present depression is merely aggravating the low earnings of the South's rural dwellers, which in normal times are very low.

These complicating factors, superimposed upon the traditional exploitative practices of this area, make it imperative that the local administration of each and all national services be conducted in conformance to the spirit and intent of the central government in creating these services.[11]

🦅 🦅 🦅

Two Landowners' Point of View

Born around the turn of the century, Harvey and Bessie Durham owned and operated a small farm in Cobb County, in the upper Piedmont. Their primary crop was cotton, but they also operated a dairy and grew corn, wheat, oats, and syrup cane. During the Depression, Mr. Durham supplemented the family income by working for the Agricultural Adjustment Administration (AAA). For twenty-nine years he was a rural mail carrier. Until they died the Durhams dwelled in a plain, one-story farmhouse in the Mars Hill community. Even when expensive subdivisions began going up near them and the value of their land multiplied many times, they remained committed to the simple life of their earlier years. The interview below, conducted by Thomas A. Scott and Mary B. Cawley, reveals a farm couple who were hardly rich, but obviously influential in their rural community.

Scott: Tell me a little bit about how tenant farming worked in this area. When somebody was working on your land, for instance, how did they pay their rent? How much rent did they pay?

Harvey Durham: Third and fourth and half. I owned my own land. I furnished the stock, my land, half of the fertilizer. They done the work and we went fifty-fifty on what they growed.

Scott: And then, the third and the fourth?

Bessie Durham: If you owned your own stock and everything, a third of the corn and a fourth of the cotton.

Scott: The main crops that the tenant farmer grew in this area were corn and cotton?

Harvey Durham: That was the main crop: cotton, corn, potatoes and syrup cane, and such as that. . . .

Bessie Durham: If the landlord furnished everything, and the tenant grew cane, he got half of it, didn't he?

Harvey Durham: Yes. Or, it was just according to what you agreed on. If he was a good man, and a poor man having a hard time, I'd say, "Go ahead." And if he made a big crop of it, well, we shared.

Bessie Durham: Everybody had their own garden and their own chickens and meat and milk. When we married, he had a hog and a cow and his horse. And we had our chickens. I had the chickens, and I think it was seventy-five jars of fruit and vegetables I canned that year. . . .

Scott: About how many bushels of corn could you produce on an acre back then?

Harvey Durham: Well, they didn't fertilize then. Some of it made ten bushels to an acre, some of it might make twenty-five, some might make thirty. We had some land rented, what we call the old Hill place. When Edward, our oldest son, was in the 4-H Club, he made 129 bushels of corn on that acre. We fertilized it yearly. . . .

Bessie Durham: We used guanner [guano] when we planted cotton. . . . [One of the black sharecroppers] lived in the little house over here where my daughter lives now. His wife was a schoolteacher, and they had a house full of children — a whole bunch of children. They lived here with us a long time. Once, he and his wife and another colored man, they got to taking off [fighting] a little. He walked right out there in front of the house, went over and shot that man. He didn't hurt him much, but George had to go to the chain gang. He didn't stay but a year, and Harvey paid him out.

Harvey Durham: No, he didn't stay but three months. "Politicked" him out.

Bessie Durham: Old George didn't ever give them any trouble. The sheriff knew him, and knew he was all right. He only did one bad thing.

Harvey Durham: He was supposed to get twelve months straight. The judge was as good a friend as I had. So, he told me, "He's gonna have to make three months at least. . . ."

Bessie Durham: Came back and raised a big family of children.

Cawley: You didn't have to pay. You just had to go talk to the judge, sort of vouch for him. Is that what you did?

Bessie Durham: "Stood" for him, that's what they called it. . . .

Scott: [When you worked for the Agricultural Adjustment Administration] what did it mean to "measure cotton?" What did you actually do?

Harvey Durham: You could just have so much cotton planted. . . . We had to go to school just about three weeks to learn how to operate those things. We had orders to be sure and watch for cotton planted where it shouldn't be. I ran into a field over here once. The little road ran out into the woods a ways. I don't know what made me do it, but I said, "I just believe I'll see where that road goes to." I walked back as far from here to the highway out there [roughly one hundred yards], and there's where a man had cleared up a four-acre field and planted it in cotton. . . . I measured it out. Carried my papers in, showed them to the head man down there. . . .

Bessie Durham: Those people sure did get mad. . . .

Cawley: Did most of the farmers cooperate pretty well?

Harvey Durham: Oh yes. We had one man down below here. Had a boy by the name of Kemp that went to measure his cotton. He took a shotgun to him. Ran him off, and told him not to come back there and not to send nobody. So Mansfield [the supervisor] talked to me about it and said, "I want you to help me out on this." He asked me for some kind of suggestion. . . . I said, "I'll measure that cotton." He said, "You'll go over there and get shot." I said, "I won't." He said, "Well, do you know the old man?" I said, "No, I don't know him, just know him when I see him, is all." He said, "I'll tell you what I'll do. I'll give you pay for a full day's work if you'll measure it. There's not but six acres of it." I said, "Give me the papers." The next day, I got in the car and drove over there. I met the old man coming out behind a pair of good mules. I kept good mules, too. I stopped, got to talking to him, looked at his mules, bragged on 'em that they was the prettiest things that ever I saw. I guess I sat there about an hour. "Mr. Jed," I said, "they tell me you and Kemp had a little trouble about measuring your cotton." He said, "Yeah, he came over here and said he was going to measure it, and I just told him he wasn't. I took my gun to him." I said, "Well, did he run?" He said, "Yeah, he got it on." I said, "What are you going to do to me? I've got the papers out there in the car." He said, "You want to measure it?" I said, "Yeah, I'll measure it." He said, "Let's go." No problem at all. I went right on, and didn't have a bit of trouble with the man. He didn't like the program. And I didn't like all of it myself. I'd tell them I didn't, [but] there wasn't no slipping around.[12]

NOTES

1. Arthur F. Raper, *Preface to Peasantry: A Tale of Two Black Belt Counties* (Chapel Hill: University of North Carolina Press, 1936; reprint, New York: Atheneum, 1968), 202.

2. In 1900 about 1,181,000 whites and 1,035,000 blacks lived in Georgia; in 1970

the respective figures were 3,391,000 and 1,187,000. While the Caucasian population grew by two million, the African-American population hardly grew at all. Due to the end of legal segregation and to the healthier Georgia economy in the late twentieth century, the Great Migration ended. The black population for two decades has been expanding at a slightly faster rate than the white population. In 1990 some 1,747,000 African-Americans made up 27 percent of the state population. The black population is no longer concentrated in the countryside, however, but in the cities.

3. Raper calls the migrants from Greene County in the early 1920s "virtual refugees" and adds: "They were *fleeing from* something rather than being *attracted to* something. They were fleeing from hunger and exposure, they were going to . . . they didn't know what." *Preface to Peasantry*, 191.

4. In 1930 only 32 percent of Georgia farm operators owned the fields they worked.

5. Quoted in Roy Edward Fossett, "The Impact of the New Deal on Georgia Politics, 1933–1941" (Ph.D. diss., University of Florida, 1960), 90.

6. The trends that began in the era between the world wars have accelerated in the five decades since. In a recent book Jimmy Carter noted the disappearance since the early 1960s of black farmowners in the area near Plains. The former president attributed the loss to fierce competition, the increasing cost of agricultural machinery, federal policies that favor larger farmers, and "the subtle discrimination of banks and other financial institutions." Jimmy Carter, *Turning Point: A Candidate, a State, and a Nation Come of Age* (New York: Times Books, 1992), 190–91.

7. Sharecroppers on halves paid half their crop as rent; therefore, the more bushels and bales they grew, the more they paid. In contrast, a fixed renter worked for a predetermined cash amount or for a set number of cotton bales.

8. Mary Ann Kimbrough Brewer, interview by Cliff Kuhn, September 12, 1986, Atlanta, Georgia, Southern Oral History Program, University of North Carolina at Chapel Hill.

9. *The Tragedy of Lynching* (Chapel Hill: University of North Carolina Press, 1933); *Sharecroppers All* (Chapel Hill: University of North Carolina Press, 1941); and *Tenants of the Almighty* (New York: Macmillan, 1943).

10. The RFC started during the Hoover administration in 1932 as a federal attempt to lend money to troubled banks and businesses and provide the states with funds for relief and public works. The program was continued after Franklin Roosevelt took office in March 1933.

11. Arthur F. Raper, "National Services in the Alabama and Georgia Rural Black Belt," Spring 1933, Commission on Interracial Cooperation Archives, box 25, "Relief Work, 1935," Atlanta University.

12. Harvey E. Durham and Bessie H. Durham, interview by Thomas Allan Scott and Mary Boswell Cawley, May 20, 1987, Cobb County Oral History Series, no. 2, transcript, Kennesaw State College, Marietta, Georgia.

15

Moving toward the Mainstream: Georgia in the 1940s

From the Civil War until World War II, the South was the nation's poorest region. Described by Franklin Roosevelt as America's number one economic problem, the old Confederacy led the nation in illiteracy, infant mortality, and virtually every other negative indicator. The 1940 census recorded a median family income for Georgia that was only 57 percent of the national average. The entry into World War II, however, carried Georgians out of their economic doldrums. The state's longtime strategy of placing key congressmen on armed services committees paid off, as the military ordered recruits south to train in military camps located in Georgia. Wherever the troops went, millions of federal dollars were pumped into the local economy.

The most spectacular change took place just north of Atlanta in Marietta, a small town that became the home of the southern branch of Bell Aircraft Company. Marietta's prewar population was about eight thousand, and the entire county of Cobb had just thirty-eight thousand, but Bell Bomber offered over twenty-eight thousand high-paying jobs. People from all over the nation flocked there to seek employment at the "bummer plant." At least poetic truth can be found in President Lawrence D. Bell's comment that "the B-29 in Georgia was probably the biggest and most successful single manufacturing enterprise in the country during the war. . . . My friends down there have repeatedly told me that the operation of Bell Aircraft probably had more influence on the rebirth of the South than anything that's ever been done."[1]

Georgia's sudden prosperity continued into the postwar era. Southerners for the first time had enough spending money to attract the attention of northern businesses, many of whom decided to establish southern branches. In Marietta, Bell closed down after the victory over Japan; but five years later, during the Korean conflict, Lockheed moved into the same facilities. With the army remaining strong during the Cold War, military bases such as Fort Benning near Columbus continued to be crucial to the nation's defense and Georgia's economic development. By the late 1960s Georgia's fifteen military bases contained over one hundred thousand men and women in uniform and forty-five thousand civilians. Defense contracts provided jobs for in excess of forty-thousand additional employees. These roughly two hundred thousand workers accounted for about 10 percent of the state's personal income. With the defense industry leading the way, by 1950 median income for all Georgia families had risen to 70 percent of the national average, and by 1980 to 86 percent.

When the war began, Eugene Talmadge was serving his third term as governor. Crude but colorful, the "wild man" from Sugar Creek had the virtue of always being entertaining. The farmers loved him. According to Talmadge, "the poor dirt farmer ain't got but three friends on this earth: God Almighty, Sears Roebuck, and Gene Talmadge."

In the spring of 1941, however, Talmadge made the greatest blunder of his political career, when he decided that the president of Georgia Teachers' College at Statesboro and a dean at the University of Georgia should be fired for allegedly advocating communism and/or racial equality. Without any evidence to back his charges, the governor demanded that the Board of Regents refuse to renew the contracts of these prominent administrators. When a divided board at first defied the governor, the offending regents found themselves under attack. Gene demanded and received resignations from two regents, then replaced them with political cronies. A stacked board then proceeded to do the governor's bidding.

For this gross political interference the Southern Association of Colleges and Secondary Schools stripped the institutions of the state university system of their accreditation. Suddenly, college students worried that their credits and degrees would mean nothing when they sought employment or attempted to complete their education in other states. The entire public became alarmed over the fate of their schools.[2]

The person who capitalized on the issue was Ellis Arnall, the young attorney general, who campaigned against Talmadge in the 1942 gubernatorial race. Arnall promised to free the Board of Regents from direct political manipulation and to restore the accreditation of the system. Defeating Talmadge on the higher education issue, Arnall kept his word.

The Newnan attorney not only reorganized the university system, but during his four years as governor achieved a national reputation for progressivism. Georgia was made more democratic through the extension of the vote to eighteen-year-olds and the elimination of the poll tax. At the same time, government was made more efficient through civil service reform. Recognizing that discriminatory railroad rates had long retarded the South's economic development, Arnall took a number of railroads to court. When the U.S. Supreme Court agreed to hear the case, the railroads caved in and agreed to equalized rates in all parts of the nation.[3]

There were limits to Arnall's progressivism. He never attacked segregation and refused to seek a tax increase to fund better schools and roads. But the need for higher taxes was considerably diminished by the expanding tax base resulting from wartime prosperity, and everyone understood that no one could be elected who challenged segregation. Moderates in the South were those who did not complain excessively when the federal courts in 1944 struck down a Texas white primary law and two years later overturned a similar Georgia statute. As a result of those decisions, black registered voters in Georgia were able to participate in the 1946 Democratic primary. Along with the repeal of the poll tax, the elimination of the white primary promised a new day for African-Americans.

It was perhaps not accidental that far-reaching political reform came at a time when Georgia was experiencing so many social and economic changes. The agricultural revolution of the 1920s and 1930s reduced the rural population and forced many blacks into cities, where their political influence would be felt. Wartime industrial expansion brought to the state northerners and westerners with different outlooks and expectations from government. In the postwar period growth would continue to be in the metropolitan areas and not in the countryside. Power would rest in the hands of white, rural lawmakers until the 1960s, when federal courts ordered the legislature to reapportion and knocked down the county-unit system.[4] But by World War II it was already clear that the old order was changing, however slowly.

Reproduced below are four documents, two giving the opinions of Arnall and Talmadge and two viewing change in Georgia from African-American perspectives. The sources shared a sense that World War II was a watershed of Georgia and U.S. history and that events afterward flowed in a new direction. Three of the individuals favored the alterations; the fourth, Talmadge, fought to maintain the old ways.

🏴 🏴 🏴

Ellis Arnall's Views
on the Expansion of Democracy

In the campaign of 1942, many young people under the age of twenty-one took an active interest. They drew the fire of the spellbinders stumping for my opponent. The young men and young women in the colleges of Georgia were aroused by the loss of accredited status of the institutions. Many of them already were in uniform; many men were waiting calls from their draft boards; but between their interest in the war and their class work, they found time to canvass thousands and thousands of Georgia homes and ask neighbors and relatives and friends, and strangers they had never seen before, to vote for me and rebuke the demagogues who had attacked education. . . .

I knew that I owed much to the audacious and vigorous campaign of Young Georgia. I knew that they represented an element in public life that deserved, somehow, to be recognized. But it was not until the campaign and the party convention were over that their real place in the political system occurred to me.

A young man, a student at Georgia Tech, who had worked hard in the campaign and shown exceptional interest in spite of his nineteen years and his disqualification as a voter, came to my office to tell me goodbye. He was being inducted into the service and expected to be stationed soon in New Mexico.

"Well, I guess I am old enough to help with the Japs, even if I can't vote," he said as he was leaving.

My young friend was old enough to fight, but he was not old enough to vote. It set me to thinking and to examining the precedents. It was easy to discover that the idea of letting a citizen of eighteen vote was not really new in America; the State of Franklin established that precedent one hundred and fifty years ago. Moreover, in England and France, the age of eighteen was a conventional age for attaining a majority, being the age at which youths normally might receive knighthood. It was the age of full citizenship in many jurisdictions in Greek and

Roman days. It was the age at which women might lawfully contract marriage without parental consent. It was the age at which a boy might shoulder a rifle or flash through the sky in an airplane to defend his country. It was an age at which both boy and girl ceased to be a "dependent" for income tax returns of parents.

In my message to the General Assembly of 1943, a proposal to reduce the voting age from twenty-one to eighteen was recommended. The idea was embodied in a constitutional amendment and attained the two-thirds majority of each branch of the Legislature for submission to the people; and in the summer of 1943, we went into a campaign to get the amendment ratified by the voters of Georgia.

The political organization that was defeated in 1942 was still alive. It singled out the "teen-age amendment" as its object of attack. Though there were many other amendments on the ballot that year, including those establishing academic freedom and removing control of clemency from the Governor's office, it was the question of youth suffrage that attracted the most attention. It was a lively campaign. In a radio talk on the amendments, I challenged the belief that American parents had failed to rear honorable and intelligent sons and daughters and defended the theory of youth suffrage by saying:

"The additional experience that these young men and women will obtain through extension to them of the right to vote will equip them better to serve their country as citizens, whether officeholders or not, throughout their lives.

"We need the idealism, the candor, the unselfishness of these young people's influence in our public affairs. We need more, I say, of the 'starry-eyed enthusiasm of youth. . . .'"

The people of Georgia responded to that plea with an overwhelming vote in favor of the amendment, a vote of slightly more than two to one. And Georgia became the first of the forty-eight States to lower the voting age to eighteen. . . .

It is a recognition of the new responsibilities assumed by American youth and of the place of young men and women in the national life that has led President Truman to urge that, throughout the Nation, they be given the right to vote. It seems to me to be an inevitability if political democracy is to retain its dynamic quality in our country.

Lowering the voting age to eighteen brought to the fore in Georgia an issue that was unexpected. Georgia had a poll tax, levied upon all male citizens above the age of twenty-one and below that of sixty, and upon such women of that age as registered for voting. The poll tax in Georgia was not originally designed, as many suppose, to limit the right of suffrage. Almost from the establishment of the State and until 1933, Georgia had required the payment of all taxes as a prerequisite to voting. This was not the practice in the typical "poll tax State."

But the younger voters were exempt from taxation under the new amendment, and the voters above the age of sixty had been exempt from poll tax since its establishment. More than half of all Georgians were free of the tax; its retention was ridiculous.

The 1943 Assembly had authorized revision of the Georgia Constitution by a commission that was to report its findings and recommendations, and if desirable, a new Constitution, to the 1945 Legislature. The Revision Commission recommended that the poll tax, as a prerequisite for voting, be eliminated. In the meantime, I prepared to ask the Legislature to abolish the tax, which was permitted by the existing State Constitution but which was not required.

There was long debate in the 1945 Assembly over abolition of the poll tax, although, even among its opponents, there were few who endeavored to turn the debate into a discussion of racial problems. Ultimately, after one defeat in the House and a successful move for reconsideration, the repeal measure was adopted. Local officeholders had little complaint against repeal; the few who had worked against it discovered suddenly that not only was the measure popular with Georgians but that it had created about 500,000 new voters overnight, whose votes they desired most earnestly in the next campaign. These former opponents became publicly the most fanatical converts to the wisdom and virtue of the measure.

The poll tax continues to be a topic of heated debate. As a prerequisite for voting, it is confined entirely to the South, today, but once was found everywhere in America. Originally it was a revenue device; today it is either an anachronism or a device for the disfranchisement of citizens whose ballots deserve to be counted in an election.

The South's present championing of the poll tax is based more upon irritation than anything else. I know this is true because hundreds of Georgians have told me that they are glad to be rid of the nuisance of the poll tax but that they resent Federal interference on the subject.

If the issue were reduced in every Southern State to the one drawn in Georgia: "No man ought to have to pay for the right to vote," removal of the poll tax would be easy except in two machine-dominated States; but zealous self-designated liberals persist in using the poll tax as an excuse for bitter attacks upon the South. Some of them are ill informed and cannot distinguish between conditions in any two Southern States; others of them are deliberately irritating at the behest of Southern Bourbons and the special Eastern interests that they serve. . . .[5]

A Black Female Employee at Bell Bomber

World War II was a liberating experience for many African-Americans. Although blacks were inducted into a segregated military, they served in great numbers in Europe and Asia and returned home with a sense of self-confidence and self-respect. The veterans were in the forefront of the fight against segregation in the postwar years. Blacks who remained on the home front also developed a new sense of freedom as economic opportunities expanded for them. A domestic worker such as Ernestine J. Slade, for instance, suddenly discovered she could earn three or four times more money working in the defense industry. The following is her story, as told to Kathryn A. Kelley.

Slade: I always managed somehow to work. And having [eight] children, it was necessary to work. When I started working out at Bell Aircraft, [my husband Horace Slade] was working on the day shift. . . .

Kelley: Now what kind of work did you do before you went to Bell Aircraft?

Slade: Housekeeping and laundry work. . . . What I did was, I would stretch curtains . . . putting curtains on stretchers and you would charge so much for each pair. And I would do linens because you could get a little more money for doing linens than you could for just doing a whole wash. Although I've done the family wash, too, but my specialty was washing and stretching curtains and doing the linens, the tablecloths and things like that—that's special work. . . .

Kelley: So what a big change, then, from you doing laundry and being more or less self-employed, to going to work at a big company like Bell Aircraft. Tell me about—how did that come about?

Slade: . . . It was a little difficult when Bell first came here for a person who had a regular job, a domestic worker, to get on. Because, see, like they had an understanding or had discussed or didn't want to take nobody's help away from them, especially a person who was working for, you know, a well-to-do family. If you went there, and you were working for one of these well-to-do families, you could not get on at Bell easily. And you made so much money at Bell—much more money at Bell than you could make working for a permanent family. So me and my friends, we didn't go to the employment office here in Marietta. We went into Atlanta to the employment office. And that's how I got hired. Then I came back, and I told this lady that I had been working for, they hired me that day, told me when I could start to work. So that weekend, I told her. I said, "Now

I'm going to start working at the Bomber Club"—that's what we called it. Well, naturally, she didn't like it, but she didn't fuss too much about. And I said, "I'll be leaving you." And so I went on that Monday morning to work out at Bell. . . .

Kelley: Now when you went to Bell, what kinds of job openings were there and what led you to the job that you took?

Slade: I can tell you what I did. It was something like the finishing department where they sent all parts that went into the airplane, regardless of how small they were, through some kind of treatment process. We would clean those parts, and they would put it in a machine and then some kind of solution and what-have-you. I don't know whether it was strengthening or just to be sure it was clean or what. And then sometimes, after they had got a part of the plane completed, we'd go inside of that plane and clean it all in the inside. Those long parts to the plane, sometimes we'd have to take something like steel wool and rub them; and then they would put them through this process I'm telling you about. And the little, bitty pieces like that, we had in the buckets we'd drop them in. They'd put them through this process.

Kelley: Did you work Monday through Friday?

Slade: Yes, yes, I did. I went on the evening shift. We would go in around 11:00 or 11:45 and work until—now my older children had started to school. And see, I'd get here early enough to see that all was well with them and that their clothes and everything were on properly and so forth, and they could get to school without being late. . . .

Kelley: So when you came home then, some of your children were just getting up and getting ready to go to school?

Slade: Yes. I'd come in from work, do my cleaning, do my wash and my laundry work, wash the children's clothes, iron whatever needed to be done, then I would lay down and go to sleep. And when they would come in the afternoon, I'd get up and do their dinner, fix their meals for them, and have that ready for them so they could eat. Then I'd lay down again and take another little nap before going to work at night. I'd comb the girls' hair at home for the next day, and I put stocking caps over their heads so their hair would stay nice, and give them their bath and get them ready for bed and get them in the bed before I'd leave. . . .

Kelley: How much money did you make at Bell, do you remember?

Slade: Oh, Lord. It was like a million dollars, my first paycheck—it was about thirty-three or thirty-four dollars [a week]. I can't tell you the exact amount. [Before then I had been paid] seven and ten dollars a week.

Kelley: Now it sounds like a very small amount, but at the time, was that enough money for you?

Slade: It wasn't enough, but we had to manage, you know. No black woman made a whole lot of money. I remember some of our neighbors and friends used to work for five dollars a week. . . .

Kelley: Where you worked in your unit at Bell, was that all black women working together?

Slade: No, black and white worked together. . . .

Kelley: I'll bet that some jobs weren't available [for blacks].

Slade: Well, you know not, no.

Kelley: Some of the women that I've talked to that worked in secretarial services, for example, there were no black women—

Slade: That's true, that's true.

Kelley: What kinds of jobs were available for black women at Bell?

Slade: Well, just they worked in the cafeteria helping to prepare food. Some of them had a little better job than I had and a better paying job. . . .

Kelley: To sum up your experience at Bell Aircraft, do you think that that experience changed your life at all?

Slade: Well, it was a help.

Kelley: A lot of money?

Slade: Yes. Well, you know, a little more money. Yes, that was a help. Oh, Lord, it just helped in every way. I remember when I started working, I first paid off all my bills. Got my bills paid off and I was able to get some things that we needed in the home. The older girls had never had Sunday shoes—they always had shoes, you know. I bought them some nice dresses, and I bought them Sunday shoes, an extra pair of shoes. And that meant everything in the world to them and me, too. When I started working out at Bell, I never could put no money in the bank. I didn't have a million dollars, however, now, I was able to save a little bit.[6]

Gene Talmadge and Georgia Tradition

In 1946 the question of race figured prominently in the gubernatorial election, where Gene Talmadge achieved his last victory over James V. Carmichael, a young attorney who ran the Marietta branch of Bell Aircraft during the later part of the war. By the end of the campaign Gene's health was failing, and he died before he could be inaugurated. For several months the nation watched with fascination as the legislature and the state supreme court struggled to determine who lawfully possessed the governor's office. The assembly gave the post to Gene's son Herman on the grounds that he had received several hundred write-in votes and thus led all living candidates. For a while Ellis Arnall thought that he might stay in office, since a successor had not been elected and qualified. Ultimately, the state's highest court gave the post to Lieutenant Governor M. E. Thompson, who clearly would have been governor if Gene has passed away in office instead of dying before taking the position. Thompson served until the 1948 election, when he was defeated by Herman.

The document below contains excerpts from Eugene Talmadge's April 6, 1946 announcement for governor.

Issues now prevailing in Georgia and the chaotic aftermath of the war, rehabilitation of veterans and the period of reconversion make the coming campaign for Governor of Georgia the most important one since carpetbagger days. . . .

Economy

I have always been opposed to increased taxes. Federal, state and local taxes are too high. The tax burden of our country is, indeed, difficult to bear and still operate a business or small enterprise. I hope and believe that the state can be operated without increased revenue. We cannot tell for certain because we do not know what the present condition of the State Treasury is. We know that there should be a huge surplus of useless state employees who draw large salaries to do nothing. . . .

Traditions and Primary

The most important issue of all now faces the people of Georgia and of the Southland—the Democratic white primary. Alien influences and communistic influences from the East are agitating social equality in our state. They desire Negroes to participate in our white primary in order to destroy the traditions and heritages of our Southland. They desire to pass the FEPC law and to defeat our Southern Congressmen and Senators who have opposed the FEPC.[7] They want Negro policemen, Negro officeholders, Negro tax assessors and many other offices, federal, state and local, that are held by the white people of this state.

If elected Governor, I shall see that the traditions which were fought for by our grandparents are maintained and preserved. I shall see that the people of this state have a Democratic white primary unfettered and unhampered by radical, Communist and alien influences.

Negroes should be protected under the law. Negroes should have good schools, the opportunity to work, protection of our health laws, the right to earn and make a living and educate their children, but they should not participate in our Democratic white primary in the Southland.

We must protect the Negroes from the Communist organizations and alien influences. The best friends that the Negroes have are their Southern friends. The best friends that the Negroes have in Georgia are their white neighbors and white public officials and the citizens of the community in which they live.

The county unit system of the state protects us from political machines that are maintained in many of the states of this Union. It serves to break up a political machine at the county line. It gives us representation to the rural sections of this state and cities of Georgia. I will preserve, maintain and protect the county unit system of this state.

If the county unit system were destroyed, a few boss politicians of the larger cities of the state would control the policies of Georgia and the rural areas would be without effective representation or a voice in the government. A county unit system is not only a protection for the rural sections but it is a protection for the population in the large cities as well.

If elected Governor, my administration of the above policies and programs will be a broad progressive one to give better jobs, opportunities and a better livelihood to the people of our State. Georgia is the Empire State of the South and the Southland is now the number one opportunity in our country. We must improve our schools, health, roads, pensions, farming conditions, labor conditions and go forward in Georgia to become the most progressive state of the Union.[8]

The Civil Rights Movement of the 1940s

It should be clear to the readers of this book that the Civil Rights movement started long before Martin Luther King Jr. articulated a philosophy of passive resistance in the 1950s. The movement involved many people in many communities throughout the region. Returning home from World War II, black soldiers were often in the forefront in registering voters and protesting the Jim Crow system. African-Americans joined the battle against fascism to make the world free. After the war they also wanted to make Georgia free. One of Savannah's foremost community activists is W. W. Law. As a young man in the late 1940s and early 1950s, he was involved in voter registration drives, the attempt to add African-Americans to the police force, and other activities. In more recent times he has gained recognition not only for his civil rights efforts, but for his work in historic preservation, helping to establish museums in Savannah's 1896 King-Tisdell Cottage and the 1865 Beach Institute, established just after the Civil War to educate free black citizens.

Law: [After the courts overturned the white primary], the resistance was in placing blacks on those voters lists. We had a registrar . . . and he and his crowd, those days you had to answer the twenty questions satisfactorily. And, of course, there were two windows, one for the white registration and one for the blacks. Oftentimes there was one person doing the registering, so they would work at the white window. And you would just stand there and stand there until there were no more white folks to register or else they just would be so embarrassed that they would come over and make an effort to get you registered. . . .

We had a method of going downtown and working the square in front of the courthouse. We would see people come through the square on other business. We would say: "Are you registered to vote? Why don't you walk over here, and take a minute to register to vote?"

But it wasn't easy. [The registrar] did not desire to see any increase in the black registrants, so he used every resistant method that he possibly could. . . . You didn't have to use violence. If you called a black man a "nigger," that was as demeaning and as hurtful as anything, because we had long been trained and taught that anybody could be a "nigger." It is a low person, and it could be white, black, or anything else. But when you went before the twenty questions and realize that the guy who is asking the questions has to look on the page in order to get the answer himself; and he is already registered and is administering the test—

. . . Many of the blacks that we were registering could write their names, but they were not sophisticated enough to know who was president, or vice president of the United States. A whole lot of people would have difficulty now recalling who is vice president, even if they knew about Bush. Then, who is the Secretary of State for Georgia; how many counties are there in Georgia; and what is the county seat, and all kinds of irrelevant questions that had nothing to do with your voting for the mayor or for the governor of the state. But these questions were there. So in 1950, we started a school in the various churches. We had the questions printed, and we would hold sessions in the churches. . . . Then, we would drill the people on the answers to the questions. Then, when they felt strong enough, we would then take them to register and to vote. . . .

You must realize that Savannah was under one-man domination. . . . This was Johnny Bouhan. He was the boss of the machine. It was the Irish control, and he was boss. And he had named all the mayors of the town from Tom Gamble, I know, Thomas Gamble on. And the way he maintained control was if he gave you a job with the City, then you had to be responsible for voting all of your family members and what-have-you, so that they remained in control. There was hardly any resistance up until the forming of the Jaycees. The Jaycees came in on the scene, young white boys, who began to advocate city management government. Finally, the idea took. And it was John Kennedy who was the city management candidate. He was the first mayor who was willing to hire a city manager and not be the figurehead and run the city with Johnny Bouhan behind manipulating. . . .

The Kennedys . . . promised that they would form a Negro Advisory Committee. It was not possible then to run a black on their slate; but they ran a whole slate of people who, with a few exceptions, were decent and did not mind coming into the black community to campaign and to dialogue with blacks. And they agreed to an agenda that was mainly formulated in the mind of Dr. Ralph Mark Gilbert, and that was that there would be an advisory committee that would begin to have them understand what things they needed to address to benefit blacks. And there was also the agreement that they would hire black policemen. . . .

There was no announcement, and on the day that the black policemen had finished their training and were to take to the streets, I was the president of the Youth Council. This was '47, and a citizens meeting was held in what was then the 4-Ss, which was a local organization . . . operated to serve the black soldiers during World War II. After the war, that building was taken over by the City as a recreational center. And on the day that the mass meeting was held in the gymnasium of the 4-Ss, the policemen, who nobody knew had been trained — other than Dr. Gilbert and the Citizens Democratic Committee — they were all marched in the building; and the news then broke on the citizens.

. . . I was the youngest speaker on the day that the policemen came into the city . . . and I objected to the fact that blacks, the police, were not allowed to arrest white folks. . . . I now realize that being young, inexperienced, and brash, that's the only way now that it could have happened; and it wasn't a bad idea because, in time, all of that changed. Being young, I was not willing to wait. . . .[9]

Mr. Law also described statewide NAACP activities of that era. The following is part of the discussion.

There was never a greater man in all of Georgia than D. U. Pullum. . . . It was Terrell County, "Terrible Terrell. . . ." The man maintained the NAACP in that community even when he was the only person who would dare let it be known that he was an NAACP member. . . . Whenever it was necessary to go before the board to speak out on school conditions or anything like that, he would make that trip, and alone, with tears in his eyes, and full up with all of the pain and what-have-you that he was feeling about the injustices done to his people. . . .

On one occasion that I personally know about when riding from town back to his farm—he was one of the biggest farmers in the county—a group of whites waylaid him—and he was not a young man—and dragged him out and whipped him. It did not deter him. He still washed himself up, and the next week, he would be back on the case again.

The blacks who would meet him in town were afraid to even be seen talking with him on the streets. They would walk by him on Saturdays when they would come to town. As they would pass each other, they would push the NAACP money in his hands and not break their steps and keep on walking.

But he kept an NAACP presence . . . and as results of his perseverance, his son is now Superintendent of Schools in Terrell County.[10]

NOTES

1. Donald J. Norton, *Larry: A Biography of Lawrence D. Bell* (Chicago: Nelson-Hall, 1981), 133–41.

2. Eugene Talmadge is discussed in William Anderson, *The Wild Man from Sugar Creek: The Political Career of Eugene Talmadge* (Baton Rouge: Louisiana State University Press, 1975), and in Herman E. Talmadge, with Mark Royden Winchell, *Talmadge: A Political Legacy, a Politician's Life: A Memoir* (Atlanta: Peachtree Publishers, 1987). For the accreditation controversy see James F. Cook, "Politics and Education in the Talmadge Era: The Controversy over the University System of Georgia, 1941–42" (Ph.D. diss., University of Georgia, 1972).

3. See Harold P. Henderson, *The Politics of Change in Georgia: A Political Biography of Ellis Arnall* (Athens: University of Georgia Press, 1991).

4. Until 1962, in the Democratic primary, the candidate who carried each county would receive all the county-unit votes of that jurisdiction. Several of the largest counties were given six votes, the middle-sized counties had four, and the small counties had two. Since Fulton County's population might be a hundred times larger than that of many small counties, the vote of the large county did not carry its fair weight.

5. Ellis Gibbs Arnall, "Experiment in Democracy," *The Shore Dimly Seen* (Philadelphia: J.B. Lippincott, 1946), 51–57.

6. Ernestine J. Slade, interview by Kathryn A. Kelley, April 28, 1992, Cobb County Oral History Series, no.28, transcript, Kennesaw State College, Marietta, Georgia.

7. The Fair Employment Practices Commission (FEPC) was created by an executive order of Franklin Roosevelt in 1941 to protect blacks from discrimination in defense industries. After the war, President Harry Truman advocated a Fair Employment Practices Act to make the FEPC permanent.

8. *Atlanta Constitution*, April 7, 1946. Much of the document consisted of a highly progressive plan, allegedly written by Gene's son and campaign manager, Herman. Included was a call for a 50-percent increase in teachers' salaries, pensions for the elderly, more rural roads, more money for health care, affirmative action for veterans, the right of collective bargaining, aid to country schools, and support for the Farm Bureau. At the same time the former governor presented a more traditional Talmadge message in explaining his economic philosophy and racial attitudes.

9. Savannah was a year ahead of Atlanta in hiring black policemen. Georgia's largest city employed its first African-American officers in April 1948, also with the stipulation that they could only arrest black suspects.

10. W. W. Law, interview by Cliff Kuhn and Tim Crimmins, October 15–16, 1990, Georgia Government Documentation Project, transcript, Special Collections, Georgia State University, Atlanta.

4 – 11

16

The Integration of Public

Schools and Colleges

Protests against white supremacy had a long history in Georgia; as far back as the nineteenth century black activists such as Du Bois, Turner, and Holsey worked tirelessly to plead their cause to an uncaring state and nation. The Civil Rights movement, clearly, had only limited success before World War II and the postwar era. Then a variety of forces persuaded whites as well as blacks that change was imperative.

Once the first cracks appeared in the walls of segregation, African Americans became increasingly impatient to breach the barriers entirely. By the mid-1950s unprecedented numbers of students, workers, and other ordinary citizens took to the streets to protest. Dr. Martin Luther King Jr. was propelled into the spotlight by a bus boycott organized in 1955 in Montgomery, Alabama, where he was ministering at the time. A few years later he returned to Atlanta to head the Southern Christian Leadership Conference, an organization at the center of the mass movement for equal rights.[1]

For the Civil Rights crusade to succeed, it was necessary for part of the nation's

208

white political elite to join the effort. Some did so because they believed the cause was just, others because they considered it to be in their or the nation's self-interest. For example, Atlanta's business and political leaders feared that civil unrest would reflect negatively on a city attempting to attract Fortune 500 companies. They advertised Atlanta as the "city too busy to hate" and worked with Civil Rights leaders to relieve tension.[2]

Despite the relatively open position of some business leaders, southern states would have maintained segregation much longer than they did if they had not been forced by the rest of the country to alter their laws. All three branches of the federal government participated in overturning southern practices, but no branch was more effective in the 1950s and early 1960s than the judiciary. An activist Supreme Court, headed by Chief Justice Earl Warren, unanimously decided in 1954 that "separate but equal" was no longer constitutional. In the landmark case of *Brown v. Board of Education of Topeka* the Supreme Court ordered the nation's schools to admit students regardless of race. The following year, however, the Supreme Court hedged on the enforcement of the decision, stipulating that the decree would be carried out not according to a specific timetable but under the vague concept of "all deliberate speed."

The reason for the Supreme Court's lack of decisiveness in enforcing the *Brown* verdict was that the governors and legislators of the southern states promised "massive resistance." In Georgia the state constitution was amended in 1954 to permit the governor to close down the school system to avoid integration. Students would then be given tuition vouchers to attend private schools, and public school property would be leased to private corporations. The state also passed a law requiring the withholding of funds from any educational district that allowed white and black children to attend school together. While the public schools were never actually closed in Georgia, they clearly became the battlegrounds of the war between Southern traditionalists and champions of a new day.

The Attempt to Desegregate Atlanta's Public Schools

With its large black middle class and history of Civil Rights activism, Atlanta, not surprisingly, became the first Georgia city to integrate its public schools. On January 11, 1958, several African-American parents, represented by the NAACP Legal

Defense Fund, brought a class action suit against the Atlanta Board of Education. Known as *Calhoun v. Latimer,* the case was heard the following year in the U.S. District Court for the Northern District of Georgia.

The first document below comes from the testimony on May 19, 1959, of Leanard Jackson, Sr., father of five African-American students in the Atlanta system. The school board attorney, Newell Edenfield, attempted to prove that the plaintiffs wanted only equal facilities, not integrated schools. In this confrontation, one glimpses a parent of limited education who, nonetheless, held his own against one of Atlanta's best attorneys.

Q: . . . In other words, you concluded that the difference in your mind was not necessarily one of race but one of facilities, that is, good teachers, good buildings, good books, good water, good sanitation, and that sort of thing, is that what you wanted?

A: No, I wanted the children to go to the schools of which it had been told to me that was better throughout. . . .

Q: Don't they use the same books in every school?

A: Well, as far as I know, I couldn't say, but I know this much, that they don't use the same grade, class of books if you would speak of them in the conditions, because I have noticed down through the past two or three years carefully the childrens coming from the high school or coming from elementary school, all the colored children mostly would have older books, and I've noticed in my books, in my childrens' books where they have been issued to some white school, but I have noticed the white children very careful, mostly they all have new books, so it seemed like that since the school is colored, it gets the old books.

Q: They have the same material in them, don't they?

A: That I can't say because I haven't looked in the books that the white children have. I looks from the outside. . . .

Q: Leonard,[3] your children are perfectly normal healthy children, are they not?

A: That's right, they is.

Q: Nothing wrong with their personalities that you know of?

A: Well, I'll say it is.

Q: Something wrong with them?

A: That's right.

Q: What is wrong with their personalities?

A: Well, I started—my son, for instance, a year or two ago he and I was together and we passed this white school of Joe Brown. At that particular time the guys [were] out there in R.O.T.C. uniforms, and his question was to me,

"Daddy, why doesn't my cousins have those kind of uniforms that go to Turner High and Washington High?"

Q: How old was your son at that time?

A: He was about nine or ten, I disremember, because he's twelve now.

Q: Leonard, let me ask you this: From what I gather from your testimony, is it true that your biggest complaint concerns the fact, one, that you have not had a school that you consider as convenient as it should have been, for example, Philadelphia School was taken away; second, that the books that your children have you consider to be inferior to the white children's books; third, that from your attendance at meetings of the Board of Education you have heard that the white children make better grades than your children; and fourth, that the white schools have R.O.T.C. uniforms that your children don't have? Is that the basis of your saying that there is some discrimination against you?

A: That's the basis and it's complete discrimination.

Q: I see. In other words, what you are complaining about are those four things, those four you have mentioned, and that is the kind of thing you are talking about?

A: That's right.

Q: Do you think that if those four things were equalized or corrected you would have just as good a school as anybody else?

A: No. The onliest correction I could see in them was to be to integrate the schools.

Q: Why?

A: Because then it wouldn't be said that the books would be shuck up and distribute seemingly. My son would become and when he reached high school he could take R.O.T.C. and wouldn't have to go in the Army like his daddy without it, and the schools throughout seems better. . . .

Q: Leonard, you are a responsible citizen of the community. What if all of us were forced to a choice of separate schools or no schools?

A: Now, that question again, please.

Q: What if it were a question of having separate schools or no schools at all?

A: Well, I would prefer no schools at all or equal schools integrated.

MR. EDENFIELD: That is all, Leonard. Thank you.[4]

The Beginning of Desegregation

On June 16, 1959, Judge Frank Hooper found the Atlanta public schools to be segregated and gave the school board six months to submit a plan to rectify the situation. Rallying around a concept of "freedom of choice," the Atlanta school board in December 1959 proposed that students be allowed to transfer to any school in the system if they could pass a battery of tests to show they were qualified. In the first year eleventh and twelfth graders would be eligible, then in future years the younger students gradually would be included. Even after the court approved the plan, however, Judge Hooper was slow to implement it.

Hooper recognized that Georgia law mandated the cessation of state funding to integrated schools. He, therefore, decided to give white Georgians time to accept the inevitability of change. Over the next year and a half, white moderates devised a strategy to preserve the essence of segregation while permitting token integration. In 1960 a legislative committee, headed by John A. Sibley, recommended that the state back away from its threat to terminate funding and permit local school districts to decide for themselves whether to desegregate. Governor Ernest Vandiver endorsed the Sibley solution in a speech to the Georgia legislature on January 18, 1961. That oration is included later in this chapter.

With the state in retreat, the first nine black students in September 1961 enrolled in previously all-white Atlanta schools. City and Civil Rights lawyers, however, met in court many times during the 1960s and 1970s, as Atlanta moved slowly toward a fully integrated system.

Because of delays in implementing *Calhoun v. Latimer*, the first victory against segregated education in Georgia actually came in 1961 on the college level, eight months before the Atlanta plan was carried into effect. In January of that year a federal court ruled that the University of Georgia must accept two black students who were denied admission despite meeting all academic requirements.[5]

The document below is the decision of Judge William A. Bootle in the case of *Holmes and Hunter v. Danner.* Bootle pointed out that the state no longer could deny qualified black students the right to attend tax-supported colleges or universities. He asserted that the only issue in the case was whether the plaintiffs had been denied admission solely due to their race. The judge argued that administrators at the University of Georgia could not be expected to make an impartial judgment because, under current Georgia law, the institution could not desegregate without losing state funding. Pointing out that the plaintiffs had always made good grades, he concluded:

After a careful consideration of all of the evidence admitted at the trial, the court finds that, had plaintiffs been white applicants for admission to the University of Georgia both plaintiffs would have been admitted to the University not later than the beginning of the Fall Quarter, 1960. . . .

No Negroes have ever been enrolled at the University of Georgia, and prior to September 29, 1950, no Negro had ever applied for admission. At the time of the trial only four Negroes, including plaintiffs, had made application for admission to the University, all on or since September 29, 1950, none of whom has yet been admitted.

"Limited Facilities"

Plaintiff Hunter was informed by defendant that she could not be considered for admission for the Fall Quarter, 1959, the Winter Quarter, 1960, the Spring Quarter, 1960, the Fall Quarter, 1960, and the Winter Quarter, 1961, "due to limited facilities." Plaintiff Holmes was given the same reason for defendant's refusal to consider his application for the Fall Quarter, 1959, the Winter Quarter, 1960, and the Spring Quarter. Therefore, it seems appropriate to consider the housing situation at the University during July 1959 and subsequently, especially since University regulations would require plaintiff Hunter, being a female student under 23 years of age, to be housed on the campus, and would have required plaintiff Holmes to be housed on the campus during the 1959–60 academic year, he being a freshman male student at that time.

Dr. O. C. Aderhold, President of the University, addressed a letter to defendant on July 16, 1959, a part of which follows:

"It is my judgment that with no additional housing in prospect for 1959 and limited laboratory facilities in certain phases of our instructional program, that we should not accept any additional new students for admission prior to the 1960–61 academic year. . . ."

Several students were accepted for admission to the Fall Quarter, 1959 whose applications were received by defendant after July 22, 1959, the date plaintiffs' applications were marked received. Some of these students did not require University housing, being students living with parents or relatives or freshman men who are veterans or married. However, others would apparently require housing. Defendant testified that these students were exceptional cases—freshman men with advanced standing, a transfer from the Rome University Center of the University of Georgia, and football players who had already received grants-in-aid from the University. . . .

Undoubtedly, housing facilities at the University of Georgia have been taxed, particularly in the Fall Quarters of 1959 and 1960. However, the reason behind the "limited facilities" preventing plaintiffs' admission is probably best expressed in a handwritten letter, dated June 15, 1960, from Dr. Harmon Caldwell, Chancellor of the University System, to President Aderhold, with reference to a request from Howard Callaway, a member of the Board of Regents, for assistance in getting a white applicant admitted: "I have written Howard that it is my understanding that all of the dormitories for women are filled for the coming year. I have also indicated that you are relying on this to bar the admission of a Negro girl from Atlanta. . . ."

Interviews

Defendant testified at the hearing on plaintiffs' motion for preliminary injunction that he was unable to consider plaintiff Holmes' application for the Fall Quarter, 1960, because Holmes had not had the required personal interview. And on November 29, 1960 defendant rejected Holmes for admission to the University "from a review of [his] records and on the basis of [his] personal interview." Therefore, some discussion of the University's personal interview requirement is particularly important.

The evidence discloses the following pertinent facts. Since the Winter Quarter, 1960, defendant has generally required a satisfactory personal interview of applicants for admission to the University, pursuant to action of the Board of Regents taken on February 11, 1959. This interview requirement has been satisfied in a number of different ways. Many freshman students have been interviewed by University representatives at College Day programs held in many white high schools throughout the State. A number of transfer students have been interviewed by University representatives at the colleges from which they are transferring. Other students have been interviewed by defendant or a member of his staff in the Registrar's office at the University. Many out-of-state applicants have been interviewed by University alumni living at or near the place of the applicant's residence. Although, in most cases, an interview record was completed on the applicant, in at least one case, a letter from an alumnus stating that the applicant was "an excellent student" and "one of the outstanding young ladies in her class" and that she "would be a definite asset to the University" was accepted in lieu of the regular interview. . . . At least one applicant was interviewed by his brother-in-law. In at least two instances, applicants were interviewed by two different interviewers who arrived at different conclusions.

Contrasted to this somewhat loose application of the interview requirement described above, is the application of that requirement to plaintiffs. Little need be said about plaintiff Hunter's interview since defendant admits in his brief that, on the basis of her interview, she has given "evidence of general fitness for admission to the institution." However, these circumstances of that interview should be noted. Plaintiff Hunter was interviewed by *three* University officials—defendant and two of his staff members, Paul Kea and Dr. Morris Phelps—for approximately forty-five minutes because, according to Dr. Phelps' testimony, it was a "difficult case" since the University had never before received a student from Turner High School, a Negro high school in Atlanta. Plaintiff Hunter was asked numerous questions, including whether she "had any apprehension concerning being the first Negro to enter the University of Georgia."

Plaintiff Holmes was interviewed by the same three University officials for approximately one hour because, in Dr. Phelps' words, his, too, "was a particularly difficult case" having "already been presented at court." The atmosphere of the interview of Holmes was entirely different from that of the interview of Miss Hunter, however. Apparently the interview was conducted with the purpose in mind of finding a basis for rejecting Holmes. He was asked, in substance, the following questions which were not asked of Miss Hunter and which had probably never been asked of any applicant before:

1) Have you ever been arrested?

2) Have you ever attended inter-racial parties?

3) What is your opinion concerning the integration crises in New Orleans and in Atlanta?

4) Give some insight into the workings of the student sit-in movement in Atlanta.

5) What are some of the activities of the student sit-in movement, and have you ever participated therein?

6) Do you know of the tea houses (or coffee houses or Beatnik places) in Atlanta, and have you ever attended any of them?

7) Do you know about the red light district in Athens?

8) Have you ever attended houses of prostitution?

9) Since you are interested in a pre-medical course, why have you not applied to Emory University, since it is in Atlanta?

It is evident from the above that the interview of Holmes was not conducted as the interview of white applicants and, from the evidence as a whole, it is also evident that, had the interview of Holmes been conducted and evaluated in the same manner as the interviews of white applicants, Holmes would have been found "to be an acceptable candidate for admission to the University. . . ."

Decree

Pursuant to the foregoing findings of fact and conclusions of law, it is

ORDERED, ADJUDGED and DECREED that the defendant, Walter N. Danner, his agents, employees, successors, associates and all persons in active concert and participation with him are hereby permanently enjoined as follows:

From refusing to consider the applications of the plaintiffs and other Negro residents of Georgia for admission to the University of Georgia upon the same terms and conditions applicable to white applicants seeking admission to said University. . . .

Inasmuch, however, as it has been made to appear, and is found by the court, that the two plaintiffs are fully qualified for immediate admission to said University and would already have been admitted had it not been for their race and color, it is a further intent of this injunction that the defendant and other persons above indicated be and they are hereby enjoined from refusing to permit the plaintiffs to enroll in and enter said University as students therein immediately for the now beginning Winter Quarter, 1961. . . .[6]

Massive Resistance

Georgia's governor in 1961, Ernest Vandiver, was elected overwhelmingly in 1958 on a pledge, almost mandatory for southern governors of the decade, that not one black child would be allowed in a white school during his watch.

Integration had already led to violence in a number of trouble spots in the South. The question after Judge Bootle's decision was whether Athens, Georgia, would be the next scene of mob action. On the night of the verdict some two hundred University of Georgia students staged a demonstration in which a blackfaced effigy was hanged over the archway entrance to the main campus. University authorities were able to stop an attempt to burn a fifteen-foot cross on the front lawn of the home of President O. C. Aderhold.

The largest demonstration occurred on Wednesday evening, January 11, when a howling mob of some two thousand students, townspeople, and outsiders rampaged across the campus. The first of the protestors came out of the basketball arena, where Georgia had just lost in overtime to Georgia Tech. They marched on Myers dormitory, which housed one of the black students, Charlayne Hunter. Shouting racist slogans, they hurled rocks through dormitory windows, injuring at least one white student in her fourth-floor room. Rocks were also thrown at the police, and dozens of small fires were set. Responding with tear gas and arrests, the Athens police force eventually quelled the riot. Eugene Patterson of the *Atlanta Constitution* referred, however, to "a heart-sickening breakdown of law enforcement" when state troopers failed to appear to help the Athens police.

Governor Vandiver's response to the violence was to suspend the two black students, ordering state troopers to carry them to Atlanta for their own safety. The governor's attempts to maintain segregation, however, could no longer work. On January 12, Judge Bootle struck down as unconstitutional the state law requiring the termination of funds to colleges that accepted black students. The following day he ordered the state to readmit Holmes and Hunter.

Having failed to keep black students out of the University of Georgia, Vandiver found himself with only two options. He could be on the wrong side of history, gesturing defiantly at federal officials while losing control of events, or he could maintain a measure of authority by accepting the new reality. Vandiver's legacy is that he never encouraged defiance of law. His solution was freedom of choice, letting each Georgia school system decide for itself whether to admit blacks and letting students decide for themselves where they wanted to go to school. "Freedom of choice" proved to be a face-saving compromise in 1961, but later in the decade it too would be swept aside by federal mandate, when it became obvious that "freedom of choice" usually meant no choice for black students. Vandiver's speech to the legislature on January 18, 1961, asking for open-school laws, follows:

The Fate of Public Education in Georgia

This evening, you and I meet together in this joint session on an occasion history will judge. I am addressing you not only as your chief executive, but as a devoted father of one son and two daughters in the classrooms of our public schools. I am speaking to them about their future, as much as I am speaking to you and your children about yours.

We meet together to proclaim to the whole world that: PUBLIC EDUCATION WILL BE PRESERVED! OUR GEORGIA CHILDREN WILL BE PROTECTED! LOCAL ADMINISTRATION AND AUTONOMY WILL BE MAINTAINED! GRANTS WILL BE AUTHORIZED! THE PUBLIC SCHOOLS, THE VERY CENTERS OF OUR COMMUNITY LIFE AND ACTIVITY WILL BE STRENGTHENED! THE RIGHT OF YOUR CHILD AND MINE TO AN ADEQUATE EDUCATION TO FIT THEM FOR AN INCREASINGLY COMPETITIVE WORLD WILL BE ENRICHED AND GUARDED AS ARE OTHER SACRED RIGHTS!

. . . In the past few days we have seen events move so swiftly that it was hard to keep them in their true perspective. My friends, under Georgia's present statutes, it has been demonstrated that it is futile even to send a lawyer into the court room to defend them. . . . Yes, in a single stroke of the federal judge's pen we have seen the state stripped of any protection whatsoever. That is why I have summoned you here in this unusual emergency session. . . .

I reject, as I know you and the people of Georgia do, any thought, suggestion, hint or encouragement of defiance of lawful processes or the subjecting of the children of Georgia to the bodily hazard of violence and mob rule. Having seen what can happen in the university system, we must move to protect the public schools and Georgia school children within the legal framework left to us. Developments in the university case raise the real peril that under certain circumstances state-funds support for the Department of Education and for the 159 county and 139 independent school systems might not be constitutionally permissible and might have to be withheld by the state.

In such circumstances there could be only one result. All of the public schools in the state could be forced to close. That is a possibility which you, and I, and the people of Georgia are unwilling to contemplate, much less permit! . . .

There is no—NO—sentiment in this state for a blind destruction of public education without offering an effective alternative. There never has been. Every legal means and resource to circumvent the effects of the decision, yes. Defiance, no. Private schools offered as a resort, yes. Destruction of education, no. That has been the policy. THAT IS THE POLICY TODAY.

There is no real sentiment in Georgia for integrating the classroom of her schools and colleges. We are the target of destructive forces beyond our borders, the evil effects of which must be neutralized by Georgians acting in concert for their best interests. The great body of our people—the masses—white and colored alike—wish, are proud of and are content with our system of separate education. Its preservation is the fundamental objective of Georgia people. It is the fundamental objective of the Vandiver administration. Separate education — segregated facilities—are our objectives, first, last and always. . . .

Our course is to evolve a sensible plan; not to engage in emotional, futile moves which accomplish nothing but further aggravate an already bad situation. Our course is lawful resistance—not defiance—not violence. . . .

The administration will present to you a freedom of association child protection defense package at this session, composed of a proposed constitutional amendment and three bills. The amendment would guarantee freedom of association. . . . Their passage is an additional and necessary step in Georgia's efforts to avoid the harmful effects of the decision in the Brown case and those which have followed. . . .

We have a great state here and the finest citizens on earth. Praying for Divine Guidance in all that we do, rededicating our faith in education, young Georgia eyes will look deeper into the world of the future. An educated youth will discover broad new horizons for the betterment of mankind. And a people, armed with knowledge, will be easy to lead, difficult to drive and impossible to enslave.[7]

🏴 🏴 🏴

Epilogue

Not until James E. Carter's inaugural address ten years later in 1971 would a Georgia governor enthusiastically embrace the concept of equal rights. Hamilton Holmes went from the University of Georgia to Emory Medical School. By the mid-1990s he was senior vice president for medical affairs of the Grady Health System and associate dean at Emory Medical School. A journalism major, Charlayne Hunter, now Charlayne Hunter-Gault, is a national correspondent on the MacNeil-Lehrer NewsHour on PBS. In June 1988 she became the first black commencement speaker at a University of Georgia graduation.

The following comes from an article written by Hamilton Holmes a year after the events described above:

My First Year at the University of Georgia

Looking back, I realize that the last year has probably been the most eventful and crucial one in my young life. After one complete year at the University of Georgia, I can't help but look back and review the things that have happened to me over the past year or more, and evaluate the effect that they have had on my life.

Perhaps I should begin my account by going back to June, 1959. Shortly after graduation, Charlayne Hunter and I decided that we would apply to the University of Georgia. We really didn't have any hopes of being accepted but we decided that there was no harm in our applying. So in early July of 1959, we sent our applications in after having acquired them from the registrar's office. Surely, at this time it was beyond our fondest hopes and expectations that we would ever attend this, the oldest of all state chartered colleges.

Certainly the actions of the University officials bore us out. We were told that we could not be accepted because all freshmen housing had been exhausted.

There is a rule at the University of Georgia which requires all freshmen to live in dormitories. We accepted this as a valid reason and promptly asked that our applications be kept on file and that they be considered for the fall term of 1960.

In the fall of 1959, Charlayne entered Wayne State University in Detroit, Michigan, and I entered Morehouse College in Atlanta, Georgia, in order that our education would not be delayed. We both had very fruitful years, but always in our minds was our newly acquired ambition—that of entering the University of Georgia.

When again our applications were turned down by the University officials, our parents decided to take the case to court, to determine if our rejection was justifiable.

In late September, a preliminary hearing was held in Macon, Georgia, in the Federal Middle District of Georgia. District Judge William Bootle was presiding. The defense (the state) asked for more time to prepare for the case, so a date was set for the trial early in December.

On December 12, the trial reconvened in Athens, Georgia, the site of the University. Once again Judge Bootle presided. The trial lasted six days, and truly was very eventful. The courtroom was packed everyday with newsmen and interested persons. Our lawyers, Mrs. Constance Motley and Mr. Donald Hollowel, handled the case masterfully, as did also the defense attorneys.

On January 6, 1961, Judge Bootle handed down his historical decision. We were ordered to be admitted immediately.

After several days of confusion and legal procedure we began classes about two weeks late. Our first few days were clouded by tremendous riots and demonstrations. After these events, however, things quieted down, and everything went back to normal.

I had completed one year at Morehouse College, so I was classified as a freshman. I had some very good grades at Morehouse, but I sincerely believe that they were not indicative of my best work. This was due partly to the fact that I participated in numerous extra-curricular activities, and that I really didn't exert myself.

Things have been totally different the past year. I have really settled down and worked hard. Although I've been under tremendous pressure all year, my grades have actually improved. This can be attributed to my increased devotion to my books. I felt that a lot of people were depending on me, and I couldn't let them down. I am very proud of my grades. In a tough Pre-medical course, I have made 2 A-pluses, 5 A's and 3 B-pluses. I've been on the honor roll once and the Dean's list twice (the past two quarters).

Last year the students adopted a cold atmosphere and made things very trying for us. I made very few friends and would often go entire days without speaking to anyone on the campus. In contrast, the teachers were most friendly and helpful. Without their help and aid, we could not have made it. We have been treated fairly in all respects by the faculty and administration.

Since leaving Morehouse I have not participated in extra-curricular activities. I did not realize until this year the sacrifices that I have really made. I live a very lonely existence in Athens. Being away from one's life-long friends is no easy thing.

I really do miss my friends at Morehouse. I miss playing football and basketball. I miss the social life and I miss my fraternity (Alpha Phi Alpha) brothers, and the fun that we always shared. However, I do go home almost weekly for a day or two, so things still aren't as bad as they could be. Although my after class life is dull and uninteresting, I do enjoy my classes very, very much.

This year things have improved a little. I've made many friends, especially among the incoming freshmen, who look up to me as an upperclassman. Much of the resentment and hostility of last year is absent, but there is still a lot present. I'm not worried about this for I realize that it will take time for everyone to adjust to the great change which has taken place.

I am very pleased to be at the University of Georgia, not because Morehouse is inferior, but because the University has more advantages. Morehouse, with its limited funds cannot compete equipment-wise with the tax-supported University. There is no comparison in the physical plant and equipment of the two schools. Morehouse is far behind in this aspect, but it is equal to the University in non-lab courses. Morehouse is a fine school and richly deserves its fame.

The past year has changed my entire outlook on life. The things that I have seen and experienced the past year have caused me to mature rapidly and perhaps prematurely. I can only hope that the events of the past year will have a positive effect on my life, and I hope that my future years will be as productive and progressive as this past one has been.

May I take this opportunity to thank all who prayed for Charlayne and me during our periods of trial and crisis. Your prayers will forever be appreciated and revered by us. Truly God has kept His hand in ours.[8]

NOTES

1. King was the author of a number of books, including *Stride toward Freedom: The Montgomery Story* (New York: Harper and Row, 1958); *Strength to Love* (New York: Harper and Row, 1963); *Why We Can't Wait* (New York: Harper and Row, 1964); *The Trumpet of Conscience* (New York: Harper and Row, 1967); and *Where*

Do We Go from Here: Chaos or Community? (New York: Harper and Row, 1967). Also available are *The Papers of Martin Luther King, Jr.*, Clayborne Carson, senior ed., vol. 1, *Called to Serve, January 1929–June 1951* (Berkeley and Los Angeles: University of California Press, 1992); and vol. 2, *Rediscovering Precious Values, July 1951–November 1955* (Berkeley and Los Angeles: University of California Press, 1994). For student involvement in the Civil Rights movement, see *The Student Voice 1960–1965: Periodical of the Student Nonviolent Coordinating Committee*, Clayborne Carson, senior ed. (Westport: Meckler, 1990); and Clayborne Carson, *In Struggle: SNCC and the Black Awakening of the 1960s* (Cambridge: Harvard University Press, 1981). For a white activist's firsthand perspective on the South and the attempt to integrate Albany, Georgia, see Howard Zinn, *The Southern Mystique* (New York: Alfred A. Knopf, 1964).

2. For the viewpoint of a central figure in the Atlanta power structure of the 1960s, see Ivan Allen, Jr., with Paul Hemphill, *Mayor: Notes on the Sixties* (New York: Simon and Schuster, 1971). One of the better general histories of the Civil Rights movement is Taylor Branch, *Parting the Waters: America in the King Years, 1954–63* (New York: Simon and Schuster, 1988).

3. Mr. Jackson's first name was spelled Leanard when the case was filed, but was spelled Leonard by the court reporter who prepared this deposition.

4. "Depositions of Mrs. Ruth Smith and Others," 19 May 1959, pp. 34–37, 39–42, *Vivian Calhoun, et al, Plaintiffs, vs. A. C. Latimer, et al, Defendants*, Civil Action No. 6298, United States District Court for the Northern District of Georgia, Atlanta Division, Box 55H, Folder 2, National Archives—Southeast Region, East Point, Georgia.

5. The two students who sued for admission to the University of Georgia were from accomplished families. Hamilton Holmes's grandfather was an Atlanta physician; his mother was a teacher and his father a businessman. His father, grandfather, and an uncle won a U.S. Supreme Court case in 1956 integrating Atlanta's public golf courses. Charlayne Hunter's father was an army chaplain who retired a lieutenant colonel. Her parents were separated, however, and Ms. Hunter lived in Atlanta with her mother, a secretary. Holmes graduated first and Hunter third in the 1959 class at Turner High School. For a journalist's account see Calvin Trillin, *An Education in Georgia: Charlayne Hunter, Hamilton Holmes, and the Integration of the University of Georgia* (New York: Viking Press, 1964; reprint, Athens: University of Georgia Press, 1991).

6. *Hamilton E. Holmes and Charlayne A. Hunter v. Walter N. Danner*, January 6, 1961, United States District Court for the Middle District of Georgia, Athens Division. All records pertaining to this case are located at the National Archives—Southeast Region, East Point, Georgia.

7. Ernest Vandiver, "The Fate of Public Education in Georgia," *Atlanta Constitution*, January 19, 1961, p. 9.

8. Hamilton E. Holmes, "My First Year at the University of Georgia," *Sepia* 11 (May 1962): 44–45. Located in Hamilton Holmes Papers, series 1, box 4, file 7, Library and Archives, Martin Luther King, Jr. Center for Nonviolent Social Change, Atlanta. Charlayne Hunter-Gault's firsthand account is told in *In My Place* (New York: Farrar Straus Giroux, 1992).

159
counties

County- unit System

1917-1962
strick down be
Supreme Ct

6 up...
4. votes

4-25 elec

urban - 8 long d
town - 30
rural - 121

Themes
change
Blacks othr
voices

17

The Rise of a Future President:

The Gubernatorial Inauguration

of Jimmy Carter

State Senator Jimmy Carter made his first race for governor of Georgia in 1966, when he came in third in the Democratic primary, behind Ellis Arnall and the ultimate winner, Lester Maddox.[1] The young businessman from Plains spent the next four years campaigning for the 1970 election. In that heated contest, he edged out former governor Carl Sanders in the primary and defeated broadcast newsman Hal Suit in the general election.

Despite a relatively liberal record in his home community and as state senator, Carter managed in 1970 to appeal to Maddox-style segregationists. He sought the support of politicians such as Alabama governor George Wallace and won endorsements from Maddox and longtime Augusta power broker Roy Harris, an archsegregationist. At the same time, he never specifically opposed integration,

224

promised to appoint blacks to top government jobs, and, unlike Sanders, campaigned publicly in African-American neighborhoods.

In the 1970 Democratic primary Georgia's liberal and black voters went to Sanders rather than Carter.[2] Nonetheless, the new governor shocked his conservative supporters by saying in his inaugural address that the days of racial discrimination in Georgia were over. Carter's speech was viewed with favor by the national media. Northern publications, such as *Time* magazine, discovering Carter for the first time, saw the erstwhile peanut farmer as a representative of a new breed of progressive southern governors. The favorable attention was essential to Carter's rise as a serious presidential contender just five years later. The text of his inaugural address follows.

☙ ☙ ☙

Carter's Inaugural Address

true self

January 12, 1971

Governor Maddox and other fellow Georgians:

It is a long way from Plains to Atlanta. I started the trip four and a half years ago and, with a four year detour, I finally made it. I thank you all for making it possible for me to be here on what is certainly the greatest day of my life. But now the election is over, and I realize that the test of a man is not how well he campaigned, but how effectively he meets the challenges and responsibilities of the office.

I shall only take a few minutes today to summarize my feelings about Georgia. Later this week my program will be described in some detail in my State of the State and Budget messages to the House and Senate.

I am grateful and proud to have with us the Naval Academy Band, because it reminds me as it did when I was a midshipman of the love of our Nation and of its goals and ideals. Our country was founded on the premise that government continually derives its power from independent and free men. If it is to survive, confident and courageous citizens must be willing to assume responsibility for the quality of our government at any particular time in history.

This is a time for truth and frankness. The next four years will not be easy ones. The problems we face will not solve themselves. They demand the utmost in dedication and unselfishness from each of us. But this is also a time for greatness. Our Georgia people are determined to overcome the handicaps of the past and to meet the opportunities of the future with confidence and with courage.

Our people are our most precious possession. We cannot afford to waste the talents and abilities given by God to one single Georgian. Every adult illiterate, every school dropout, and every untrained retarded child is an indictment of us all. Our state pays a terrible and continuing human and financial price for these failures. It is time to end this waste. If Switzerland and Israel and other people can eliminate illiteracy, then so can we. The responsibility is our own, and as Governor, I will not shirk this responsibility.

At the end of a long campaign, I believe I know the people of our state as well as anyone. Based on this knowledge of Georgians North and South, Rural and Urban, liberal and conservative, I say to you quite frankly that the time for racial discrimination is over. Our people have already made this major and difficult decision, but we cannot underestimate the challenge of hundreds of minor decisions yet to be made. Our inherent human charity and our religious beliefs will be taxed to the limit. No poor, rural, weak, or black person should ever have to bear the additional burden of being deprived of the opportunity of an education, a job or simple justice. We Georgians are fully capable of making our own judgments and managing our own affairs. We who are strong or in positions of leadership must realize that the responsibility for making correct decisions in the future is ours. As governor, I will never shirk this responsibility.

Georgia is a state of great natural beauty and promise, but the quality of our natural surroundings is threatened because of avarice, selfishness, procrastination and neglect. Change and development are necessary for the growth of our population and for the progress of our agricultural, recreational, and industrial life. Our challenge is to insure that such activities avoid destruction and dereliction of our environment. The responsibility for meeting this challenge is our own. As governor, I will not shirk this responsibility.

In Georgia, we are determined that the law shall be enforced. Peace officers must have our appreciation and complete support. We cannot educate a child, build a highway, equalize tax burdens, create harmony among our people, or preserve basic human freedom unless we have an orderly society. Crime and lack of justice are especially cruel to those who are least able to protect themselves. Swift arrest and trial and fair punishment should be expected by those who break our laws. It is equally important to us that every effort be made to rehabilitate law breakers into useful and productive members of society. We have not yet attained these goals in Georgia, but now we must. The proper function of a government is to make it easy for man to do good and difficult for him to do evil. The responsibility is our own. I will not shirk this responsibility.

Like thousands of other businessmen in Georgia, I have always attempted to conduct my business in an honest and efficient manner. Like thousands of other citizens, I expect no less from government.

The functions of government should be administered so as to justify confidence and pride.

Taxes should be minimal and fair.

Rural and urban people should easily discern the mutuality of their goals and opportunities.

We should make our major investments in people, not buildings.

With wisdom and judgment we should take future actions according to carefully considered long-range plans and priorities.

Governments closest to the people should be strengthened, and the efforts of our local, state and national governments need to be thoroughly coordinated.

We should remember that our state can best be served by a strong and independent governor, working with a strong and independent legislature.

Government is a contrivance of human wisdom to provide for human wants. Men have a right to expect that these wants will be provided by this wisdom.

The test of a government is not how popular it is with the powerful and privileged few, but how honestly and fairly it deals with the many who must depend upon it.

William Jennings Bryan said, "Destiny is not a matter of chance, it is a matter of choice. Destiny is not a thing to be waited for, it is a thing to be achieved."

Here around me are seated the members of the Georgia Legislature and other State Officials. They are dedicated and honest men and women. They love this state as you love it and I love it. But no group of elected officers, no matter how dedicated or enlightened, can control the destiny of a great state like ours. What officials can solve alone the problems of crime, welfare, illiteracy, disease, injustice, pollution, and waste? This control rests in your hands, the people of Georgia.

In a democracy, no government can be stronger, or wiser, or more just than its people. The idealism of the college student, the compassion of a woman, the common sense of the businessman, the time and experience of a retired couple, and the vision of political leaders must all be harnessed to bring out the best in our State.

As I have said many times during the last few years, I am determined that at the end of this administration we shall be able to stand up anywhere in the world—in New York, California, or Florida and say, "I'm a Georgian"—and be proud of it.

I welcome the challenge and the opportunity of serving as Governor of our State during the next four years. I promise you my best. I ask you for yours.[3]

Reaction of the Atlanta Constitution

Through the efforts of editors such as Henry W. Grady in the post-Reconstruction period and Ralph McGill in the Civil Rights era, the *Atlanta Constitution* had long enjoyed throughout the nation a progressive, probusiness, proreform reputation. Since Atlanta's and the newspaper's goals and aspirations often ran contrary to those of rural Georgia, the *Constitution's* endorsement of candidates for statewide office was sometimes viewed outside the capital city as a "kiss of death." Thus, it is not surprising that the *Constitution* was skeptical of Carter's vacillation on the race issue in the 1970 campaign and that Carter often chose in rural areas to campaign against the *Constitution*. The next two editorials, by senior *Constitution* writers, reveal something of that controversy.

Carter's Pledge to End Bias Shows Times have Changed, by Bill Shipp

Jimmy Carter made a little history in front of the state Capitol Tuesday.

He got up in front of 5,000 people and said: ". . . I say to you quite frankly that the time for racial discrimination is over."

Now, in many states that would be like saying apple pie is good and so is motherhood. But for a Georgia governor to come out four-square against racial discrimination in his very first speech as governor was, to say the least, precedent-shattering. And for George Wallace's old pal, Jimmy Carter, to say such things was unheard of.

As Carter unfolded his 12-minutes of Kennedyesque rhetoric, at least two other men on the inaugural platform must have remembered their own inaugural addresses in other times.

Former Gov. Ernest Vandiver, now decked out in the uniform of Carter's adjutant general, must have recalled that Tuesday, Jan. 13, 1959, when he took the oath as governor.

Much of his address was similar to Carter's. Vandiver called for economy in government, and reform and reorganization.

But he had some other things to say, too, that were in stark contrast with the inaugural day speech of 1971.

Vandiver pledged to his enthusiastic supporters in the winter of 1959 that he would work to preserve the county unit system. It was a promise he kept, but the county unit system died anyway.

And he said: ". . . the great rank and file of both races are fully aware of the fact that separate schools is best for all."

Oddly some present day political thought has come almost full circle on that point—from segregation to de-segregation to re-segregation.

Sen. Herman Talmadge also sat up there Tuesday and listened as Carter announced his intention to see an end to racial discrimination and called for programs to help the underprivileged. Carter's speech sounded quite different from the strident, super-conservative phrases of Talmadge in the late 1940s.

But the times change and so do the words that make successful politicians.

In the era of the Talmadges and Vandivers, Carter's speech would have been denounced as the talk of wild-eyed liberals or Communists or race mixers or worse. In the context of Tuesday, Jan. 12, 1971, Carter's inaugural address sounded simply like the proper words at the proper time.[4]

Carter's Inaugural Speech: Like 1966, by Reg Murphy

Gov. Jimmy Carter threw away his querulous campaign speeches and spoke of ending racial discrimination in his inaugural speech Tuesday.

He sounded more like the admirable young candidate of 1966 than the waspish stinger of the 1970 campaign.

He seemed to be trying to live up to State Senator LeRoy Johnson's assessment that he had to run a racist campaign but would change once in office.

Frankly, the state will not know for several months which is the real Carter. There are clues leading in all kinds of directions.

One looks first to his appointments. There are some first-class men in that group and some men with records of appalling administrative jobs.

Then one looks to the legislative program, and it does not exist at the moment. His widely heralded state reorganization bill is as toothless as an old mule. The rest of the program is hidden behind the panoply of inauguration.

But if one looks solely at his inaugural speech, and forgets all the whining and carping of the summer, there is an impressive beginning.

He said for everybody to hear that "the time for racial discrimination is over." Some of the crowd standing under the thin winter sun in Washington Street applauded, and others groaned.

Without flinching, he said, "No poor, rural, weak or black person should ever have to bear the additional burden of being deprived of the opportunity of an education, a job or simple justice."

With Atlanta Mayor Sam Massell standing there listening, he said, "Governments closest to the people should be strengthened." That means giving them the power to raise taxes from new sources, and if Carter relents on this point some of the agony of the cities could be helped.

He claimed to believe this: "The idealism of the college student, the compassion of a woman, the common sense of the businessman, the time and experience of a retired couple, and—the vision of political leaders must all be harnessed to bring out the best in our state."

If he means it, it will mean a lot more than his pledges last summer to lead troops onto campuses to snuff out disorder.

Yet he did strain credibility. He asked people to believe that four months could make such a tremendous difference in his approach to politics. He asked them to forget a summer of speaking favorably of George Wallace, of deliberately splitting Atlanta off from the rest of the state, of meeting with Roy Harris, of consoling Long County.

Perhaps they can, and perhaps he never meant to get into all those strange alleys last summer.

If it can be assumed for the moment that the real Jimmy Carter was speaking Tuesday, without the encumbrances of a political campaign or the necessity of getting to the right of any other candidate, then his administration could rank with the good ones in Southern history.

At the beginning of a new term, the only fair thing is to believe that Carter meant what he said at the inaugural. There will be plenty of time later to adjust that judgment if it turns out to be wrong.

A witness to the inaugural guesses that Carter could use some help in getting the summer's extravagances off his back while he settles into the office. Fair enough. We wish him luck.[5]

Why Not the Best?

Written in 1975, Why Not the Best? *was an attempt by presidential candidate Jimmy Carter to present his views and record to the nation. The following is his assessment of the controversy with the* Constitution *and of his civil rights record as governor.*

My biggest problem and worst mistake [during the 1970 election] involved one of the Atlanta newspapers. The editor early in the campaign began to characterize me as an ignorant and bigoted redneck peanut farmer. Editorial cartoons showed me standing in the muck of racism while all the other candidates disappeared into the sunrise of enlightenment. These attacks had a serious effect on some of our tentatively committed, liberal, and idealistic supporters who did not know me personally, particularly those in the Atlanta area who might have helped us financially. Since the newspaper strongly supported former Governor Sanders, I presume that the editors had recognized me as his major potential opponent and wanted to destroy me early in the campaign. The attack actually backfired, because it projected me into a position of prominence among the many candidates in the race.

I wrote an ill-tempered letter attacking the newspaper, but it was not published. When all the candidates were invited to address the annual convention of the Georgia Press Association, I used my time on the program to read the letter to all the state's editors. It was a mistaken and counterproductive action.

This altercation also hurt me among the black voters in the primary. Throughout the campaign I had established a standard practice of working among them on an equal basis with whites. I was the only candidate who visited all the communities in the cities, and who spent a large part of my time within the predominantly black stores, restaurants, and street areas. Although I did poorly among black citizens in the Democratic primary, I did well in the general election. . . .

After I was elected governor, and other new governors like Reubin Askew, Dale Bumpers, and John West were elected in Florida, Arkansas, and South Carolina, there were a rash of articles written about the "New South." Reporters came to see us all, from over the nation and from many foreign countries. Yet, there was often an insinuation that somehow a few progressive candidates had misled the Southern voters, and had captured the governors' offices by subterfuge. Nothing could be further from the truth. As accurately as possible, we represented the people who had elected us. The "major and difficult decision" had already been made.

Now it was time for the challenge of the "hundreds of minor decisions," and they surrounded me during four years as governor. We were lucky not to have any major racial conflagrations during my term, but there were still many actions to be taken during those years following the end of legal segregation in the South.

During the years before I was elected, massive efforts had to be mounted by the Georgia State Patrol to maintain order in the communities of our state, as threats of racial disturbance arose and were assuaged by demonstrations of uniformed force. From 1968 through 1970, just before I took office, the number of man-hours of uniformed patrolmen's time spent on civil disorders per year rose from 12,113 to 45,910. Instead of using state patrolmen to such an extent, we formed a biracial civil disorder unit. It consisted of three persons, and we trained them to go into a community when any threat to peace was detected. This crew, dressed in civilian clothes, entered a community quietly, used a maximum of communication and persuasion, a minimum of publicity, and no force. By 1973 only 177 man-hours of our state patrol officers' time were spent in civil disorder work. In the aftermath of any potential racial disturbance, there was often left a permanent local organization or committee to assure continuing communications between black and white leaders in a community. Because of their success, our CDU members were asked to visit several other states to explain their methods of operation. . . .

It was my privilege as governor to appoint dozens of qualified black citizens to major policy board positions, so they could participate fully in official deliberations such as those concerning the university system, the corrections system, state law enforcement, all aspects of human resources, the pardon and parole system, and the professional examination boards for dentists, physicians, nurses, funeral directors, beauticians and barbers, and many more.

One appointment which was particularly well received involved State Senator Horace Ward. When he accepted his appointment to a judgeship, he quietly pointed out that he had tried unsuccessfully to enter the Georgia Law School several years ago, but had been denied admittance because he was black. Although his lawsuit for admission was ultimately successful, he had already completed law school outside the state before the decision was final.

There were thousands of school children each week visiting the State Capitol building to learn about our history and our government. Portraits of famous Georgians—governors, senators, poets, authors, editors, industrialists, educators, and founders of national organizations—almost cover the walls of the building. Every single portrait was of a white citizen, though it seemed obvious that many black leaders had played major roles in the shaping of our state's society. As both a substantive and symbolic gesture, I decided to select several notable black citizens and honor them by hanging their portraits in the State Capitol. At the first meeting of the selection committee there was an immediate and unanimous decision that Nobel Laureate Martin Luther King, Jr., should be included and a thorough assessment procedure was devised to select the others.

This was a proper and long-overdue action, and it received approval from the vast majority of our people. But there were a few vocal dissenters. Lester Maddox announced that when he was elected governor to succeed me that the King portrait would be instantly removed. (He was soundly trounced in the 1974 election.)

On a Sunday afternoon on February 17, 1974, a small band of Ku Klux Klansmen straggled around outside the capitol while the portrait of the black civil rights leader was unveiled. The capitol was packed as Secretary of State Ben Fortson recounted the accomplishments of Dr. King.

Fortson, a white-haired veteran of many years in the State Capitol, has long been a glorious speaker to groups of school children visiting the capitol, talking to them of American history and American ideals. That day he was eloquent in talking about Dr. King and the meaning of his life, especially for black Americans, and in the end Fortson led the white and black audience in singing the anthem of so many civil rights marches, "We Shall Overcome."

The two other black Georgians whose portraits were unveiled that day were Lucy Laney [an educator] and Bishop Henry McNeal Turner, both influential nineteenth-century figures.

This was a small gesture in a way, the hanging of these portraits, but it seemed especially significant to those who had assembled for the ceremony. It seemed to me that everyone was aware of how far we had come during the last few years, but were much more cognizant of how far we had to go. There was a dramatization of the good will that had long existed between the black and white people of our state, and the realization that no matter what the future holds we must face it together.

A new degree of freedom for both black and white Southerners evolved from the trauma of desegregation. Instead of constant preoccupation with the racial aspect of almost every question, public officials, black and white, are now at liberty to make objective decisions about education, health, employment, crime control, consumer protection, prison reform, and environmental quality. . . .[6]

NOTES

1. Jimmy Carter has written a number of books. Of greatest value on his career in Georgia politics are his presidential campaign autobiography, *Why Not the Best?* (Nashville: Broadman Press, 1975); and his description of his first state senate race in 1962, *Turning Point: A Candidate, a State, and a Nation Come of Age* (New York: Times Books, 1992).

2. In the primary runoff Sanders received 93 percent of the black vote, while Carter won three-fourths of the white vote. For a good analysis of the 1970 election see Randy Sanders, "'The Sad Duty of Politics': Jimmy Carter and the Issue of Race in His 1970 Gubernatorial Campaign," *Georgia Historical Quarterly* 76 (Fall 1992): 612–38. Randy Sanders shows that Carter used dirty tricks to smear the reputation of former governor Sanders and to obscure both candidates' positions on the race issue. Historian Sanders argues that Carter felt pangs of conscience over his behavior, apologized after the election to his opponent, and confessed that he "prayed for forgiveness" (637–38).

3. James Earl Carter, *Addresses of Jimmy Carter, Governor of Georgia, 1971–1975*, comp. Frank Daniel (Atlanta: Ben W. Fortson Jr., Secretary of State, 1975), 79–81.

4. *Atlanta Constitution*, January 13, 1971, p. 3-A. Reprinted with permission from *The Atlanta Journal* and *The Atlanta Constitution*.

5. Ibid., 4-A. Reprinted with permission from *The Atlanta Journal* and *The Atlanta Constitution*.

6. *Why Not the Best?*, 102–3, 106–10. For Carter's tenure as governor see also Gary Fink, *Prelude to the Presidency: The Political Character and Legislative Leadership Style of Governor Jimmy Carter* (Westport, Conn.: Greenwood Press, 1980).

4. 25

18

Economic Development and Quality of Life: The Debate over a Hazardous Waste Facility for Taylor County

In the last quarter of the twentieth century Georgia was closer to the national mainstream than it had been for years. The people usually voted for the winner in presidential elections. In 1976 they helped send to the White House a Georgia native. Atlanta was known internationally as the host of the 1996 Olympics. Especially in the metropolitan suburbs, one could find many transplants from other states. Attracted by climate and expanding opportunities, the newcomers brought the state fresh perspectives.

Yet commentators spoke of two Georgias. A few affluent urban and suburban counties experienced population explosions and building booms. In stark contrast, blighted inner cities suffered from multiple social and economic problems, and rural communities fell further behind metropolitan areas in population and influence.

A late-twentieth-century controversy that illustrates the promise and problems of modern Georgia is the question of hazardous waste disposal. Dynamic urban communities produce much of the state's industrial waste, yet they are reluctant to dispose of harmful materials in their own backyards. Poorer counties are so starved for economic development that they sometimes are willing to do anything to create jobs. From the latter perspective concerns about the potential danger of waste disposal are a lower priority than bringing new business to one's community.

At the beginning of his second term in 1987, Governor Joe Frank Harris announced that the building of a hazardous waste management facility was a major priority. The facility would include an incinerator to dispose of used solvents, paint sludges, drycleaning fluids, materials contaminated with metals such as lead, and pesticide waste products. It would *not* receive nuclear or radioactive wastes, and it would not be a landfill. The system was supposed to operate so efficiently that only an insignificant portion of the burned material would escape into the atmosphere. Advocates claimed there would be no odor. Whatever remained would be stored in a structure above ground, so that there would be no groundwater contamination. The site would include at least three thousand acres, although construction would occur on only one hundred acres. If things worked as the proponents said they would, the public would hardly notice that the facility existed. Some environmentalists, however, questioned whether it was possible to build and operate a totally efficient, error-proof system. From their perspective, spills of dangerous substances were inevitable.

In his 1987 "State of the State" message, Gov. Harris argued that

> Georgia has numerous responsible and essential industries throughout the State, including agribusiness, public utilities, and national defense contractors, which are important to our economy, that produce hazardous waste.
>
> I realize the controversial and sensitive nature of any discussion of this topic and the misinformation that abounds; however, if Georgia is going to be competitive in the future, if we hope to expand our manufacturing sector, we must be able to safely dispose of our own wastes, not depend on others to handle our problems.
>
> Over the past 10 years, Congress has enacted legislation mandating procedures for the disposal of such waste. Technological advancements in this field provide high temperature incineration, detoxification, and solidification,

which coupled with permanent dry storage facilities, preclude the need for any landfills.

We must provide this type facility to assure protection of our vital environmental resources and protection of our jobs. . . . [1]

Harris called on interested counties to submit bids to the Georgia Hazardous Waste Management Authority, a body that at the time consisted of the governor and other high-ranking state officials. In October 1987 eleven counties formally requested such a site. Most of them were poor and had a high black population.

In December 1987 the hazardous waste authority awarded the facility to Taylor County, a rural, sparsely populated entity between Macon and Columbus. According to the 1987 property and utility digest, Taylor ranked 135th in wealth of Georgia's 159 counties. The population was 43 percent African-American, far above the state average of 27 percent. Some critics saw a measure of racism in the state's determination to dispose of hazardous waste in a poor, heavily black county. They pointed out that the African-American community of Carsonville was next to one of the sites considered. Allegedly, places of this sort had little influence and were unable to protect themselves from the manipulations of the politically powerful. On the other hand, prominent African-American leaders of Taylor County actively and enthusiastically campaigned for the facility and the jobs it would create. Indeed, two of the five Taylor County commissioners seeking the facility in 1987 were black. One of them was Rufus Green, whose speech before the hazardous waste authority is printed below.

The county commission and, at first, the local newspaper, viewed the facility as a badly-needed form of economic development. Nonetheless, some people were outraged at the lack of citizen involvement in the selection process and at the potentially harmful impact on the environment. Thus began a five-year controversy that divided the people of Taylor County and involved the courts, governments at all levels, state and national media, and environmental organizations such as Greenpeace and the Georgia Conservancy.

After much turmoil, the authority in February 1988 voted to rescind its initial acceptance of the Taylor County site and reopen the bidding process. At the end of the year, however, the board decided to place the facility in a second Taylor County location.

In 1987–88 Lieutenant Governor Zell Miller had gone along with the rest of the hazardous waste body in selecting Taylor County. Nonetheless, as governor in 1991, he pushed a bill through the legislature that changed the authority's composition. The governor, other elected officials, and chief administrative heads were removed from the board. They were replaced by fifteen citizens appointed by the governor, the lieutenant governor, the speaker of the house, and the chancellor of the Board of Regents. Former congressman Elliott Levitas, now a private citizen, was selected to chair the authority. For the first time the board was assisted by a permanent professional staff.

After a year-long study the authority voted in July 1992 to rescind the selection of Taylor County, deciding that the process by which the site was selected was unacceptable. In November 1992 the authority determined that Georgia did not need a hazardous waste treatment facility anywhere at this time, thus ending the Taylor County saga, at least for the immediate future.

☙ ☙ ☙

The Advocates

The Taylor County Commission

Below is a speech by Rufus Green, chairman of the Taylor County Commission, to the Georgia Hazardous Waste Management Authority. In addition to heading the commission, Mr. Green was associate superintendent of the Taylor County School System.

. . . Each and every person in Taylor County wants the same thing. We all want a place with clean air and clean water and we will fight anything that threatens to take that away from us. We also want a place with sufficient economic growth to provide the jobs to permit our children to remain in the County if they desire. The only difference between the Members of Citizens for Safe Progress and the rest of us is that they believe that you are going to build a facility that will poison our air and water and bring about death and disease, whereas, we have complete confidence that neither you nor Governor Miller nor Lt. Governor [Pierre] Howard nor Speaker [Tom] Murphy, who appointed you, nor Mr. [Harold F.] Reheis at EPD [Georgia Environmental Protection Division] nor EPA [the federal Environmental Protection Agency] are going to approve, permit or allow to operate any facility that would not be an asset to The Community in which it is located. . . .

When this authority announced in 1987 its intention to build a hazardous waste treatment facility and invited any counties interested in hosting this facility to submit a list of potential sites that met listed criteria, we were immediately interested. The facility was described as a $50 million plant that would employ approximately 200 people. In addition, the county would receive a host fee of 1 percent of the gross revenues. When you consider that the total tax digest in 1987 was less than $100 million and the total county budget was less than $1.5 million, this was and *still* is a high economic plan for Taylor County. Taylor County, along with eleven other counties, submitted potential sites for consideration. Taylor County listed three sites that met the criteria set by the Authority and in December of 1987 site #1 in the West Central portion of the County was selected as the site of Georgia Hazardous Waste Treatment Facility.

Shortly thereafter things started to become unglued. The Authority was accused of making its selection on the basis of a "windshield survey" made from a drive-by of the sites by the consultants. The EPD was strongly criticized for being involved in the site selection process and also being the agency responsible for permitting the site and regulating the facility. The Taylor County Commissioners were accused of violating the open meeting laws because we failed to record the decision to submit a proposal for the facility in our minutes. We were even taken to Court and found guilty of failure to comply with the Open Meeting Act. As a result, the Authority in January, 1988 voted to throw out the entire selection process and start over from scratch.

On February 24, 1988 the Authority again sent requests to all of the counties to submit proposals to host the State Hazardous Waste Treatment Facility. Taylor County submitted a new proposal, this time being extremely careful to make sure that every "I" was dotted and every "T" was crossed. We even went to the extremes of having not only our local paper, but also Macon, Columbus, and Atlanta papers represented when the motion was made to submit a proposal and again when the proposal was approved by the Board. We also had at least five TV crews to record the event.

The Authority took the EPD out of the site selection process altogether, hired a new consultant firm and once again began examining sites, and once again Taylor County was selected. However, this time the site chosen was Site III in the Northwestern part of the County. . . .

I have been asked whether or not I was concerned that this plant would pose a threat to the health and safety of the citizens of Taylor County, the answer to that is "NO, not in the least." We fully are confident that any proposal submitted by this group and that survives the permitting process will be designed and built properly. We also are confident that Mr. Reheis and his people at EPD will insure that it will be run properly. We also believe that if you should happen to slip up somewhere that Mrs. [Debbie] Buckner or some of the members of her organization [Citizens for Safe Progress] will be there to point out the error of your ways.

Although we as elected officials have at times been the object of Mrs. Buckner's wrath, we recognize that the groups that she is representing have legitimate concerns that should and must be addressed. Although I personally feel that some members of her organization go overboard looking for a conspiracy behind every bush, the environmental concerns they raise are valid.

If you get your information from the newspapers or TV or from representatives of the advocacy groups, you would be led to believe that the issue of this facility is the #1 burning issue in Taylor County. In truth when you exclude the members of Citizens for Safe Progress for whom it is the #1 issue, it is hardly an issue at all. I go for weeks at a time and the subject of a Hazardous Waste Plant never comes up and when it does it is most often the question "are they ever going to get around to building that plant up in the North part of the County?"

I did some checking before I came up here. In our Society Election results are usually a reliable indicator of the mood of the citizens. Taylor County held elections for County Commissioners in 1986, the year before the issue arose and again in 1988 right in the middle of the Second Site selection process, the comparison of the results of these two elections is enlightening.

In 1986 the Commissioner representing the area of the County in which all three of the potential sites were located received 59 percent of the votes. In 1988 he received 47 percent of the votes, reflecting the dissatisfaction of the residents who lived near the proposed sites. This was District 3, in the other districts, the results looked like this:

District 1—1986	Unopposed
(Green) 1988	Unopposed
District 2—1986	61%
(Bentley) 1988	Unopposed
District 4—1986	54%
(Amos) 1988	62%
District 5—1986	Unopposed
(Gaultney) 1988	Unopposed

As you see all of the incumbent Commissioners except District 3 either ran unopposed or won by larger margins in 1988 than they did in 1986. . . .

In conclusion, let me say that although at times the road has been Rocky, and we have made some mistakes along the way, we have also made some progress. You have a host county that wants you, you have a site that to this point has met the technical and environmental tests. You have a long way to go to reach your objective, but it is not as far as it has been. If we in Taylor County can be of any help, please feel free to call on us. Speaking for Government of Taylor County, the citizens of [the towns] of Butler and Reynolds and the members of Development Authority, I promise you our continued support.

(Signed by four of the five members of the Taylor County Commission.)[2]

The Local Newspaper

Throughout the hazardous waste crisis, Jim Cosey was the publisher, editor, and chief reporter for the local weekly newspaper, the *Taylor County News and the Butler Herald.* As indicated in the editorial "Take Close Look!" (1987) reprinted below, he initially favored the construction of the hazardous waste facility. Later he took a more neutral stance. From beginning to end, he kept his newspaper open to the diverse views of his local readership.

This county is buzzing lately with talk of sanitary landfills and hazardous waste sites.

People are getting confused over the two issues and it's understandably so.

The county has signed a contract with a firm to construct a sanitary landfill in the county that will take care of our own garbage, plus that of other counties, but in the meantime pay the county for allowing such an operation to be built.

In the meantime, the county made application, along with nine other counties, to be considered for the site for a proposed hazardous waste facility in the county. Details and possibly some answers to questions are on the front page of this week's edition.

Let me say at the start, that I'm FOR both of these facilities! Now, you may agree or disagree, that's your privilege. I see the sanitary landfill as an answer to a county's prayer. Folks got up in arms over this proposal, but I wonder how many of those who got all excited have visited our present landfill? Talk about a mess! Nothing could be worse than what we already have!

If you haven't visited our present sanitary landfill, then I suggest that you do! The state is on the verge of fining the county thousands of dollars if something isn't done. And why isn't something being done? Because it's too costly for a poor county such as ours! The proposal from the firm in Smyrna is like manna from heaven. It will take care of our garbage plus pay the county money! Besides that, it will create new jobs and it will be strictly regulated by the state.

Then comes this hazardous waste business!

Now, I'll be the first to comment that I don't like the way our county commissioners handled this! I really feel that they tried to sneak it through and by the people. I happened to find out about it and revealed it on the front page earlier this month.

But, after careful study (and I've done quite a bit), I've discovered that this could be the answer to many more prayers for our county.

I'd like to say now that I don't think the county commissioners give the people of this county enough credit. If they had come out in the open to begin with, I think it would have been considered seriously much more readily.

But, now that the county has made application for this facility, I feel that we should look at all the facts before jumping the gun.

First of all, when you merely mention "hazardous waste," we immediately think of radioactive materials that will contaminate our water, our land and our very lives. This is not so!

The facility will be rigidly controlled by the state.

But, the main thing that I see is progress! That's right! Progress! Such a facility in our county would create some 200 to 400 jobs. And, good paying jobs. Why, I'm considering applying for something!

Just think! Jobs, new buildings, new people, we now have Hardee's, how about McDonald's, Wendy's, Shoney's? Think about how much taxes such a facility would pay. That would mean lower taxes for us homeowners and those struggling to get their children through college.

We now have in our future a new Community Services Center, a State Detention Center, a nursing home (if the land deals can ever be ironed out), a sanitary landfill, a hazardous waste facility—there seems to be no limit!

We could be on the threshold of a new era. But, that seems to be our problem. There are so many people in Taylor County who don't want to see change, who don't want to see growth. They want to become stagnant! They want to just remain as we have been for over 100 years.

I may be wrong, but I want to see us grow. I want to see us rise above being on the list of one of the 10 poorest counties in the state.

I think it's time to look to the future. Whether it be detention centers or hazardous waste. None of the projects will be detrimental to our community. Rather, they will be pushing us into the 21st century where we belong.

Come to the hearing set for Friday, Oct. 30. Ask questions and listen. Make your own decisions. But, don't go spouting off your mouths before you hear the whole story.

And, county commissioners—Don't hide things from us! Let us in on what you're thinking! Most of us are intelligent. Don't you know that when you appear sneaky, it looks as though you have something to hide? We're on your side![3]

☙ ☙ ☙

The Opponents

A Fourth-Generation Resident

Below is a speech by Terry J. McCants, spokesperson for Citizens for Safe Progress, the community organization which led the fight against the facility.

. . . For 22 months we have spent thousands of hours educating ourselves about this issue, written hundreds of letters, made thousands of phone calls, spent tens of thousands of dollars and made numerous trips to Atlanta at our own expense trying desperately to keep Taylor County from being sacrificed on the altar of expediency. I think all of us here today can agree that Georgia *must manage its own hazardous waste*, but it is high time that you as Authority members quit allowing yourselves to be held hostage by the EPA and by multi-national waste disposal companies that have a vested interest in building as many incinerators for profit as possible. This rush to burn must be halted. And it can . . . right here in Georgia. . . .

There are many areas of concern about the siting process of the proposed incinerator. Specifically, we are calling for a 3-year moratorium on any further action by this Authority on siting an incinerator until:

1. A comprehensive waste audit of industries in Georgia be performed to see *if* there is enough hazardous waste to warrant such a large-scale facility. The Weston Report indicates there will not be enough hazardous waste to justify such a facility without out-of-state waste being utilized. The [proposed] Regional Compact Agreement [with seven other Southern states] should be held in abeyance until this audit is performed.

2. Strong reduction and minimization laws [to reduce hazardous waste emissions by industry] should be enacted with the appropriate penalties to back them up.

3. Recycling should be encouraged by tax incentives and freeport legislation. A Hazardous Waste Clearinghouse should be established so that one industry's

hazardous waste could be routed to another company that could recycle it in their processes.

4. Examine the nine existing commercial hazardous waste disposal facilities (including incinerators) now operating in Georgia to determine if they can be enlarged and/or modified to take care of Georgia's hazardous waste. We are accepting out-of-state waste now at some of these facilities.

5. A comprehensive, in-depth, fair and unbiased study should be done. . . . We want the best minds in the University System with the foremost credentials *agreeable to all* to prepare and perform the environmental studies. The study should include:

A. Botanical and zoological studies of rare and protected plants and animals. The Linda R. Chafin report commissioned by Citizens for Safe Progress clearly identified rare and endangered species of plant life on the site.

B. Geological and hydrological studies to show the impact of massive amounts of toxins on the Cretaceous Aquifer system that is around and directly under the site. (New Jersey already has laws that protect any area above an aquifer or water source from being used as a disposal area.)

C. Pertaining to Taylor site III, wetland delineation studies should be done to determine just how extensive they are. The U.S. Army Corps of Engineers report asked for by our group clearly shows these wetlands to be present. Photographs and maps (which many of you have seen) prepared by Mr. Jack McGlaun proves beyond a shadow of a doubt this is a major aquifer recharge area. In his own words, "a blind hog could find these wetlands. . . ."

The people in opposition to this facility have felt a lot like John the Baptist, the voice of one crying in the wilderness. We have been dubbed radicals, greenies, Communists, environmentalists (as if that were a dirty word) and dirty words. But the one term that sticks in my craw was used by Mr. Leonard Ledbetter [Commissioner of the Georgia Department of Natural Resources] in the minutes of the October 29, 1987, meeting of the Hazardous Waste Management Authority. He says much of the controversy is generated by "outsiders." I am a lifelong resident of Georgia and Taylor County. My sons will be the fifth generation on the same land. My family genealogy dates back to the late 1700s in Georgia. How long do you have to live here before you are *not* considered an outsider? If *you* are going to call us names, how about "good stewards of God's earth"? . . .

In concluding my prepared presentation before you today, I would like to end with some personal thoughts. I could tell you how it feels to be deceived by elected officials, threatened physically by those less tolerant of an opposing view, frustrated by the use of political pressure to intimidate opponents to the facility and sorrowed by the loss of friends and the divisions in families and churches across Taylor County. But, I could also tell you how gratifying it is to have people stop you on the street and tell you to keep up the fight or "God Bless You." Yes, it has been a long, hard fight and I know it will not be over anytime soon. The government that is supposed to protect us has been coercing us to take something no one else wants. In the final analysis, all we want in Taylor County is our environment left intact and to be *left alone*. . . .[4]

Another View from Citizens for Safe Progress

The next document from Citizens for Safe Progress includes excerpts from a 1991 speech by Debbie Buckner, one of the most active opponents of the hazardous waste facility.

. . . The State of Georgia has tried to site and build a hazardous waste facility since the 1970s. Throughout this entire process the emphasis has always been on "dumping the waste" so it would be cost-effective and attractive to industry.

It was through citizens' actions that the emphasis of this authority was redirected to focus on source reduction due to legislative action in the 1991 General [Assembly] Session. In order for this Authority to be taken seriously by the citizens of Georgia and by Georgia hazardous waste generators you must abandon the Taylor County site and actively pursue an established goal of reduction. As long as a site remains in escrow to be pulled out for use as a disposal site—no one will believe you are dedicated to toxics use reduction. . . .

The siting process in Georgia has been a huge mistake politically, economically, and environmentally. . . .

I believe the real criteria for the site was to find a place:

sparsely populated,

with a poorly educated population,

with little political power,

that is economically deprived,

rural, reasonably priced land,

and majority black population.

The reasoning for this criteria (used in other SE states) was to expedite the construction of the facility with the least public opposition. There being no Blacks or women on the old [Hazardous Waste Management Authority prior to 1991] seems to indicate the lack of concern for these segments of the population. . . .

The economic outlook is what first hooked the Taylor County Commissioners.

A poor county, high unemployment, the sole banker serving as a county commissioner and a letter from then-governor Harris with the promise of economic prosperity was too much for these commissioners. They chose to apply without study, investigation or thought for anything like health, safety, or the environment. . . .

Decision makers have made some inaccurate assumptions such as:

The past Authority assumed the Fall-Line Freeway would be funded and go right by the site when in fact neither is true. . . .

They inaccurately assumed that continued hazardous waste production at current levels is inevitable. . . .

They ignore that "state of the art" incinerators have contaminated groundwater.

They ignore that we do not have the technology to monitor incinerator emissions.

They ignore the expense of spills. . . .

To continue with the Taylor County Site, a site many believe must be the worst site in the state, cannot be justified. Only people standing to make a profit from it or people who are ignorant of the detrimental effects of incineration can support this facility and this site.

This site is in the transition area known as the Fall Line.

The soil is porous—with sand and clay marbled together.

The surface water flows directly into the Flint River, which is less than two miles away.

The largest known concentration of the federal and state endangered plant the Fringed Campion is located on the site.

Within the "new" site of roughly 500 acres the wetlands are extensive. I have walked the site, or should I say trudged through the site knee-deep in wetlands. . . .

A U.S. Geological Survey map shows that the cretaceous aquifer, the vast underground water supply that the Growth Strategies Commission is relying on to supply south Georgia's water needs until the year 2010, runs beneath the Taylor County site. Much of Taylor County is an aquifer recharge area making spills extremely dangerous. Complicated by the fractured bedrock that lies beneath the site if water is contaminated by hazardous emissions or spills, it could seep through the fractured rock undiluted and undetected. . . .

I know it has been a long day and you have listened well. In closing I must tell you an old saying of my Grandmother's—she said timing is the difference between a wise person and a fool. For you see a fool does last what a wise person does first.

I think in Georgia in relationship to the management of hazardous waste we have been foolish enough. Let's abandon the Taylor County site today.[5]

Report of the Site Selection Analysis Work Group

In July 1991 the newly constituted Hazardous Waste Management Authority created a Site Selection Analysis Work Group to determine whether the old board had followed proper procedures in choosing Taylor County. The work group included three authority members and four representatives of the public. The chair was Dr. Wade L. Nutter, a faculty member at the University of Georgia. The vice-chair was Dr. Deborah S. Wallace, a dean at Kennesaw State College. Ex-officio members of the work group were authority chair Elliott Levitas and executive director G. Robert Kerr. Their twelve-month study persuaded the hazardous waste authority in July 1992 to reject the Taylor County site. The executive summary of their report follows.

The Site Selection Analysis Work Group (SSAWG) was established by the Georgia Hazardous Waste Management Authority to review the process whereby Taylor County Site III was selected as the location of a proposed hazardous waste management facility.

In the process of carrying out its mission, the SSAWG solicited written public comments, held public hearings, interviewed invited persons, reviewed documents, viewed video tapes and deliberated issues in open public meetings. The SSAWG held 14 public meetings and hearings since its inception in July, 1991. More than 175 written statements from interested parties were received and reviewed by SSAWG members. Representatives of three groups and 59 citizens gave voluntary verbal statements to SSAWG in seven public hearings conducted in Atlanta, Taylor County and Talbot County. Fourteen persons were interviewed by SSAWG, including members and support staff of the former Authority.

During its review, the SSAWG compiled a chronology of important events pertaining to the selection of the two sites in Taylor County. The SSAWG also collected and reviewed more than 400 pieces of information which included memos, letters, court records, newspaper articles and video tapes.

After reviewing information derived from more than 225 written and verbal statements, approximately 100 issues and/or allegations were identified and evaluated by SSAWG members. Following deliberations, which were held in open public meetings, 26 findings were established by the SSAWG.

The SSAWG unanimously determined, that: *taken as a whole, the process by which Taylor County Site III was chosen as the site of a hazardous waste management facility is unacceptable.*

While the Georgia Hazardous Waste Management Authority was legally empowered to site a hazardous waste management facility, the SSAWG concluded that:

Public participation in the siting process was neither required nor actively sought.

The Authority sought local governmental and political support and did not screen for environmental factors.

Members of the Authority were designated by law and not for their expertise in hazardous waste management, and the Authority lacked sufficient fulltime staff to adequately carry out its work.

Officials and citizens of Talbot County, adjacent to the selected site, were not consulted by the Authority.

Due to the actions of certain Taylor County officials, an atmosphere of intimidation toward opponents of the facility existed in Taylor County.

The SSAWG unanimously recommended that: *the newly reconstituted Authority rescind the selection of Taylor County Site III as the location of a hazardous waste management facility.* The SSAWG recommended that: *a new site selection process be developed, if the Authority determines that a hazardous waste management facility is needed.*[6]

NOTES

1. Joe Frank Harris, *Addresses of Joe Frank Harris, Governor of Georgia, 1983–1991* (Atlanta: Stein Printing Company, 1990), 151–52.

2. Speech of Rufus Green to Georgia Hazardous Waste Management Authority, July 23, 1991, attached to minutes of meeting, Office of Hazardous Waste Management Authority, Atlanta.

3. Jim Cosey, "Take Close Look!" *Taylor County News and the Butler Herald,* October 22, 1987.

4. Speech of Terry McCants to Georgia Hazardous Waste Management Authority,

August 24, 1989, attached to minutes of meeting, Office of Hazardous Waste Management Authority, Atlanta.

5. Speech of Debbie Buckner to Georgia Hazardous Waste Management Authority, July 23, 1991, attached to minutes of meeting, Office of Hazardous Waste Management Authority, Atlanta.

6. Site Selection Analysis Work Group, "Executive Summary," July 1992, report submitted to Hazardous Waste Management Authority, Atlanta.

APPENDIX:
QUESTIONS TO CONSIDER

For those using this book in the classroom, the following may be helpful in generating discussion:

Chapter 1

1. What did Juanillo fear the Native Americans were losing by adopting Spanish culture and religion? Do you think his analysis was correct? What do you think of his motives and tactics?

2. How did Father Ávila describe his treatment during captivity? What do you think was the model for his story of suffering and endurance? Why did the Indians not kill him?

3. Do you think that either the missionaries or the Indians understood the culture of the other?

4. Why do you think that the history of the Spanish presence in Georgia is not better known?

Chapter 2

1. What seemed to be the message of the Cherokee myths about the proper relationship between humans and the rest of nature? What was man's responsibility for disease? What do you think the Cherokees were trying to explain in their creation story?

2. What do the myths suggest about proper gender relationships? How does the Cherokee version of the origin of sin compare to the story of Adam and Eve and the expulsion of humankind from the Garden of Eden?

3. Do you think that Musgrove was a friend more of the whites or of the Indians? Why do you think she was able to do such unconventional things for an eighteenth-century woman?

4. Did Benjamin Hawkins describe Creek culture in a positive or negative way? In his activities as Indian agent, of what did he seem proudest? Do you think that his influence was good for the Creeks or bad?

5. How does Benjamin Hawkins's description of Creek domestic relations compare or contrast with the Cherokee myths? Do you think that Indian women were better off before they adopted white civilization or after?

6. Do you think that Georgians today can learn anything of value from the Cherokees and Creeks? If so, what?

Chapter 3

1. Do you think the arguments of the malcontents (Talifer, Anderson, Douglas, and Stephens) are plausible?

2. How convincing were the points made by Benjamin Martyn in justifying the trustees' policies?

3. How did Thomas Stephens attempt to rebut Martyn's arguments? Who do you think made the stronger case?

4. What moral and practical concerns did the Highlanders and Oglethorpe raise? How would you explain the presence of human rights concerns in Georgia in the 1730s?

5. What do you think Georgia gained and lost by permitting slavery?

Chapter 4

1. Do you think "Mercurius" made a convincing case not to support the northern colonies in their protest against the Tea Act?

2. Where did "A Freeholder" agree with "Mercurius," and on what issues did they differ? In your opinion, who made the stronger argument? Does "A Freeholder's" letter provide any clues as to why he eventually chose not to support the Revolution?

3. How did Governor Wright play on the fears of the colonists in pleading for their cooperation? On the issue of liberty, how did he differ from the Sons of Liberty? Do you think Wright was an advocate of liberty?

4. How did the answers to Wright's address from the two houses of the assembly differ in tone and content? How would you account for the differences?

5. How would you assess the areas of agreement and difference between Georgia's loyalists and patriots? Did Wright and the Council differ from the Commons House or the Sons of Liberty on the question of American rights? Did they differ in their opinions on how best to redress grievances? Which side do you think had the stronger arguments?

Chapter 5

1. According to Rep. Wilson Lumpkin, why would the Cherokees be better off in the West? How did he try to use race and class differences among the Cherokees in making his argument? Do you think that any of his arguments were convincing?

2. On the Indian removal question what evidence of Northern hypocrisy did Lumpkin present? Does the speech anticipate in any way the coming conflict between the North and South?

3. Judging by Chief John Ross's first annual message, how much had the Cherokees become like whites? How persuasive were his arguments against Georgia's claims to Cherokee lands? Why do you think the Cherokees were forced to move west?

4. Why do you think that the story of Cherokee removal has received more attention in American history textbooks than the removal of most other eastern nations?

Chapter 6

1. What conclusions about slavery could one reach from the John Brown narrative and the Leah Garrett interview? Do you think their accounts are accurate?

2. How did Charles Colcock Jones use the Bible to justify slavery? What did he think the Bible called on masters to do? Did Jones and Georgia Baker make a persuasive case for slavery as a paternalistic institution?

3. How would you explain the major differences in Garrett's and Baker's descriptions of slavery? Were there any implied criticisms of slavery in the Baker oral history? Do you think that the interviewer influenced either erstwhile slave's testimony?

4. If you had no more evidence than the documents in this chapter, what judgments would you make about slavery?

Chapter 7

1. According to Joseph E. Brown, why was the northern position on slavery hypocritical? What was his case for secession? Which of Brown's arguments did you find most convincing and which were least plausible?

2. Why did Alexander H. Stephens think Georgia should wait before seceding? Do you think he built a convincing case for staying in the Union?

3. On what matters did Brown and Stephens agree? Why do you think that Brown and the secessionists opposed Stephens's cautious policy?

4. How did Brown contrast the labor systems of the north and the south? How did racism influence his views?

5. Who do you think had the stronger arguments in Georgia's 1860–61 debate over the Union: the secessionists or the cooperationists?

Chapter 8

1. How would you evaluate the conduct of Union soldiers toward civilians? Did the greatest danger seem to come from soldiers following orders or from lawless troops acting on their own?

2. What can we learn from the documents about Georgia women during the war? Why did Frances Howard believe that submission to the North was easier for southern men than women?

3. How did the account of Unionist Louisa Fletcher differ from the others? Did her treatment by Union soldiers differ from the others? How was her family treated by the Confederacy? What does she reveal about the attitudes of Georgians?

4. What attitudes were white southern women liable to carry into the postwar period? What feelings would they probably have about the North, states' rights, white supremacy, and Republican rule?

Chapter 9

1. According to the 1865 constitution, why was slavery abolished? How did this constitution limit the rights of the freedmen? What conclusions could you reach about the racial attitudes of its authors?

2. How did the 1868 constitution differ from the 1865 document regarding civil rights? How would you explain the difference?

3. Do Daniel Howard and Alfred Richardson offer persuasive evidence that blacks were innocent victims of white terrorism? Why did they think that whites attacked them? During Reconstruction do you think that black power was real or imagined?

4. How did Augustus R. Wright and John B. Gordon justify the white South's violent resistance to Republican rule? Why do you think they refused to admit the existence of the Klan? Do you think their arguments were convincing?

5. Why do you think the Federal government was unable to protect Republicans and former slaves in the South? What do you see as the consequences (negative or positive) of Georgia's decision to reject Radical Reconstruction?

Chapter 10

1. What did Joseph E. Brown want northerners to think about the South? What did he see as the solution to southern poverty? Do you think that cooperation with northern businessmen was in the South's best interest?

2. How did Clare de Graffenried describe the women who worked in the mills? What did she think of the men? Do you think she understood these people? Why do you think many southerners resented her article?

3. How did housing conditions for Dougherty County black farm laborers compare to those of De Graffenried's white mill workers? According to Du Bois, what was the impact of rural poverty on black workers? Do you agree with his analysis?

4. How did Tom Watson explain poverty in a land of plenty? In your opinion how accurate was his analysis? Would Populist solutions have helped the South?

Chapter 11

1. What did Henry McNeal Turner think blacks would gain by emigrating to Africa? Do you think his plan was feasible?

2. In 1899 what qualifications did W. E .B. Du Bois place on his support for the Hardwick bill? Why do you think that in a few years he would oppose literacy tests under all circumstances?

3. How did Hoke Smith link disfranchisement with other causes that progressives favored? Why do you think he made this issue central to his campaign? How would the 1908 amendment disfranchise blacks without also hurting poor, illiterate whites?

4. What did blacks dislike about their treatment on streetcars and in other public places? Do you think that Ray Stannard Baker's description of Atlanta was objective? Did he find any evidence of African-American progress?

5. Do you think there was a possible solution to Georgia's race problem of the late nineteenth and early twentieth centuries? If so, what would have worked?

Chapter 12

1. What theory did Solicitor-General Dorsey develop to explain Frank's motives? How did the prosecutor appeal to the jury's emotions?

2. Do you think Frank received a fair trial? Why do you think the U.S. Supreme Court upheld the conviction?

3. What evidence is there that Tom Watson was anti-Semitic? To what type of reader would Watson's article appeal? What fears and frustrations did Georgians have

in 1915 that perhaps would explain why many wanted to believe that Frank was guilty?

4. How did Dorsey and Watson view women? What did they seem to say about the ideal relationship between men and women?

5. On what grounds did the Georgia Board of Pardons and Paroles grant Frank a pardon? Did the board say he was innocent? Do you think the board made a wise decision?

Chapter 13

1. Did Rebecca Latimer Felton make a convincing case for the historic subjection of women in Georgia? With what other issues did she link the question of female suffrage? Do you disagree with any of her arguments?

2. Was there anything on which Felton and Dolly Lamar seemed to agree? What evidence did Lamar provide that the vote for women would not lead to moral reform? Do you find her argument convincing?

3. What connection did Lamar and Rutherford find between the suffrage amendment and the destruction of white supremacy? Do you think their argument was plausible? Were Felton and McLendon less racist in their advocacy of woman suffrage?

4. Why do you think the State of Georgia rejected the Nineteenth Amendment?

Chapter 14

1. How did life change in the 1920s for people such as Mary Ann Brewer? What evidence did this interview provide of the breakdown of the old plantation system? Do you view the exodus from counties such as Greene as a positive or negative step for African-American tenants?

2. Did Arthur Raper provide convincing evidence of abuse in the loan and relief programs in the Black Belt? Do you think that the practices of the planters were defensible? Do you think the planters had legitimate reasons to fear the impact of relief programs on the availability of labor?

3. What does the Durham interview reveal about relationships between owners and tenants, blacks and whites, and farmers and the government in rural Georgia during the 1920s and 1930s?

Chapter 15

1. Do you think that Ellis Arnall made a convincing case for the eighteen-year-old vote and the abolition of the poll tax? How did he try to avoid the race issue in the latter debate? Why do you think Georgia was willing to make these two changes in the voting laws?

2. How did political and economic opportunities for blacks change during the 1940s? Do you think there is a connection between Georgia's economic transformation and the beginning of the end of the Jim Crow system?

3. To what degree was Georgia in the 1940s still wedded to the practices and traditions of earlier days? How did Gene Talmadge reflect Georgia's traditional values?

4. How would you evaluate Arnall and Talmadge as political leaders? What traditional Georgia values did each seem to reflect? To what degree did each advocate change?

Chapter 16

1. What seemed to be the central issues in the cases of *Calhoun v. Latimer* and *Holmes and Hunter v. Danner*? Do you think that Judge Hooper and Judge Bootle handled these cases properly?

2. In Governor Vandiver's January 18 address to the legislature, how did he try to resolve the integration crisis? How would you evaluate his handling of the situation?

3. According to his own account, why did Hamilton Holmes want to attend the University of Georgia? How was he treated there? What does the article tell you about Holmes's personality and character?

4. The year 1961 was the centennial of the start of the Civil War. What similarities were there between Georgia in 1861 and Georgia in 1961? How had the state changed?

Chapter 17

1. What does the inaugural address tell you about Jimmy Carter's values and character? Do you agree with him that Georgia suffered from "the handicaps of the past?" Why was it necessary to end his speech with the hope that in four years Georgians could stand up anywhere in the world and say with pride that they were Georgians?

2. How did Bill Shipp explain the difference between Carter's inaugural address and those of former governors? Do you agree with Shipp? Why was Reg Murphy skeptical of Carter? How would you assess Carter's explanation of his controversy with the *Constitution*? Do you agree with Murphy's evaluation of the speech?

3. Do you think that Carter's civil rights record helped him become president? How significant do you think his civil rights record was? How liberal do you think he was?

Chapter 18

1. Why did Gov. Harris believe that Georgia needed a hazardous waste management facility? Why do you think he let the counties bid for the site rather than selecting the location himself?

2. What was the case for a hazardous waste facility in Taylor County? Do you think that commission chairman Rufus Green and newspaper editor Jim Cosey gave reasonable arguments for placing the facility in their county? Do you think there are "two Georgias," one affluent and one poor?

3. What were the environmental risks of placing the facility in Taylor County? How serious do you think the environmental concerns were?

4. Do you believe that environmental regulations should be strong or weak? Do you think Georgians historically have been good stewards of natural resources? What do you see as the proper balance between development and the environment?

INDEX

🐦 🐦 🐦

Aderhold, O. C., 213–14, 216
African-Americans: and slavery, 26–36,
    63–85; and emancipation, 107–9; and
    Reconstruction, 107–20; and self-
    government, 116–17, 138–39, 140–45; as
    farm laborers and sharecroppers, 130–
    31, 181–91; and Civil Rights, 136–37,
    140–42, 202–6, 208–10, 215, 232–33; and
    segregation, 136–50; and black
    nationalism, 137; and the back-to-Africa
    movement, 137–40; and the American
    Colonization Society, 138–39; and the
    Leo Frank case, 151–53, 155; and the
    woman suffrage issue, 170–77; as
    percentage of Georgia population, 180,
    191–92; and the Great Migration, 180–
    81, 184–85; and Depression era relief
    programs, 186–89; and the Tuskegee
    Negro Red Cross chapter, 187; as
    domestic servants, 199–201; and World
    War II, 199–201, 203–6; as police
    officers, 205, 207; and the
    administration of Gov. Carter, 224–26,
    228–34; and the 1970 gubernatorial
    election, 225, 231, 234; and racial unrest
    in the 1960s and 1970s, 232; and the
    hazardous waste issue, 237, 245
African Methodist Episcopal Church, 137
Agricultural Adjustment Act, 180–81,
    189–91
Akin, Warren, 97
Albany, Ga. (Dougerty County), 110,
    130–31, 222
Altamaha River, 9, 18–20, 39
American Revolution: causes, 38–49;
    Stamp Act crisis, 39; Sons of Liberty,
    39–40; patriot viewpoint, 39–40, 42–43,
    48; Tea Act and tea party, 39–43;
    loyalist viewpoint, 41–49

Anderson, Hugh, 27–29
Anthony, Susan B., 164
Anti-Semitism, 132, 151–63
Arnall, Ellis, 195–98, 202, 224
Arnold, Reuben R., 157–58
Arp, Bill, 98
Askew, Reubin, 231
Athens, Ga. (Clarke County), 52, 112, 176,
    178, 215–17
Atlanta Campaign, Civil War: Georgia
    women during, 92–105; battle of
    Pickett's Mill, 93; fall of Atlanta and
    march to the sea, 93, 102, 104; battle of
    Kennesaw Mountain, 93, 103;
    occupation of Cassville, 97–98;
    occupation of Marietta, 100–104
Atlanta Constitution, 122–25, 175–77, 217,
    228–31
Atlanta, Ga. (Fulton County), 52, 93, 117,
    122–23, 147–51, 157–59, 163–65, 185,
    199, 207, 209–12, 215, 230–31, 235, 247;
    1906 Atlanta riot, 150; National Pencil
    Company, 151, 154–56; Atlanta school
    system, 210–12; Turner High School,
    211, 215, 222
Atlanta Journal, 142, 165
Augusta, Ga. (Richmond County), 69, 105
Au-put-tau-e, 21
Avila, Francisco de, 2–10

Baker, Georgia, 72–75
Baker, Ray Stannard, 147–50
Barnsley, Godfrey, 94–95
Bartolome of Tolomato, 9
Bartow County, Ga., 93–94, 97; Cassville,
    Ga., 97–98; Cartersville, 98, 165
Beck, James B., 117–20
Bell Aircraft Company, Marietta, Ga.,
    193–94, 199–201

Economy of Georgia: land distribution, 26, 38; antebellum economic expansion, 88–89; economic policies, Reconstruction era Republicans, 122; post-Civil War poverty, 122–35; economic policies, New South Democrats, 122–25; convict lease system, 123; colonial status with the North, 123–25, 131–34; moderation of Atlanta leaders, 124–25, 150, 209; cotton mills, 125–29, 134, 180; agriculture, 129–34, 179–92; crop lien system, 129–30; impact of tariff legislation, 133–35; impact of boll weevil, 179–80, 182–85; impact of Great Depression and New Deal, 180–81, 186–93; agricultural diversification, 181, 183; decline of the plantation system, 185; median family income, 1940–1980, 194; railroad rates, 142–45, 195; impact of World War II, 193–94, 199–201; economic development and the environment, 226, 235–48; "two Georgias" concept, 235–36; economic development in poor counties, 235–43, 245
Edenfield, Newell, 210–11
Environmental Protection Agency, U.S., 238, 243
Environmental Protection Division, Georgia, 238–39
Environment of Georgia, 10–14, 226, 235–48

Farm Security Administration, 181
Federal Writers' Project, 69, 76
Felton, Rebecca Latimer, 135, 165–70, 176–77
Felton, William Harrell, 165
Ferguson, Helen, 155
Finney, Sterling (or Starling), 64–65, 76
Fleming, W. H., 166
Fletcher, Dix, 103–5
Fletcher House (or Kennesaw House), 103–5

Fletcher, Louisa Warren Patch, 93, 103–5
Fort Benning Military Reservation, 24, 194
Fortson, Ben, 233
Franciscan missions, 2–9
Frank, Leo, 151–63
Freedmen's Bureau, 110–11, 119, 137
French and Indian War, 39

Gaines, Frances Elizabeth (Lizzie), 97–99
Gamble, Thomas, 205
Garfield, Captain, 99
Garrett, Leah, 69–71
George II, 25
Georgia Association Opposed to Woman Suffrage, 170, 176
Georgia Board of Pardons and Paroles, 153, 162–63
Georgia Conservancy, 237
Georgia Federation of Women's Clubs, 170
Georgia Gazette, 40–43, 49
Georgia Hazardous Waste Management Authority: Taylor County controversy, 237–48; Site Selection Analysis Work Group, 247–48
Georgia Institute of Technology, 196, 216
Georgia Military Institute, Marietta, Ga., 100–102
Georgia Press Association, 231
Georgia Prison Commission, 160
Georgia Rural Rehabilitation Corporation, 181
Georgia State Patrol, 232
Georgia Teachers' College, Statesboro, 194
Georgia Woman Suffrage Association, 164–65, 175
Georgia Woman Suffrage League, 165
Georgia Woman's Christian Temperance Union, 170
Gilbert, Ralph Mark, 205
Gold rush of 1829, 51
Gordon, John B., 117–20, 123
Grady Health System, 219

McClatchey, John, 102
McClatchey, Minerva Leah Rowles, 100–102
McGill, Ralph, 228
McGlaun, Jack, 244
McLendon, Mary Latimer, 165, 175–76
Menendez de Aviles, Pedro, 1
Mic-co thluc-co, 21
Milledgeville, Ga. (Baldwin County), 153, 162
Miller, Zell, 237–38
Moore, Betty, 75
Morehouse College, 220–21
Motley, Constance, 220
Mount Venture (trading post), 18
Murphy, John, 110, 120
Murphy, Reg, 229–30
Murphy, Tom, 238
Musgrove, Johnny, 17
Musgrove, Mary, 17–20

National American Woman Suffrage Association, 164–65
Native Americans: Guale Indians, 1–9; customs and traditions, 2–16, 21–24; women, 7, 15–20, 23–24; reverence for nature, 10–14; Cherokee myths, 11–16; Cherokees, 11–16, 39, 50–62; agriculture, 15–16, 21–24; Creeks, 17–24, 39, 41, 44–46, 48–51, 57; Yamassee Indians, 20, 26, 36; government, 22–23, 58–60; marriage and divorce, 23–24; 1835 Cherokee census, 50; Cherokee constitution, 51, 58; *Worcester v. Georgia*, 51–52; Trail of Tears, 52; Treaty of New Echota, 52; slavery, 56; Cherokee press, 58–59; National Academy at New Echota, 59
New South movement, 122–25
Nutter, Wade L., 247

Oglethorpe, James Edward, 17–20, 25–26, 28, 32, 34–36, 63
Olympics, 235
O'Neal, Walter, 185

Paine College, 137
Pardo, Juan, and Hernando Boyano expedition, 1
Parks, J. B., 182–83
Patterson, Caroline, 170
Patterson, Eugene, 217
Penn, W. F., 148
Phagan, Mary, 151–56, 160–62
Phelps, Morris, 215
Pierce, William P., 109–10, 120
Poland, Luke P., 115, 120
Ponce de Leon, Juan, 1
Pool, John, 117, 120
Populist Party, 131–32, 179
Progressive era, 142–50, 179
prohibition, 26–27, 168, 171–72
Pullum, D. U., 205–6
Putney, Francis Flagg, 110

Raper, Arthur F., 186–89, 192
Reconstruction, 107–22, 167; and constitutional revisions, 108–9, 167; and Klan activities, 109–20; and alleged need for self-defense, 116–17, 119–20; and carpetbaggers, 119; and Republican economic policies, 122
Reconstruction Finance Corporation, 186, 188, 192
Red Cross, 187–88
Reheis, Harold F., 238–39
Republican Party, 78, 80–81, 84–85, 88, 103, 109–12, 122–23, 136
Richardson, Alfred, 112–15
Roan, L. S., 157–58
Rome, Ga. (Floyd County), 52, 115
Ross, John, 52, 58–62
Ross, Quatie, 52
Rosser, Luther Z., 154, 158
Royal rule, colonial era, 36, 38–49; Council, 38, 44, 46–48; Commons House of Assembly, 39, 43–44, 48–49
Rural Electrification Administration, 181
Rutherford, Mildred, 176, 178

Saint Augustine, Florida, 1–2, 6, 9, 19, 30–33
Saint Catherine's Island, 1, 17
Saint Simon's Island, 18
Sanders, Carl, 224–25, 231, 234
Santa Elena (Port Royal), 1
Savannah, Ga. (Chatham County), 17, 27, 29, 93, 185, 203–5, 207; Independent Presbyterian Church, 40; Beach Institute, 204; King-Tisdell Cottage, 204; Irish political machine, 204–5; Jaycees, 205
Sax, Bill, 185
Scots Club, 27–28
Secession debate: states' rights issue, 54, 78–82, 84; nullification crisis, 77; Compromise of 1850 and Georgia Platform, 77, 85; case for secession, 78–85; reaction to John Brown's raid, 79–80; patronage as an issue in the secession debate, 81; fear of slave revolts, 81–83; white supremacy argument, 83–84; cooperationist argument, 85–90; economic argument against secession, 88–89; popular sovereignty, 90
Sequoyah (George Guess), 51, 57
Sherman, William T., 92–93, 104, 115, 147
Shipp, Bill, 228–29
Sibley Committee, Georgia legislature, 212
Sibley, John A., 212
Silva, Juan de, 2
Slade, Ernestine J., 199–201
Slade, Horace, 199
Slaton, John M., 152–53, 160–62
Slavery: debate over its establishment, 26–35; human rights issue, colonial period, 34–35; treatment of slaves, colonial era, 36; and Native Americans, 56; paternalism, 63, 65–69, 72–75; abolitionists, 63, 78–85; antebellum era, 63–76; interstate slave trade, 64–65; religious instruction of, 65–69; in the Bible, 66–69; African slave trade, 79–

80; emancipation, 107–9; southern compensation claims, 108; involuntary servitude, 109; allegedly a providential institution, 138
Smith, Haddon, 40–42, 49
Smith, Hoke, 137, 142–46
Smith-Lever Act, 142
South Carolina, 1, 17, 25, 28, 31, 33, 39, 41, 44, 77–78
Southern Association of Colleges and Secondary Schools, 194
Southern Railroad, 143
Spanish colonization, 1–9, 18–20, 25, 30–31, 39
States' rights: and Cherokee removal, 51, 54–57; and secessionist controversy, 54, 78–82, 84, 90; and opposition to Reconstruction, 111–20; and Gene Talmadge, 201–3; and massive resistance, 208–9, 216–19
Stephens, Alexander H., 72–75, 85–90, 116
Stephens, Lordnorth, 73–74
Stephens, Thomas, 31–33
Stephens, William, 31
Stirling, Hugh, 29
Suit, Hal, 224

Talbot County, Ga., 247–48
Talifer, Patrick, 27–29
Talmadge, Eugene, 194–96, 201–3, 207
Talmadge, Herman, 202, 207, 229
Taylor County, Ga., 235–48; Carsonville, 237
Taylor County News and the Butler Herald, 239, 241–43
Terrell County, Ga., 205–6
Terrill, John A., 97
Terry, Alfred H., 109
Thomas, Ella Gertrude Clanton, 105
Thomas, George H., 101
Thompson, M. E., 202
Thomson, Ga., 131
Thrasher, John O., 113
Tilly, Britt, 72
Tilly, Mary and Grandison, 72

The Passery
1988
Jenel Sams

Away Down South
Janes Cobb